# PUERTO RICO

## Commonwealth or Colony?

# Roberta Ann Johnson

# PUERTO RICO

## Commonwealth or Colony?

PRAEGER

PRAEGER SPECIAL STUDIES • PRAEGER SCIENTIFIC

Library of Congress Cataloging in Publication Data

Johnson, Roberta Ann.
    Puerto Rico, commonwealth or colony?

    Bibliography: p.
    Includes index.
    1.  Puerto Rico--Politics and government.  I.  Title.
F1971.J63          972.95          80-16879
ISBN 0-03-053576-X
ISBN 0-03-053581-6 (pbk.)

Published in 1980 by Praeger Publishers
CBS Educational and Professional Publishing
A Division of CBS, Inc.
521 Fifth Avenue, New York, New York 10017 U.S.A.

090785

23456789  038  98765432

Printed in the United States of America

*for my father*

Human beings do not live forever... we live less
than the time it takes to blink an eye, if we measure
our lives against eternity. So it may be asked what
value is there to a human life. There is so much pain
in the world. What does it mean to have to suffer so
much if our lives are nothing more than the blink of
an eye?... I learned a long time ago... that a
blink of an eye in itself is nothing. But the *eye* that
blinks, *that* is something. A span of life is nothing.
But the man who lives that span, *he* is something. He
can fill that tiny span with meaning, so its quality
is immeasurable though its quantity may be insignificant....
A man must fill his life with meaning, meaning is not
automatically given to life. It is hard work to fill one's
life with meaning.... A life filled with meaning is
worthy of rest.

A father talking to his child, from Chaim Potok, *The Chosen*.

# FOREWORD
## by Gordon K. Lewis

Dr. Johnson has written an informed, sympathetic, and exhaustively documented book on post–1898 Puerto Rico. It seeks to explain to an American audience why Puerto Rico, so late in the day, remains a tropical colonial possession within the Caribbean Third World region. Since that audience, generally speaking, is ignorant of the topic, knowing Puerto Ricans only as migrants to the North American industrial cities, the book will perform a useful service.

It explains, among other things, how and why Puerto Rico became a dependent territory under the American flag. Senator Henry Jackson has called the island a piece of "war booty," and the chapters of this book that deal with the long chronology of U.S.–Puerto Rican relationship over the last 80 years will tell the American reader of the consequences of that process. Economically, it has meant a deceptive economic growth generating a capital-intensive industrialization program. This has resulted in continuing mass unemployment, huge private and public indebtedness, forced migration, and, perhaps most important of all, a continuing structural economic dependency on the American capitalist market. Thus, Puerto Rico remains a classic dependent colony that imports its goods and exports its people. The market integration with the mainland means that Puerto Rico is unable to defend itself against mainland recession.

Culturally, it is perhaps an even more dismal story. Americans suffer from a cultural ethnocentrism and a moral egocentricity that makes them bad colonial masters. Hence, the long story of cultural penetration of the colonized people. There are few chapters more distressing to read than Dr. Johnson's brief chapter on the symbolic figure of the Puerto Rican *jibaro*; the independent highlands peasant whose virtues, frequently romanticized, have become the ideal of what it means to be a Puerto Rican. Today the Americanizing process has almost obliterated the type, replacing it with the tragic figure of the Neorican; the migrant who has become so Americanized that on return to the island he finds himself an unwanted stranger in his own home. Dr. Johnson quotes the observation of the older Puerto Rican leader Antonio Barceló, to the effect that Puerto Ricans might embrace the immense benefits to be derived from the American connection but do not wish to become shapeless hybrids where they would resemble the old Puerto Rican in nothing and yet differ from the American. But that is exactly what has happened, and Puerto Rico today is nothing more than what one Puerto Rican commentator has called a requiem for a culture. All that is made worse by the American incapacity to understand what has happened. Despite all of the cultural emaciation, Puerto Rico still remains indubitably Latin and Antillean in much of its life. That is why it is misleading to see the mainland Puerto Rican group as just another American minority group struggling to inherit the full promise of American life. It is in cultural terms a separate nation, or, rather, literally one-third of a cultural nation that lives in exile.

The political story of Puerto Rico reflects all this, for politics are deeply rooted in the ecology of class formation and class struggle. Dr. Johnson succinctly traces the 80-year history of Puerto Rican political parties. Most of them have been and still are pro-American colonial parties, asking at the most for enlarged *autonomia* or internal self-government. There has been no major movement for real independence, only minority *separatista* groups. In her chapter entitled "The Failure of Independence," Dr. Johnson explains that the reasons for this failure include Puerto Rican colonial docility, psychological colonialism, and official harassment of *independentista* movements. This is intensified by massive propaganda coming out of both Washington and San Juan that identifies independence with communism. The final reason is a deeply structured economic dependency, and I wish Dr. Johnson had emphasized it more. Modern-day Puerto Rico, where more than 70 percent of all families live off the U.S. food stamp program, is nothing much more than a huge colonial welfare state in which the average Puerto Rican is taught that separation from the U.S. would mean immediate massive poverty along Haitian lines. Thus the economic appetite destroys the political appetite. American colonialism in Puerto Rico, in brief, is probably the first colonial experiment in modern history that buys off the colonial victim-client by a largesse of material benefits (many of them socially and culturally debilitating), on a scale that the previous colonialisms in the Caribbean—British, French, and Dutch—have been unable to match.

In sum, modern-day Puerto Rico is a theater of the absurd. Economically, it is a dependent tropical economy that could easily grow its own rice—the Puerto Rican staple diet—but imports it from California. It is a colonial economy that produces what it does not consume and consumes what it does not produce. Culturally, it is a Spanish-speaking society, but the prestigious language in most areas is English. Politically, it is an American territory whose people are U.S. citizens, but who are second-class citizens. They can vote in the newly inaugurated local primaries of the national Democratic and Republican parties, but cannot vote in the national Congressional and Presidential elections. It is small wonder that Puerto Rico is a standing joke in Latin America and the Caribbean.

In all of this Dr. Johnson writes as an American academic, but one with a difference. Most books written by North Americans on Puerto Rico have been exercises in unctuous self-congratulation, praising what they see as a liberal colonial policy. Dr. Johnson explodes that myth, oftentimes in sharp commentary that betrays her disgust with that sort of literature. Nor does she write in the modern social-sciences jargon that frequently mistakes obscurity for profundity. All in all, this is a book for the intelligent North American lay reader who genuinely wants to know what the Puerto Rican problem is all about. It is more than anything else a North American problem. This book clearly and unequivocally tells the reader why.

# PREFACE

In an article that appeared early this year in the New York Times Travel Section, Manny Suarez said of Puerto Rico, "It is a land of marked contrasts with opulent high rise office buildings casting their shadows over dismal shanties built on stilts over fetid streams."* For the tourist as well as the scholar, we have a choice whether to focus on the high rise or on the shanties. This book attempts to include both, and to paint for the reader as fair a picture as possible of Puerto Rico.

Chapters 1 and 2 are designed to provide background information. Chapter 1 starts with Columbus's voyage in 1493 and focuses on Puerto Rico under Spain, which colonized, "not to change but to endure." Chapter 2 focuses on Puerto Rico under the United States, which promised "to put the conscience of the American people into the island of the sea." This chapter chronicles 80 years of events, from the military landing of 1898 to the 1976 statehood victory, Ford's "Grito de Vail," and the "Carter Connection."

Chapter 3 inquires as to why Puerto Rico, in a decolonized world, is not demanding independence, and finds much of the answer in attitudes and aspirations implanted by colonial rule. Chapter 4, devoted to Luis Muñoz Marín and based, in part, on an interview with him in January 1978, views his life and politics in terms of a war waged within him between concern for material well-being and concern about the island's dignity and political status. It sees him as the architect of modern Puerto Rico.

The fifth chapter, on the Puerto Rican jibaros, witnesses the demise of the independent and simple rural Puerto Ricans as Muñoz, who rode to power on the shoulders of the jibaros, then created modernization forces that destroyed them. This chapter also focuses on the Neorican, the mainland Puerto Rican who has come home.

Chapter 6 reviews the controversies and issues of the status plebiscite held in 1967 to decide, once and for all, if the people of Puerto Rico want commonwealth, statehood or independence, and examines the plebiscite results. The last chapter is a summary that links past with recent events and focuses on Puerto Rico as well as on the U.S. Congress, the White House, and the United Nations.

---

*"What's Doing in Puerto Rico," New York Times, January 7, 1979.

# ACKNOWLEDGMENTS

The number of people I would like to thank for helping me during my dozen years of doing research on Puerto Rico would itself fill a volume. From the Puerto Rican children I tutored in Harlem who shared their world with me, and the Puerto Rican graduate students at Harvard who encouraged and assisted me when I first started my research, to the countless number of people on the island, whose generosity and hospitality always made me feel welcomed when I lived in Puerto Rico and each time I returned—to all those names I remember but have no room to write—I say thank you.

But there are some I must acknowledge more personally. Luis Muñoz Marín kindly granted me an interview, and spoke with me for hours, and I am most grateful to him. I was also fortunate to meet, on a more informal basis, Senator Rafael Picó and former chancellor of the University of Puerto Rico Jaime Benitez. Among the many political leaders I interviewed were Gilberto Concepción de Gracia, former president of the Independence Party; and Rubén Berrios Martinez, present president of the Independence Party; Hector Alvarez Silva, Independence representative in the 1967 plebiscite; Juan Mari Bras, a leader of the Movement Pro Independence; and Juan Antonio Corretjer, former Nationalist leader and head of the Puerto Rican Socialist League. I am most grateful to them for their time and insights.

I thank also the many government officials who talked with me when I was first starting my research, including former Secretary of State Carlos Lastra, former Secretary of the Treasury Jenaro Baquero, Juan Manuel Garcia Passalacqua, when he was special assistant to Governor Roberto Sánchez Vilella, and Representative Luis F. Camacho.

At the University of Puerto Rico dozens of FUPI members offered their friendship and assistance; and the following are only a small part of the list of professors who helped me: Robert W. Anderson, Raul Serrano Geyls, Milton Pabon, Manuel Maldoñado Denis, Antonio Gonzalez, Gordon K. Lewis, and Sybil Lewis. Also, John Zebrowski, editor of *Revista/Review Interamericana*, has assisted me in countless ways.

Finally, I would like to thank Professor James Q. Wilson at Harvard for his encouragement, Bill McClung, editor at the University of California Press for his advice, Professors Emily and Arnie Stoper for their friendship, and my mother and father for their confidence and support.

# CONTENTS

# LIST OF TABLES, FIGURES, AND MAPS

# LIST OF ACRONYMS

| | |
|---|---|
| ACPR | Anti-Colonialist Congress of Puerto Rico |
| ADA | Americans for Democratic Action |
| CORCO | Commonwealth Oil Refining Company |
| CPI | Congreso Pro Independencia (Congress for Independence) |
| ELA | Estado Libre Asociado (Free Associated State) |
| FALN | Fuerzas Armada de Liberacion Nacional Puertorriqueño (Armed Forces of Puerto Rican National Liberation) |
| FUPI | La Federacion de Universitarios Pro Independencias (University Federation for Independence) |
| MPI | El Movimiento Pro Independencia (Movement Pro Independence) |
| PDP | Partido Popular Democrática (Popular Democratic Party) |
| PIP | Partido Independentista Puertorriqueño (Puerto Rican Independence Party) |
| PRRA | Puerto Rican Reconstruction Administration |
| STACOM | United States Puerto Rico Status Commission |
| US | United Statehooders |

# PUERTO RICO

## Commonwealth or Colony?

# *1* SPANISH COLONY: A CHRONOLOGY OF EVENTS

*All of these islands are very handsome and very good earth, but this one seemed to everybody the best.*

Christopher Columbus describing Puerto Rico in 1493

The discovery and settlement of Puerto Rico were typical. Columbus sighted the island, stayed overnight, and claimed it for Spain in 1493. Europeanization began soon after.

Like those before and those to follow, the Spanish who settled in Puerto Rico in 1508 came in search of gold. However, by 1540 the production of gold had declined, and by 1570 it ceased altogether.[1] Yet Puerto Rico's importance did not diminish; strategic location was its wealth.

Situated between the Caribbean and Atlantic, Puerto Rico was the logical stopping and storing point for Spanish ships laden with treasures and supplies. The island "became a bastion for the attempted exclusion of enemies from Spain's *Mare Clausim*, a sentry box for guarding...,"[2] and she was the essential link between the two worlds. No nation could win or woo this strategic treasure from Spain.

For the next two centuries the tropics became the battleground for Europe. Nations large and small ignored Alexander's Papal Bull as they fought to control the Caribbean.[3] But Puerto Rico's "El Morro," the famed stone-sentry, held its own for Spain. Not only warring nations but cutthroat pirates such as Captain Kidd and vicious groups of Carib Indians bombarded, invaded, and tried to control Puerto Rico.

Its position as fortress of the Caribbean at least partially explains why Puerto Rico never fought Spain for independence. For centuries, Spanish soldiers armed the fortress island, with a resulting high ratio of military to non-military men (see Table 1). The Spanish troops, centered in San Juan, the capital, created what Gordon Lewis calls a military society and what Anderson describes as a strict absolutist military rule. Even the governors of the island were appointed from the military aristocracy of Madrid.[4]

There is, perhaps, no better example of the Puerto Rico military in action than the rigid control against "subversives" during the last two decades of Spanish rule. Not only were newspapers censored and confiscated, but men were arrested without being told why, were held incommunicado, and were regarded as guilty until proven innocent. Puerto Ricans were so much in terror of the "civil guard" that they would give false testimony, according to Puerto Rico District Judge Fulladosa.[5]

Persecutions, called *componte*, a word borrowed from the Negroes of Cuba, were particularly severe when General Romualdo Palacio González was governor. Puerto Ricans were arrested at midnight and tortured, sometimes with *palillos*. Even the demand for autonomy was met by "the fearful persecutions."[6]

If revolt was unlikely in such a garrison state, it was almost impossible because Puerto Rico was so small.[7] Smallest of the Greater Antilles, the island measures little more than thirty by one hundred miles, and is therefore easy to control.

Though the strongest of Spain's outposts, Puerto Rico was the poorest Spanish possession. There are several reasons for this. Geographic location made the island vulnerable to periodic destruction from epidemics and hurricanes. In addition, military attacks and piracy interrupted the flow of commerce. For an island dependent on the outside, this was a particularly impoverishing hardship.

An important eighteenth century Spanish official reported that the

### TABLE 1
### Totals of Population, Census of 1897

| | |
|---|---:|
| Total general population | 890,820 |
| Spanish military forces | 7,014 |
| Spanish naval forces | 368 |
| Prisoners | 1,001 |
| Total | 899,203 |

*Source:* Henry K. Carroll, *Report on the Island of Porto Rico*, p. 196.

island's population was the poorest in America.[8] There are even some comic stories that authors have used to dramatize its poverty, such as an incident in 1583 involving Governor Mendez's exchange of clothes for a shipment of food to feed his troops. After the trade the soldiers' clothes were so scanty, it is reported, that they had to march through the woods to cover their nakedness.[9] Puerto Rico suffered from the poverty of circumstance—the invasion of storms and diseases and the attacks of soldiers and pirates—yet Christopher Columbus described the lush green island as the "most handsome" and "the best."[10]

## THE ARAWAK

The Puerto Rican natives who greeted Columbus were Taino-Arawak Indians—"a peace loving nation."[11] "They go quite naked as their mothers bore them," wrote Columbus of his first encounter with the Arawaks. "They are so ingenious and free with all they have, that no one would believe it who has not seen it. Of anything they possess, if it be asked of them, they never say no."[12]

Estimates of how many Indians there were vary from a high of "2 to 3 million of them on the islands of Puerto Rico, Hispaniola and the Antilles"[13] to Puerto Rico, "thinly populated by 30,000 tribesmen."[14]

Experts also differ as to what happened to the Indians. Most say they died off, killed by the Carib raids, Spanish "domination of the natives, extensive race fusion and ravages of imported European disease."[15] Hancock suggests that "the Indians did not disappear as a race before 1600."[16] According to one official report, "the whole island of Puerto Rico had only 60 native Indians in 1543";[17] and by 1797 an official military report pronounced: "The major part of the population indigenous to Puerto Rico was exterminated by the conquistadores."[18]

What probably happened is that the Indians moved inland, and "there, for nearly three centuries after the first settlement, they remained without molestation. The mountainous interior remained unexplored and unwanted by White settlers."[19] Today, names of cities are reminders of an Indian heritage. In fact, the term *Borinquen* itself is a Taino Indian term meaning, "land of the Haughty Lord."[20]

## THE SUGAR PLANTOCRACY

The sugar plantocracy was organized when the Puerto Rican economy shifted from its short-lived mining base to agriculture in the middle of the sixteenth century. The sugar planers were able to develop the narrow, but rich, coast into sugar *latifundia* (large estates), because of its climate and flatness of land (See Map 1). These Spaniards created a

**MAP 1**
**Topography Map of Puerto Rico**

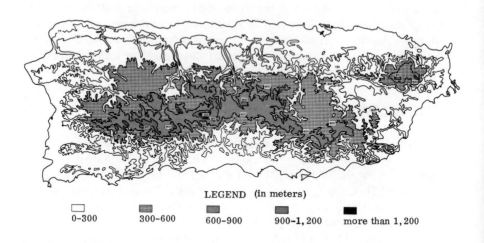

LEGEND  (in meters)

| 0–300 | 300–600 | 600–900 | 900–1,200 | more than 1,200 |

*Source:* Rafael Picó, *Geografía de Puerto Rico.*

closed feudal type of society, and worked their land with imported Negro slaves.

Because the sugar planters lived on the coast, trade, especially with San Juan, was relatively easy. Flat terrain, not the hilly and mountainous inland roads, separated the plantocracy from the main city and seaport. A system of trade enabled the planters to enjoy European imports bought with their sugar profits. The sugar growers were neither economically nor culturally isolated from San Juan, but were part of the Spanish ruling elite.

These owners of slaves were probably the least revolutionary class of all. Culturally, their style of life, entrenched in a feudal plantation system, complemented nicely the authoritarian military rule of the government centered in San Juan.[21]

The Negro slaves the Spaniards imported for the sugar harvest and tilling along the coast, introduced African strains of music, African ceremonials, African witch doctor medicine, and a new infusion of blood for the island's ethnic melting pot.[22] In the late nineteenth century the Puerto Rican "total colored population" was 257,709[23] (more than 20 percent of the population).

## THE INLAND FARMER

By the end of the seventeenth century, all of the arable coastal land had been organized by the sugar plantocracy. Thereafter, those who wanted to farm moved inland. The coffee growers planted their first beans in the rich but hilly soil of the West over a century after sugar cane first covered the coast.

Culturally their economic dealings did not Europeanize the coffee planters or make them sophisticated and urban like the sugar planters. The coffee growers grew apart from the San Juan-latifundia Spaniards, and developed their own mountain culture. The same was true for the subsistence and semi-subsistence level farmers known as the jibaros.

The jibaros lived inland, independent from the Europeanized coastal culture and their jaunty self-sufficiency came to symbolize the indigenous Puerto Rican. What the jibaros came to represent and what has happened to them in the twentieth century, is the focus of Chapter 5.

Unlike the jibaros, the coffee growers were more than merely self-sufficient; they were flourishing economically. By the nineteenth century, Puerto Rican coffee was recognized as "the finest in Europe," and by 1898, coffee represented 70 percent of the island's trade.[24] That same year a mere 5,000 acres of the coffee land was claimed to be worth over one million dollars.[25] In fact, Puerto Rican coffee, enjoyed and appreciated all over Europe, was marketable without Spain.

Thus by the nineteenth century the Puerto Rican coffee growers, although rich, were separated from the ruling class. Their connection with it was economic but not necessary to their economic well-being, since there was a market for their beans all over Europe. It is no surprise, therefore, that the largest attempted revolt against Spain was the ill-fated *Grito de Lares* in coffee country.

## GRITO DE LARES

During the nineteenth century there was some rebellious activity in Puerto Rico. Belief in independence was associated with the belief in the abolition of slavery and the right of representation, and there was often a merging of autonomist and independentist feelings. Puerto Rican governors banished many patriots from the island.[26] In 1868, in New York City, Ramon Emeterio Betances, banished for the second time, founded the Revolutionary Committee of Puerto Rico. It had a number of Puerto Rican chapters, including one in Lares. The committee began work, raising money for an armed rebellion. However, because the Spanish authorities learned of the conspirators' activities from lists found on a rebel arrested in Mayaguez, the rebellion for independence was forced to start before the participants were fully armed and organized. Their victory, El Grito de Lares, was short-lived, lasting just a few days in September 1868.[27]

The Lares attempt was planned to coincide with the Cuban revolution. It was not the first time attempts were made to link the fate of Puerto Rico with that of other Spanish colonies. More than half a century before, Venezuela tried such a linkup.

In 1810, when the municipality of Caracas became a revolutionary junta, Venezuela proclaimed its independence from Spain. "Anxious to include the island in the movement towards independence as well as to forestall the strategic advantage which the island's geographic position could offer the metropolis, the Venezuelans immediately sought to gain Puerto Rican support."[28] Envoys were sent to urge San Juan to join the insurrection.

Another attempt to link the freedom-fighting in the south with Puerto Rico was made in 1825 and was also organized completely from without, this time by Colombians. They were described as having been "inspired by the desire to free Porto Rico as they had freed their own country under the leadership of Simon Bolivar, landed at Aguadilla and captured some of the defenses."[29] But the Spanish military beat them off and they gave up their enterprise.

The attempts of 1810 and 1825 differ from El Grito de Lares in that they were attempted revolts by South Americans, not Puerto Ricans. But all three incidents share one important feature: all were explicitly connected with revolutions of other Spanish colonies—with Venezuela in 1810, with Colombia in 1825, with Cuba in 1869. Thus, Puerto Rico considered itself, and was considered to be, not the isolated filling station and sentry box, the role it was forced to play, but a part of Spain's new world of colonies.

However, in an ironic twist of events the results of revolution to the south prevented revolution in Puerto Rico. In 1775, Puerto Rico's population was 70,000; in 1800, 155,426; in 1832, 330,000; and in 1899, 953,243. This dramatic increase is explained as an influx of immigrants from the "neighboring trouble spots,"[30] as a royalist invasion.

From South and Central America, the Spanish royalists fled to Puerto Rico and made it the "Canada of the Caribbean." (I refer, of course, to 1776 and Canada's role in accepting American loyalists during and after the American revolution.) Whether called "royalist" or "loyalist," the first allegiance of these new immigrants was to the mother country. The political result is obvious. While South and Central America were cutting their respective apron strings, Puerto Rico was strengthening its own; and to an increasing degree the politics of the island were being linked with those of the peninsula.

The link was direct. Puerto Rico's liberals and conservatives not only correspondended to but cooperated with Spain's liberals and conservatives. For example, a liberal political victory in Spain ensured the Puerto Rican liberals' program of representation in the Spanish Cortes. As a matter of fact, one can plot Spanish liberal victories of that century by just knowing whether or not Puerto Rico was sending representatives.[31]

No doubt, the large numbers of royalists in Puerto Rico directly discouraged any independence sentiment. (One could argue that the tremendous influx of anti-Castro Cubans into Puerto Rico after 1959 has had a similar effect.) In a more subtle way, though, the very presence of thousands of royalists helped to submerge and shape any Puerto Rican radical tendencies. Instead of the usual choice between complete independence and complete dependence, the terms of the political debate centered around the form of dependence—complete dependence or dependence with some home rule.

Home rule dependence was called "autonomy" and was the liberal solution to the status problem. The presence of increasing numbers of royalists moved the whole political spectrum to the right. Therefore, what might have been an *independentista* emerged as an *autonomista*, and the platform of the liberals as well as of the conservatives was premised on the continued dependence on Mother Spain.

Throughout the nineteenth century, periodic successes provided the liberals sufficient incentive to work with, rather than against, Spain, and also convinced them of the viability of autonomy as an acceptable solution to the status problem. It is not surprising, therefore, that the idea of autonomy, "began to appear in Puerto Rico as far back as 1808 when the island gained a measure of representation in the Spanish Cortes," and that "it gained strength and appeal after the establishment of the Dominion of Canada...."[32] And so while the influence of royalists made autonomy the liberal's status solution, periodic successes provided them the positive feedback. In this way the Hispanic Tories who emigrated to the island during the nineteenth century prevented Puerto Rico from being completely liberated from Spanish rule—and from a Spanish world-view.

Up to the beginning of the nineteenth century, isolation and insulation from the world preserved in Puerto Rico and all of the Spanish Caribbean the outlook of 1492.[33] An influx of royalists could not be expected to revolutionize this Old World view; on the contrary, it only helped to preserve it. During the centuries of isolation it is not surprising that a colonial child continues to reflect the ideas of the mother country. The colonizer gives the new nation life. Even a twentieth century independentista recognizes the fact that Puerto Rico was a "gesto americano de la cultura de España."[34] What is most interesting is how this Spanish outlook was preserved, first through centuries of isolation, and then by the invasion of South Americans loyal to Spain. And what is most relevant about this ideology, preserved intact, is its antirevolutionary, antiliberal character.

It was antiliberal in that it began, not with a definition of Man, but with a definition of society. The feudal system, based on castes, rigid and hierarchical, was the political idea with which Puerto Rico entered the world. The colonial order did not begin with the Anglo-American rights of Man; "it was a society ruled by divine right and an absolute monarchy... an immense, complicated artifact designed to endure but not to change."[35]

The philosophy that Spain transported to the New World was antirevolutionary as well, because the social structure was legitimized by the Church. Catholicism gave unity to the whole and created the "true order" in which "form and substance were one."[36] Everything harmonized. Nothing was questioned. Spain did not seed rebellion when it planted a "world that denied the value of doubt and inquiry."[37]

This harmonizing whole had built into it neither the ability nor the propensity to change. Its rigid philosophy and "petrified faith" were antiliberal and antirevolutionary; for Spain did not invent but extend, did not colonize for the future but to endure.

It is in spite of Spain's world view, not because of it, that South and Central America fought for their independence. They fought for reasons that were practical, not ideological; they wanted creoles, not peninsulares, to rule. They changed neither the game nor the rules, only some officials and players. The nineteenth century independence movement was really the "prolongation of the feudal system,"[38] and the revolutionary leaders, like the conquistadores, took over the state as if it were medieval booty.

Even so, by the end of the century, Puerto Rico had won from Spain a new government charter. The granting of the Charter of Autonomy in 1897, and the beginnings of an indigenous creole self-consciousness were the most important developments for the island as it entered the twentieth century.

The Spanish Charter created an autonomous regime in Puerto Rico providing the Puerto Ricans with the same constitutional rights as peninsular Spaniards and providing secret ballot elections for the newly created 32-member House of Representatives. The governor general would be appointed by the Spanish king and would have extensive powers, including the power to appoint 7 of the 15 members of the upper house, the Administration Council, and the power to protect rights, suspend laws, and to choose a cabinet. The Charter also revised the mercantile relations between Spain and Puerto Rico, freeing the island to negotiate commercial treaties with foreign countries.

Luis Muñoz Rivera single-handedly negotiated for this charter with Práxedes Mateo Sagasta, head of the Liberal Party of Spain, alone at a southern vacation resort in Spain, in the summer of 1896. The agreement was ratified by the Spanish Liberals and by Muñoz's party and it became law when the Liberals came to power the next year.[39] What the Charter accomplished, according to José de Diego, "represented the most important event in the Antilles since its discovery and settlement."[40] By the summer of 1898, the elected insular Puerto Rican Parliament had met and Luis Muñoz Rivera presided as president over a Liberal cabinet.

Puerto Rico's move towards more political autonomy had the same historical roots as her growing cultural self-consciousness—Spain's war during the first decade of the nineteenth century.

Spain had requested financial asistance for her colonies to help her in her military resistance to Bonaparte. In 1809, in recognition of their support, the colonies were declared to be an integral part of the Spanish monarchy with the right of representation in the Supreme Council of Spain. A creole, a Puerto Rican soldier born in San Juan in 1775, Ramón Power Giral, was elected to represent Puerto Rico.

Bishop Juan Alejo de Arizmendi, the first Puerto Rican to attain that high post, presided over the public ceremony bestowing benedictions on the newly elected representative. According to one account:

> Although both the bishop and the representative had been cautioned by the Spanish authorities not to give any political implications to the ceremony, Bishop Arizmendi did something unheard-of at the end of the benediction. Taking his episcopal ring from his fingers he gave it to Power, saying in a loud voice: "As a token of confidence that you will not forget your duty to sustain the rights of our countrymen...."
>
> That day, in 1810, the conscience of a country was publicly born.[41]

According to another source, "It was this ceremony, attended by leading figures of both Spanish and local origin, which represented the awakening consciousness of a Puerto Rican identity, a unique society born of three centuries of a common insular existence."[42] Monclava documents for the arts and letters, in nearly every field, "devotion to the cause of Puerto Ricanness."[43] I will refer to this important theme again in Chapter 6, when I argue that what was growing and what continued to grow was not a political commitment to nationhood but rather a romantic attachment to a people. In fact, it is important to note that at the same time that Puerto Rico welcomed Spain's offer of a Charter of Autonomy, Cuba turned it down. Cuba would accept nothing less than independence. Then, in 1898, the United States "liberated" both islands.

## NOTES

1. Earl Parker Hanson, *Puerto Rico: Land of Wonders*, p. 22.
2. *Ibid.*
3. For a description of the scramble to control and the countries involved, *see* Hanson, pp. 22–25; Gordon K. Lewis, *Puerto Rico: Freedom and Power in the Caribbean*, p. 28; and José C. Rosario, *The Development of the Puerto Rican Jibaro and His Present Attitude Towards Society*, pp. 26–27.
4. Lewis, op cit., p. 48; and Robert W. Anderson, *Party Politics in Puerto Rico*, p. 3.
5. District Judge of Humacao, Fajardo, Neguabo, Vieques, Yabucoa,

Juncos, Las Piedras: Henry K. Carroll, *Report on the Island of Porto Rico*, p. 25.

6. *Ibid.*, p. 15: Gaetano Massa and José Luis Vivas call 1887 "a year of terror": see *The History of Puerto Rico*, p. 82.

7. Area, in square miles, is 3,435.

8. "...los vasallos de esta Isla son hoy los mas pobres que hay en America...," in "Memoria de D. Alexandro O'Reylly La Isla de Puerto Rico Año 1765," in *Antologia de Autores Puertorriqueños*, Eugenio Fernández Mendez, ed., p. 248.

9. For a description of the island's pre-1898 poverty, see Rosario, op. cit., pp. 26–27.

10. "All of these islands are very handsome and very good earth, but this one seemed to everybody the best." Christopher Columbus in 1493. Ralph Hancock, *Puerto Rico: A Success Story*, p. 65.

11. Walter Sullivan, "Scientist Seeks Story of Indians Who Greeted Columbus," *New York Times*, April 11, 1968, p. 47; see Earl Parker Hanson, *Puerto Rico: Ally for Progress*, pp. 22–23; Ralph Hancock, *Puerto Rico: A Success Story*, pp. 33–34; Edward B. Lockett, *The Puerto Rican Problem*, p. 60.

12. Sullivan, "Scientist Seeks Story of Indians Who Greeted Columbus." According to Morison, however, "The Arawaks of Puerto Rico lived in constant terror of Carib raids; and having no canoes in which to escape, took to the mountains as soon as they saw strange craft approaching by sea. Columbus never met a single native of Puerto Rico." Samuel Eliot Morison and Mauricio Obregon, *The Caribbean as Columbus Saw It*, p. 148.

13. Dr. Fred Olsen, quoted in Sullivan, ibid.

14. Lockett, op. cit., p. 60.

15. Ibid., pp. 61–62.

16. Hancock, op. cit., pp. 33–34.

17. Hon. Federico Degelau, *The Political Status of Puerto Rico*, p. 7.

18. Andres Pedro Ledru, *Viage a La Isla de Puerto Rico en El Año 1797 Ejecudado Por Una Comision de Sabios Franceses de Orden de Su Govierno y Bajo La Direccion del Capitan N. Baudin.*

19. Hancock, op cit., pp. 33–34.

20. Massa and Vivas, op. cit., p. 28; *"tierra del altivo señor,"* José Luis Vivas, *Historia de Puerto Rico*, p. 63.

21. Lewis describes the Caribbean plantocracy as unyieldingly parochial. *Puerto Rico: Freedom and Power in the Caribbean*, p. 31.

22. Hanson, *Ally for Progress*, op. cit., pp. 83–85.

23. Degelau, op. cit., p. 12. See Sidney W. Mintz, "The Cultural History of a Puerto Rican Sugar Cane Plantation: 1876–1949," in Eugenio Fernández Méndez, ed., *Portrait of a Society*, pp. 122–42.

24. Exports in pesos: coffee, 7,000,000; sugar, 4,5000,000;

tobacco, 500,000. Brig. Gen. George W. Davis, *Industrial and Economic Conditions of Puerto Rico*, pp. 5, 26. (I cannot reconcile Gen. Davis's 70 percent estimate with his export figures.)

25. Ibid., p. 46.

26. *See* Chapter VIII, in Gaetano Massa and José Luis Vivas, op. cit.

27. *See* ibid., pp. 78–79; Vicente Geigel Polanco, *El Grito de Lares*; Hanson, op. cit., pp. 41–43: Rafael Ruiz, "The Independence Movement of Puerto Rico, 1898–1964." (Master of Arts Thesis #2562, Georgetown University, 1965), Chapter 1: Luis Llorens Torres, *El Grito de Lares*; Federico Ribes Tovar, *A Chronological History of Puerto Rico*, pp. 302–8.

28. Lidio Cruz, Monclava, "The Puerto Rican Political Movement in the 19th Century," in *Status of Puerto Rico. Selected Background Studies*, 1966, pp. 44–45.

29. Carroll, op. cit., p. 14.

30. Hanson, *Puerto Rico, Land of Wonders*, op cit., p. 73.

31. In 1809, Puerto Rico gained representation only to be rescinded a few years later; the right was renewed in 1820 and lost in 1823. In 1869, Puerto Rico again was sending representatives. Robert J. Hunter, "Historical Survey of the Puerto Rican Status Question, 1898–1965," *Status of Puerto Rico. Selected Background Studies*, 1966, p. 51.

32. Hancock, op. cit., p. 304.

33. "...until the closing decades of the eighteenth century, the Hispanic Caribbean was to undergo a period of lengthy and almost complete isolation." Sidney W. Mintz, "Puerto Rico: An Essay on the Definition of a National Culture," in *Status of Puerto Rico. Selected Background Studies*. 1966, p. 364.

34. Antonio S. Pedreira, *Insularismo Ensayos de Interpretación Puertorriqueña*, p. 14.

35. Octavio Paz, *The Labyrinth of Solitude: Life and Thought in Mexico*, p. 110.

36. ibid., p. 166.

37. Ibid., p. 114.

38. Ibid., p. 120.

39. Thomas Aitken, Jr., *Luis Muñoz Marin, Poet in the Fortress*, pp. 31–32.

40. Cruz Monclava, op. cit. p. 42.

41. Massa and Vivas, op. cit. p. 65.

42. Cruz Monclava, op. cit.,p. 15.

43. Ibid., p. 15f.

# 2 UNITED STATES COLONY: A CHRONOLOGY OF EVENTS

> In the prosecution of a war against the Spanish Crown, the people of the United States, inspired by the cause of liberty, justice, and humanity, have sent the armed forces to occupy the island of Puerto Rico.

> Major General Nelson A. Miles in 1898.

According to a contemporary Cuban writer, "Puerto Rico was neither discovered, won nor colonized by the United States. It was intervened."[1] On July 25, 1898, the S.S. Gloucester with General Nelson A. Miles in command landed at Guánica. President William McKinley announced his desire "to put the conscience of the American people into the island of the sea,"[2] and General Miles proclaimed:

> We have not come to do battle with the people of this country who for centuries have been victims of oppression, but to offer you protection of your persons and your possessions, to stimulate prosperity and grant you the rights and benefits offered by the liberal institutions of our system of government.*[3]

But those liberal institutions did not come. As soon as Spain ceded Puerto Rican sovereignty to the United States (in a treaty which almost failed to pass the Senate),[4] the United States established military occupation.

---

*See Appendix A for the full text.

12

Even more disrupting, however, than military rule, was a hurricane, San Ciriaco, that hit the island a year after the United States did. This natural assault helped to put Puerto Rico at the economic mercy of the new mother country. The hurricane of August 8, 1899, killed 3,000, stripped a quarter of the island's population of everything but their lives, and destroyed both the sugar and the coffee crops. In his report of the incident an American general wrote, "It is doubtful if any land or district populated by nearly a million souls has, in modern times, been so devastated and overwhelmed as was Puerto Rico...."[5]

The hurricane was the death blow for coffee. Not only the coffee bushes but the shade trees necessary for their protection were uprooted. Since it took years for the trees to grow, coffee, unlike sugar, could not be replanted the following year.[6]

United States business took advantage of the natural disaster. Mortgage foreclosures over the next few years were caused not only by the disastrous hurricane[7] but also by United States economic policy. Called "systematic exploitation" by Maldonado Denis, the economic measures included freezing long- and short-term credit, devaluating the Puerto Rican peso, and land price-fixing.[8]

In the sugar industry, San Ciriaco and United States economic policy opened the way to consolidation and American monopoly. The losses from the hurricane made the sugar estate owners even more anxious to sell.[9] United States business bought up the sugar land quickly and efficiently. In the year of the hurricane there were 21 sugar centrals (central units used for processing the cane for the area) and 239 individual sugar-raising farms. Two years later the centrals and farms had been merged into 41 modernized sugar units.

United States rule was soon characterized by sugar monopoly, absentee ownership, and the creation of a Puerto Rican bourgeois class dependent on the United States. However, most Puerto Ricans were untouched by most of these economic changes.

In 1900 the majority of Puerto Ricans were isolated and independent jíbaros whose lives were as unaffected by the 1897 Spanish Constitution as by the 1898 military landing and occupation. Eighty percent of the island was illiterate, and 85.4 percent of the civilian population was rural.[10]

## FORAKER

On April 12, 1900, after two years of military occupation, President McKinley signed the Foraker Act providing Puerto Rico with a civilian government.[11] According to the provisions of the Foraker Act, the United States president would appoint the Puerto Rican governor, the members of an Executive Council (upper house), and the justices of the Puerto

Rican Supreme Court. The House of Delegates (lower house) would be popularly elected, as would a resident commissioner, who would represent Puerto Rico in Washington. In debate on the bill, Senator Joseph B. Foraker explained to the Senate that the Organic Act would not give Puerto Rico complete local self-government but a government republican in form with as much island participation as "it was safe to give them."[12]

Not only did the Foraker Act not provide local self-government, but it did not include citizenship rights and privileges for the million or so island residents. By the terms of the Foraker Act, Puerto Rico was called an "unincorporated territory"[13] and Puerto Rico's population was called "The People of Puerto Rico."[14] In 1901 the United States Supreme Court validated the right of Congress to literally choose at will which constitutional rights it wanted to extend to Puerto Rico.[15]

## 1900–17

The Foraker Act came as a blow to the Puerto Rican political parties. After the United States landing, in 1898, Jose C. Barbosa's orthodox Autonomy Party dissolved itselt to become the Puerto Rican Republican Party, while Luis Muñoz Rivera's Liberal Party disbanded to become the American Federalist Party. Both parties aimed at political absorption of the island by the United States as a way of achieving political self-rule. The Foraker Act was a real disappointment. Says Ralph Nader, "This colonial-style enactment transformed into despair the enthusiasm nurtured by the promises of complete self-government under liberal and democratic institutions which were made by responsible Americans."[16]

But Puerto Rican politicians continued to petition for change. The main petitioning organ for the island became Muñoz's Federalist Party which had, in 1904, reorganized under the name of the Union Party.[17] Their efforts were directed towards pressuring for increased autonomy and self-rule, and were largely ignored.[18]

## UNITED STATES RULE

The United States government was ill-equipped to handle Puerto Rican affairs. There was no governor and staff to represent Puerto Rican interests in Washington. There was no group of experts to champion Puerto Rico's interests in the executive. Only an uninterested, badly informed, and often prejudiced Congress had final decision-making authority.

No colonial office was established in the executive to assume administrative responsibilities for the island. There was only a Bureau of Insular Affairs set up in the War Department and, in 1934, moved to the

Department of the Interior. Its work was of a routine nature. As late as 1944 the administrative functions for all territories of the Interior Department were carried on with a total budget of $108,620.[19] There was thus no active administrative organ that was responsible for the welfare of Puerto Rico.[20] In fact, it was the misfortune of Puerto Rico to have been invaded during the hey-day of congressional rule. For, in truth, "the island became... a dependent ward of the Congress."[21]

The "real rulers of Puerto Rico" were the House Committee on Insular Affairs and the Senate Committee on Territories and Insular Affairs.[22] These two insular committees were not only not competent to handle Puerto Rican affairs because of their rapidly changing membership and their generally sketchy knowledge of the island[23] but they were also not motivated by, nor did they respond to, the needs and interests of the island. They did not have to. Puerto Rico had no power to pressure, no votes or money to withhold, and so had no political leverage.

Nor did (or could) the Puerto Rican governor, appointed by the U.S. president, effectively champion Puerto Rico's interest.* Few appointees "had more than mediocre ability,"[24] and the appointee was usually a "shoddy third-rate politician," a lame duck from Congress, or a minor claimant to patronage.[25] Henry Wells gives quite a candid but a more mixed review of the U.S. governors, using descriptions like "pro-American boor," and "bungling ignoramus."[26]

This was the situation confronting the Puerto Rican politician: no governor and staff to represent Puerto Rican interests in Washington; no group of experts to champion Puerto Rico's interests in the executive; and a nonresponsive and incompetent Congress with final authority on all Puerto Rican affairs. Chapter 3 will focus on the psychological consequences of this kind of rule. The important political fact of life here, however, is that the Puerto Rican politicians had no political leverage, that is, no power to threaten or persuade. After all, members of Congress did not depend on Puerto Rico to elect them. Even the threat of "no cooperation" was not an effective tool for the Puerto Rican.

The majority Union Party in the Puerto Rican House of Delegates precipitated a crisis in 1909. Out of a desire to force Congress to discuss Puerto Rican reform, the House of Delegates refused to pass the island's budget and appropriation bills. Instead of giving Puerto Ricans more power the action had the opposite effect. Dubbing it an act of "anarchy," Congress passed a bill that stripped Puerto Rico even further of its insular power.[27] Without political leverage, Puerto Rican commissions and delegations pleading for reforms were largely ignored.

As the Foraker Act seemed more and more permanent, statehood as

---

*See Appendix B for list of appointed governors.

an acceptable third status alternative had been removed from the Union platform and the independence issue was debated with more frequency within the party. The Union Party was the majority party, and its platform would determine priorities for the island.

Within the Union Party a schism was developing, whose factions were led by Luis Muñoz Rivera and José De Diego. Muñoz, who had struggled to achieve Puerto Rican self-rule in 1897 and who had mastered English at the age of 51 to serve in Washington as a resident commissioner, headed the moderate wing for autonomy. Although Muñoz, when he talked or wrote about politics, seemed, at times, to be for independence, he usually used the term to mean self-rule.[28] Muñoz clearly expressed his political preference in a much quoted statement, made in 1911, at the Annual Lake Mohonk Conference of Independent Peoples. Of the three possible status solutions, statehood, autonomy, and independence, the first, statehood, was to him preferable but unattainable; the second, autonomy, was acceptable; and the third, independence, was "held in reserve as a last refuge of Puerto Rican honor."[29] The goal, therefore, that Muñoz Rivera sought for the Union Party was autonomy or self-rule for the island.

José De Diego headed the independence wing of the party. He was a lawyer, and a poet, and he was nominally the official head of the Union Party. For him, independence was not a last alternative but the only acceptable alternative. De Diego and Muñoz also divided over whether to accept U.S. citizenship.

## MIRAMAR SHOWDOWN

In 1915 the Union Party met at Miramar to decide priorities. Muñoz was very influential. Noted for his success with Spain, respected for his knowledge of the United States, he engineered a resolution at the October Union Convention prohibiting the party from propagandizing for independence.[30] He was successful because of his personal influence and masterful politicking but also because of the absence of many independentistas at the Miramar meeting, and because of economic profits from World War I.

On February 9, 1912, the *Partido de la Independencia* was founded. Part of the independence wing of the Union had broken away to work for independence, a popular plebiscite that they were sure would decide for political independence, and a "second independence"—economic freedom from the United States.[31] The Union convention vote did not include this group of independentists.

In addition, World War I brought an economic boom to the island, especially in the price of sugar. Economic association with the United States was starting to be profitable for some Puerto Ricans, and profits made moderates. At Miramar it was decided that autonomy, not independence, would become the Union Party goal.

## JONES ACT

It was not until two years later, 1917, that Congress passed the new Puerto Rican Organic Law, the Jones-Shafroth Act. The long-awaited reform provided for the popular election of the 19-member Senate as well as U.S. citizenship for the island's residents.[32] By providing for a popularly elected Senate, the new law placated the Puerto Ricans, whose frustration was threatening to erupt in a massive anti-American protest vote. (Shaforth, the bill's co-sponsor, had the year before attached a rider to an appropriation bill suspending Puerto Rican elections indefinitely because he feared such a protest vote.)

But far more important than extending some self-rule was the fact that against the wishes of many Puerto Rican leaders the Jones Act made U.S. citizens of a million islanders. Congressional hearings in 1916 had indicated that many Puerto Ricans preferred to be designated Puerto Rican citizens. The Union's priority of reform, however, compelled the party to accept the new citizenship attached to reform. Muñoz Rivera's death on November 15, 1916, was another factor in the Union's acceptance.

It was known that Muñoz had worked tirelessly in Washington trying to influence various members of Congress to increase Puerto Rican self-government. His last official speech before going home to Puerto Rico to die was a dramatic appeal on May 5, 1916, in which he said, "Give us now that field of experiment which we ask of you, that we may demonstrate that it is easy for us to constitute a stable republican government...."[33] He was dead by November 15 of that year. A political contemporary remarked, "There is no doubt that many Puerto Ricans considered Muñoz Rivera a martyr, and that his death greatly strengthened sentiment in favor of the Jones bill...."[34]

## POVERTY AND ELECTORAL ARRANGEMENTS

A new political era was about to begin in Puerto Rico. The great leaders were dead—not only autonomist Muñoz Rivera, but independentist De Diego, who died in 1918, and statehooder Barbosa, dead in 1921. The political parties in this new era were interested in little more than filling offices and did so by making electoral arrangements as well as by rigging elections and buying votes.[35] Santiago Iglesias, labor crusader and head of the Socialist Party, seemed at first to be charismatic and principled,[36] but by 1924 he, too, would be playing the political game of maneuvers and alliances. By the 1930s an unholy coalition of Republicans and Socialists controlled the Insular government.

During this period the platforms of the Puerto Rican parties continued to ask for increased self-government and all took a stand on the political status of the island. Indeed, the island parties debated questions over which they had no power rather than address the fact that the Puerto Rican people were suffering from the effects of a great economic depression.[37]

Actually, the island was suffering economically even before the 1929 Depression. Puerto Rican trade was declining in the 1920s—20 percent between 1921 and 1931.[38] And the 1928 hurricane of San Felipe destroyed all but ten percent of the coffee production that was slowly being replanted.[39] The worst hurricane of the century, it killed 300 islanders and destroyed 50 million dollars worth of property, a value four times the amount spent to run the island's government for the year.

> Shattered by the San Felipe hurricane of 1928, the island was still struggling to recover from widespread devastation when the Depression struck. By December, 1929, thirty-six percent of the male population of working age were unemployed and over sixty percent had been out of work at least part of the year.[40]

The New York Herald Tribune of December 8, 1929, carried Puerto Rican Governor Theodore Roosevelt, Jr.'s personal account of the island's poverty and suffering:

> I write not of what I have heard or read, but what I have seen with my own eyes.
> I have seen mothers carrying babies who were little skeletons.
> I have watched in a classroom, thin, pallid boys and girls trying to spur their brain to action when their bodies were underfed.
> I have seen them trying to study on only one scanty meal a day, of a few beans and some rice.
> On the roads time and again I have passèd pathetic little groups carrying home-made coffins.
> I have looked into the kitchens of houses where a handful of beans and a few plantains were the fare for the whole family...
> Riding through the hills, I have stopped at farm after farm where lean, underfed women and sickly men repeated time and time again the same story—little food and no opportunity to get more. From these hills the people have streamed into the coastal towns, increasing the already severe unemployment situation there....
> Sixty percent of the children of the entire island are undernourished. Many are literally slowly starving.
> Of the 710 boys and girls in one public school in San Juan, 223 come to school each day without breakfast—278 have no lunch.[41]

A report by the Brookings Institution revealed that most of the people of the island lived in shacks without plumbing or lights and with at least two and as many as five persons to a room, and that poverty and malnutrition made the major causes of death by disease diarrhea and enteritis (21.8 percent) and tuberculosis (12.1 percent).[42] At this time, the island was still primarily rural. Sixty-seven percent of the population depended upon Puerto Rico's agricultural economy.[43] By 1933, 65 percent of the Puerto Rican work force was unemployed,[44] and Puerto Rico in the mid-1930s "was a scene of almost unrelieved misery."[45] The suffering of this period was exacerbated by a continual increase in population—21 percent between 1931 and 1935.[46] By 1940 the Puerto Rican population was nearly two million.

During this time Puerto Rican politicians offered no promise of relief. They were merely interested in getting into office.[47] As already suggested, their view was statewide. They debated "ultimate questions" of status and political reform, issues over which they had no control anyway. Although the status of Puerto Rico was the source of its powerlessness, in many ways Daniel Boorstin is right. The status issue became a prison for Puerto Rican thinkers.[48]

Elections were meaningless. Parties debated the status issue and offered no program for economic relief. Political identification meant little as politicians casually switched from one party to another,[49] and masses of Puerto Ricans sold their votes for a pair of shoes or a five-dollar bill.[50] In addition, many of the insular politicians were "sugar men," bought off by the absentee interest on the one-crop island. As early as 1910, 11 of the 35 members of the Puerto Rican House of Representatives were sugar men;[51] and a decade later, the leaders of the island's major parties, the Union Party and the Republican Party, were linked to sugar interests— Antonio Barceló "as a brother-in-law of the vice president and general manager of the Fajardo Sugar Company and Tous Soto (Republican) as a corporation lawyer, later attorney for the South Porto Rico Sugar Company."[52]

By the 1930s, "most of the best land was given over to cane and seventy percent of the island's income from exports was derived from sugar and its products."[53] Powerful North American-owned sugar became the perfect proof that there was a colonial system. The Depression hurried the Puerto Rican sugar workers' realization of their dependency on the powerful sugar industry.

There were sugar strikes throughout 1933, the largest in Fajardo. If effectiveness is measured by provoked response, they were effective. A Citizens' Committee for the Preservation of Law and Order was being planned while the fear of anarchy caused some concern about the island's next governor.

Jorge Bird Arias, then general manager and vice president of the

Fajardo Sugar Company, wired Secretary of War Stern that "existing conditions both economic and political demand... an exceptionally good, strong and capable man," while Col. James Beverley, a Texas sugar corporation lawyer and former governor of Puerto Rico, mentioned Winship in a letter to General Cox (January 1, 1934), which stated "I strongly favor an ex-Army officer for the next Governor."[54]

## THE NATIONALISTS

Meanwhile, the Nationalist Party, at this time over ten years old, was trying to tap the residue of anti-American resentment. Initially, the Nationalist Party was just another political party. In 1920 two Unionists, José Alegria and José Coll y Cuchi, formed the Nationalist Association. Two years later, when the Union Party formally favored a commonwealth status, the Nationalists became a party; and at its official assembly in Rio Piedras, Coll y Cuchi was named President. Originally the Nationalist Party sought independence by organizing rallies and lectures and by participating in elections. Their rallies and lectures were open, non-violent, and usually had the flavor of a membership made up mostly of professionals and intellectuals.

The Nationalists entered partial slates in the elections of 1924 and 1928 and did very poorly. In 1929, in the major realignment of the Puerto Rican parties, many moderate Nationalists left their party to join the Liberals. According to some historians, "Their departure left the Nationalist Part in the hands of a more radical group...."[55] On May 11, 1930, Pedro Albizu Campos, vice president of the Nationalist Party since 1925, was elected president; and the Nationalist Party was to become "no more than the shadow cast by Albizu Campos."[56]

On November 8, 1932, the Nationalists participated for the third and last time in island elections. The party polled 5,275 votes out of 383,722 votes cast. Pedro Albizu Campos, who ran for the office of senator at large, polled 11,882 votes (3 percent). According to Lovenjo Peniero Rivera, former secretary of the Nationalists, by 1933 there were close to 20,000 "members and active sympathizers."[57]

The Nationalist Party, which had once organized elitist meetings now began to organize mass rallies. Parades, not lectures, would be used to evoke a desire for independence. Mass demonstrations, not votes, would be used to measure the strength of the independence sentiment. In December 1935 the decision was formalized when the party convention voted not to participate further in "colonial elections." The Nationalist Party became the Nationalist Movement. Its "fiery leader,"[58] Pedro Albizu Campos, had the charisma to inspire his following to sacrifice and suffering.[59] According to Juan Antonio Corretjer, fellow party member and one of Alibizu's most intimate friends, "Albizu came forward as the movement's brilliant and courageous leader at a moment when the influx of the people into the independence movement required precisely such brilliant and courageous leadership."[60] An acquaintance of Albizu's described him as "gifted in his ability to foretell the past and to look back at the future,"[61] and a 1936 article described the group as "reactionary in every sense except the fierce idealism that inspires its demands."[62]

The Nationalist rhetoric lauded the Spanish tradition. For them, Catholicism was an important symbol of Puerto Rican identity. For example, in 1936, Albizu referred to the Americanization of the island as the "foolish arrogance to pretend to guide spiritually a nation whose souls had been created in pure Christianity."[63] And in his stand against the United States birth control program, he said:

> A stupid assault has been made against our Christian social order in a brutal attempt to dissolve our family structure and destroy the morality of a chivalrous race by forcing through governmental agencies the diffusion of practices of prostitution under the misleading guise of birth contol.[64]

However, to see the exaggerated pride in Puerto Rico's Spanish heritage as merely a lauding of the past, is to miss its full significance. It was also an answer to as well as protection against the clumsy and insensitive program of Americanization.

Generations of Puerto Ricans could not even read because all subjects in the public schools were taught in English;[65] the United States was deciding unilaterally to abandon the old Puerto Rican national flag;[66] and the island's very name was Anglicized and spelled incorrectly (Porto Rico) for the non-Spanish-speakers' benefit (until 1932).

The Nationalists hoped to provoke police action, not only to bring publicity to their cause, but to eventually force the U.S. courts to decide on the question of the legality of the U.S. presence in Puerto Rico.[67] Albizu argued that Puerto Rico was a sovereign island dating from the Spanish Royal Decree of 1897 granting Puerto Rico an autonomous government. The Treaty of Paris imposed on Spain, he believed, was null and void.[68]

Nationalists clashed with police throughout the Depression years. It seems unclear whether the first incident was formally planned; nevertheless, it was highly publicized. Near the University of Puerto Rico in Rio Piedras, on October 24, 1935, a car filled with Nationalists, purportedly going to a protest meeting at the university, was stopped by the police. The incident ended in a gun battle in which five were killed. Albizu's wife, the former Laura Meneses, gave an excellent account of the Nationalist version of the incident.[69] It appeared in a letter she hoped would be used in the class report for her husband's twenty-fifth Harvard reunion in 1941.*

The Rio Piedras incident was just the beginning. On February 23, two Nationalists, Beauchamp and Rosade, who had been close friends of the murdered five, shot Police Col. Francis E. Riggs. While in police custody and within an hour after this incident, the two Nationalists were shot to death at police headquarters. The incident resulted in the arrest and conviction of Pedro Albizu Campos and seven other Nationalist leaders.[70] They were indicted not for murder but for sedition, illegal recruiting of soldiers, and conspiracy to incite rebellion; and served over half their ten-year prison sentences in the federal penitentiary in Atlanta, Georgia. Albizu's hope that the trial would force a decision as to the legality of the American presence on the island was never realized.

The incarceration of the Nationalist leadership did not prevent more clashes or, as the party referred to them, uprisings. The pattern became, with the dramatic exception of the Ponce Massacre, assassination attempts. Three are well-known.

At a rally in Mayagüez, a Nationalist youth attempted to assassinate Santiago Iglesias, who was seeking reelection as the resident commissioner. A year later, June 1937, two Nationalists tried to kill Federal Judge Robert A. Cooper, the presiding judge in the Albizu conviction. And then in July of the following year, during a parade to celebrate the fortieth anniversary of the United States' landings on Puerto Rico, Nationalists tried to assassinate Governor Blanton Winship. A Puerto Rican bodyguard and a Puerto Rican national guardsman were both killed, and nine Nationalists were indicted for murder.

The most dramatic confrontation between Nationalists and police was the "needlessly brutal"[71] Ponce Massacre. The event began routinely. On Sunday, March 21, 1937, a Nationalist parade went on as scheduled, although the permit for it had been revoked at the last minute.[72] Fifty to seventy marchers as well as scores of onlookers were trapped between 17 or 18 police in front of them and 15 police behind. No one knows who fired the first shot.[73] There were about ten minutes of cross-fire in which the police shot at the onlookers as well as at the Nationalist marchers. By the end, 20 were dead and over 100 wounded.[74]

## NEW DEAL

During the 1930s unemployment, poverty, and assassination attempts charged the atmosphere of this one-crop colony. Washington's reaction was an inadequate New Deal. From 1933 to 1935 the general

---

*See Appendix C for Laura Meneses Campos's account of the incident.

aim of the New Deal was relief. Then in May 1935 the Puerto Rican Reconstruction Administration (PRRA) was established. Since the Division of Territories had been moved from the War Department into the Department of the Interior, the PRRA had come under the general aegis of Interior Secretary Harold Ickes. Dr. Ernest Gruening was the "overzealous administrator" for the PRRA.[75]

The original impulse and inspiration for a complete change and a long-range Puerto Rican economic project came in March 1934. At a round-table discussion of Puerto Rican and U.S. officials, Carlos Chardón, chancellor of the University of Puerto Rico, suggested basic economic changes for the island. The Puerto Rican Policy Commission then submitted the Chardón Plan to the Roosevelt administration in June;[76] the same month President Roosevelt created the Interdepartmental Committee on Puerto Rico to analyze the plan and evaluate the situation.

Even at this formative stage, the idea of a New Deal was very unpopular on the island. The rich landowners and political conservatives were unhappy with what they thought were forces of disruptive change. According to Hanson, they resented the New Deal and opposed social and economic changes under which their own powers were threatened.[77]

The direction of the Chardón Plan was approved of in principle by the president of the United States in a speech, the translation of which was read by Muñoz Marin and broadcast throughout the island. But it was the basic direction of the Chardón Plan that was so distasteful to the more conservative Puerto Rican leaders. Basically they disliked it because the plan called for some redistribution of land, public ownership, and governmental control of the sugar industry.

Second, Chardón's political affiliations ensured opposition. He was identified with the Liberal Party, and there were rumors that he would be appointed regional director of the PRRA. It is not surprising, therefore, that there was strong opposition to the Chardón Plan from the coalition of Republicans and Socialists. Since the coalition controlled both the Insular House (30 of 39 seats) and Senate (14 of 19 seats), they believed that they were entitled to run the aid program, not the Liberals.[78]

The coalition opposed the plan on ideological grounds as well as on political grounds since they tended to ally with the more conservative economic elements. According to Wells, "the Coalition majority in the Legislature worked hand-in-glove with the sugar interests and the Puerto Rican Chamber of Commerce to obstruct the program at every turn."[79] Thus economic interest, ideological commitment, and party affiliation created an opposition to the New Deal even before the program began.

While the Puerto Rican conservatives thought the New Deal was too radical, many Puerto Rican reformers found it too conservative. As a program it was certainly slow in starting. The Interdepartmental Committee created by Roosevelt did not report its findings for almost a year, and when it did, it had cut the Puerto Rican New Deal drastically. The Committee insisted not only that no Puerto Rican agency should be created but that the estimated expenditure of $100 million should be reduced to $40 million.[80] And even "by the end of 1938 the total expenditures for five years of New Deal operations amounted to [only] $57 million."[81]

Slow to get started, narrower in concept, and smaller in conception, the Puerto Rican New Deal was more conservative than the Chardón Plan. Land reform, public ownership, and basic changes in the sugar industry were questioned, reduced, or eliminated by the Interdepartmental Committee. What is more, the economic program that the plan retained of implementing the 500 Acre Law and creating government-operated sugar centrales (central units for processing sugar cane) was drastically slowed by court litigations and conservative political attacks.[82] The 500 Acre Law would be ready for implementation by the time Luis Muñoz Marin and the Popular Democratic Party (PDP) came to power during the next decade. However, in the 1930s "legal and financial snags delayed the start and limited the scope of the reconstruction effort."[83]

Attacked by the conservatives for being too radical and the reformers for being too slow, the Puerto Rican New Deal unwisely established political ties with Governor Winship. Actually, Dr. Ernest Gruening began by cooperating with a leader of the Liberal Party, Luis Muñoz Marin, but the working relationship did not work long.[84] The formal break was caused by the Nationalists' assassination of Police Chief Riggs.

On February 23, 1925, when the two Nationalists who shot Police Col. Francis E. Riggs were themselves shot to death at police headquarters,

> Muñoz Marin was in Washington at the time, and Dr. Gruening asked him to make a public statement condemning the Riggs assassination in order to show that the Puerto Ricans as a whole were not behind it. Muñoz refused to make such a statement on the grounds that he would also have to condemn the lynching of the two Nationalists, and such condemnation would, in effect, be an attack on the federal government. He did not believe that any purpose could at the time be served by attacking Washington. Gruening accused him of putting his own political destiny ahead of his people's welfare. Muñoz is reported to have answered that his personal destiny *was* that of his people. Quite probably Gruening regarded the answer as arrogant and egotistical. At any rate, there was a violent quarrel.[85]

Soon after Gruening's break with Muñoz Marin, the New Deal Administration broke with the Liberal Party. During the summer of 1936, Gruening purged the PRRA of employees "who had been found, on investigation, to be engaging in political activity."[86] He was really purging the agency of Liberals, and as will be shown in the next chapter, of independentists. Gruening then set up relations with Governor Winship and "friends,"[87] and thus began cooperating with the unpopular American governor.[88]

Some authorities also suggest administrative reasons why the Puerto Rican New Deal failed. Because the basic decisions were made in the United States, planning on the island seemed to be no more than a "sterile intellectual exercise" that "failed for want of execution."[89] According to Wells, the New Deal failed because there were so many "confused and contradictory directives";[90] and according to Hanson because U.S. arrogance seemed to ensure its failure. The PRRA, Hanson says, "was dominated by a corp of eager young lawyers, shipped down by Washington.... They were crusaders for social welfare, but nevertheless they were ignorant of the Puerto Rican whose welfare they had set out to improve. The continental lawyers were everywhere; they mixed into every operation, large or small; they altered policies and contracts at will; they overrode high Puerto Rican officials again and again."[91]

> [The PRRA programs] included a low-cost housing and slum-clearance program, the development of an island-wide hydroelectric system, the establishment of rural resettlement communities and demonstration farms, a reorganization of coffee and fruit production, an experience in government ownership and cooperative control of a sugar plantation and factory (central), the establishment of a government-owned cement plant, and the development of a program of planning and research. But, with the exception of the hydroelectric system and the cement plant, these projects failed to produce the results intended, and by 1939 the PRRA was all but defunct.[92]

## TYDINGS

From Washington came an independence bill, criticized because of its history and design, and all but ignored by the Puerto Rican parties. In March 1936, following the Riggs assassination, Ernest Gruening and Senator Millard E. Tydings quietly discussed the idea of an independence bill for Puerto Rico. For Tydings, according to the *New York Times*, "The recent killing of Colonel Francis E. Riggs, American Chief of Police, who was shot down by two terrorists while unarmed, was a factor in deciding that the time had come for decisive action."[93]

Tydings had been Riggs's Maryland neighbor and friend, and it was Tydings who had induced Riggs to take the Puerto Rican police post.[94] It is for this reason that some called the Tydings Independence Bill "the act of an angry man."[95]

"In offering his bill to the Senate, Mr. Tydings charged that Puerto

Rican elections were largely fraudulent, recalled the assassination of Col. Riggs, and added that 'the facts must lead us strongly to believe that the American system is not functioning properly in Puerto Rico.' "[96] His bill for independence called for a referendum to be held in November 1937 on the question: "Shall the People of Puerto Rico be sovereign and independent?" If a majority voted yes, a constitutional convention would be convened and its work presented to the U.S. president for approval, after which Puerto Ricans would vote on the document. The most debated substantive issue of the bill was the provision for a four-year transition period, in which the United States would gradually withdraw her "grants and benefits."

The Tydings Bill might have had a very different history had it gone through usual channels before being drafted. But similar to President Ford's 1977 statehood proposal, described in Chapter 7, the Tydings Independence Bill was a complete surprise to American and Puerto Rican officials. "Apparently, every effort was made to draft the bill quietly, and even administrative officials closely in touch with Puerto Rican affairs had not seen the measure until Mr. Tydings introduced it."[97] This had two effects: it caused doubts about the motivation and wisdom of the policy and it was interpreted as an affront to Puerto Ricans.

The wisdom of granting independence within only a four-year span was criticized by *The Nation* as a "Hobson's choice between domination by American absentee interests and certain economic catastrophe."[98] (The *New York Times* called it an "obnoxious choice.")[99] The bill was particularly scrutinized because there was "no impartial investigation of conditions on the island and its relation with America, no open consideration of the grounds of policy."[100] In addition, because of the bill's abnormal route and the fact of authorship, the motivation for the act was also questioned. "Some called it an act of vindictiveness,"[101] or "Tydings' punishment for Riggs' assassination,"[102] and it was referred to by *Business Week* as "window trimming for the coming Pan American conference."[103] The Tydings Bill was explained in terms of domestic interests,[104] and was excused because its plebiscite would "give the United States a fresh mandate to deal firmly with a terroristic minority (Nationalists) without being accused of being an imperialist oppressor by the rest of Latin America."[105]

If Americans were surprised, Puerto Ricans were shocked when the Tydings Bill was presented. Congressional hearings had not even been held on the independence issue as they had on the issue of Puerto Rican statehood during May and June, the year before.[106] And "Tydings made no attempt to enlist the counsel or support of the Puerto Rican leaders."[107] The political leaders were insulted;[108] the resident commissioner, Santiago Iglesias of the Socialists, thought that "common courtesy would have dictated that Puerto Rico be informed of the proposal before its presentation," and Republican Bolivar Pagán was "affronted by the attitude of superiority displayed by the administration and Congress."[109]

While the leadership of the Nationalist Party was serving time in an Atlanta penitentiary, the Puerto Rican parties played down the importance of the Tydings Independence Bill. By the November election, 1936, the Socialist Republican coalition began renewing its demand for statehood and the Liberal Party, which, traditionally had been for independence, split. Liberal Party leader Antonio Barceló and Luis Muñoz Marín divided over whether to participate in the election; Muñoz's position lost out, and eventually Muñoz was expelled from the party. A group of pro-independence Liberals left the party with him and formed Acción Social Independentista. Chapter 4 offers a fuller account of these events which led, in 1938, to the creation of the Popular Democratic Party (PDP).

## POPULAR DEMOCRATIC PARTY

Muñoz Marín conducted a grassroots campaign in which he promised specific economic changes. By July 1940, Muñoz could boast, "During the last two years I have been constantly in contact with my people. I have spoken personally with almost half a million of them."[110] His campaigning paid off. In the November election the new party received 38 percent of the total vote, control of the Insular Senate, and near control of the House.

While the new party's grassroots technique accounts for at least part of the victory, the dramatic lack of opposition offers an additional explanation for Muñoz's electoral success. It was the end of an era; old political leaders were dead, and parties were reshuffling.

By 1938 the strong party leaders were dead or dying. Antonio Barceló of the Liberals died in 1938; Santiago Iglesias of the Socialists died in 1939, and by 1940 Martinez Nadal of the Republican Union Party was in declining health. What is more, two years after the Liberal split of 1936, the other parties split and formed new sets of coalitions. Muñoz's Popular Party, therefore, was running against two new coalitions: the combination of the Republican Union Party of Martinez Nadal and the Socialist Party of Bolivar Pagán, and a coalition made up of dissident groups, proclaiming statehood as a fundamental goal.[111] Thus the election of 1940 pitted the vigorous party of Muñoz Marín against new coalitions and only the memory of old leaders.

In addition, the 1936 election law helped Muñoz's new and poorer party by inhibiting vote-selling. The law prevented the fraud of multiple-voting by establishing one polling place for 150 persons.[112] On election day, voters would assemble and, under a system called *colegio cerrado*, were "herded" into their assigned rooms at 1:00 P.M. Doors were locked, and voters were called, one by one, in alphabetical order to enter the booths in full view of their neighbors to cast their secret ballots. Says Anderson, "only a tolerant and gregarious people would tolerate the physical discomfort and inconvenience involved."[113]

The timing of the new party was perfect. Muñoz had a cooperative governor with whom he could work and a 500 Acre Law that was ready for enforcement. Both were essential.

In 1941, Rexford G. Tugwell was appointed Governor of Puerto Rico, not as a political favor but because of his political commitment. Tugwell, in fact, seemed so committed to economic change that in conservative circles he was known as "Rex the Red."[114] Governor Tugwell was Muñoz's "first real ally."[115]

> In his inaugural address Tugwell had expressed his basic philosophy as governor, which differed in no respect from that of Muñoz the political leader, in the following words: "In bettering public health, in educating children, in bringing power, light, sanitation into people's homes, in building more homes for the under-privileged, in providing all kinds of needed work, in the conservation of soil and other resources, in the use and tenure of the land, in the search for higher wages and greater social security—in all these we shall find work enough crowding in upon us in the years to come."[116]

Enforcement of the 500 Acre Law had been the major theme in the *Popular* campaign, and the most important of Muñoz's campaign pledges. The law had never been enforced since its passage by the U.S. Congress in 1900, as a part of the Foraker Act. During the New Deal the law was held up in litigation;[117] it took insular legislation and a test case that went up through the courts, reaching the U.S. Supreme Court, to prepare it for implementation. With constitutionality decided, the groundwork was laid for creating a land authority, and implementation legislation was signed by Governor Guy J. Swope on April 12, 1941. Muñoz was able to fulfill his campaign pledge,

> to put an end to the existing corporative *latifundia* in this island...provide the means for the *agregados* (squatters) and slum dwellers to acquire parcels of land on which to build their homes.[118]

Muñoz had begun his rise to power during World War II. Ironically the misery and danger of wartime brought political prosperity to the *Populares* and, in still another way, Muñoz was the beneficiary of his own timing.

World War II made the poor island poorer.[119] Puerto Rico had no war industries and almost half of her population was unemployed. What is more, the island had sunk to one-third her prewar shipping rate, "the importation of foods was drastically curtailed, and prices rose sharply."[120]

Because of the decline in trade, the needlework industry collapsed, the citrus fruit industry was seriously impaired, and all but the newly established rum industry suffered.[121] An unemployed, discontented "stricken island" is a serious threat during wartime. This is especially true if the island is strategically located, and Puerto Rico was considered with strategic interest, being central in the Caribbean, and central in the arc from Florida to Trinidad (see Map 2). When Germany threatened the Panama Canal, Puerto Rican bases were essential.[122]

For Puerto Rico, the war years were basically a combination of long bread lines and air raid alarms. Since "military men knew that a large unemployed, discontented civilian population is a serious military problem in a location of strategic importance,"[123] there was generally more U.S. support for Muñoz and his campaign pledge of economic innovation and change, and support for "Rex the Red," whose very appointment can probably be explained by the U.S. fear of growing Puerto Rican discontent.

Muñoz's Popular Democratic Party was overwhelmingly victorious in the 1944 election. Of the 581,978 votes cast, the PDP got 383,280 and won 17 of the 19 Senate seats and had 37 of the 39 representatives in the lower house. Muñoz seemed to be striking the right chord with his constituents.

During the election Muñoz tabled the status question, focusing instead of economic issues. He did so, he told me in an interview (January 1978), because the Puerto Ricans' main concern was with their economic situation. But many political activists refused to table independence.

With Muñoz's emphasis on Puerto Rico's economic well-being, the liberty in the PDP slogan "bread, land, liberty" seemed more and more to be defined as "liberty from hunger." But the new party, the PDP, had drawn to its fold independentists for whom the "liberty" in the party slogan, meant political independence. This was, in fact, according to Maldonado Denis, "a generation of men believing in independence."[124]

A variety of sources suggest that independence was the preference of the majority of the PDP activists. Speaker of the House Francisco M. Susoni estimated in October 1946 that at least 80 percent of the Popular Party was for independence ("*es partidario de la independencia*").[125] The year before, 22 of the 39 Insular House members and 11 of the 19 Puerto Rican senators had voted to endorse another of Tyding's independence bills, S. 277,[126] and according to Laura Menses de Campos, during this period, 66 of the 77 mayors of Puerto Rico sent a cable to the U.S. Senate "endorsing a bill in favor of independence" and declaring themselves "in accord with the sentiment of the majority of Puerto Rican people."[127]

## MAP 2
## Strategic Location of Puerto Rico

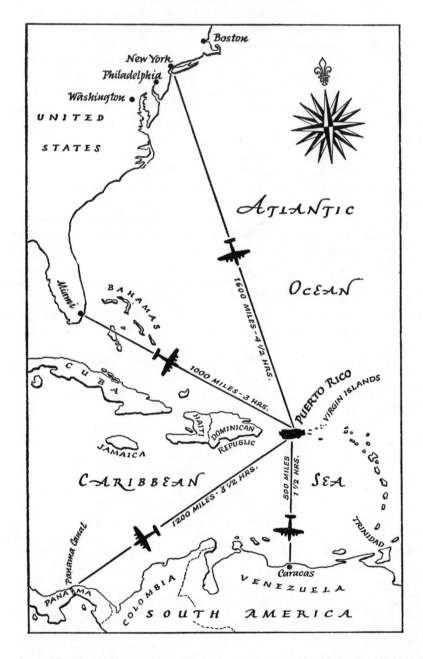

*Source:* Earl Parker Hanson, *Puerto Rico: Land of Wonders* (New York: Alfred A. Knopf, 1960).

While Muñoz got overwhelming electoral support by tabling the status question and focusing on economic issues, political activists would not postpone the independence question.

## THE INDEPENDENCE PARTY

In August 1943, a small Mayagüez group, *La Agrupación Patriótica Puertorriqueño*, called the first meeting of the *Congreso Pro Independencia* (CPI).[128] Over 1,800 independence-minded delegates, most of them from the Popular Democratic Party, attended. Luis Muñoz Marin sent a message of felicitation.

The CPI's stated aim was to gain Puerto Rican independence by "all legal and peaceful means."[129] The group called its Washington delegation a "diplomatic mission," and the CPI emphasized that it was not a political party but a patriotic organization.

More than a year after the original San Juan meeting, Gilberto Concepción de Gracia was elected president of the Congress for Independence. Concepción had been a member of the Nationalist Party during the 1930s and had helped prepare the legal defense for Albizu Campos and the Nationalist leaders during the trials of 1936 and 1937.

The first CPI meeting was prompted by another one of Tydings's independence bills. Senator Millard Tydings had become chair of the Senate Committee on Territories and Insular Affairs. During the 1940s he introduced several more bills designed to lead to Puerto Rican independence; otherwise, he thought, "Puerto Rico will remain a perpetually unsolved problem always dangling before Congress."[130] The nonpartisan CPI was forced to become an independence party in just three years because the independentist reaction to each of the Tydings bills differed from the official Popular Democratic Party line. The Elective Governor Act of October 1943, introduced by Senator Tydings, created a rift between Muñoz's party and the CPI; in January, 1945, another Tydings independence bill widened the rift; and in May, the Tydings-Piñero bill made the chasm uncrossable.

The Elective Governor Act (S. 1407), introduced by Tydings on October 1, 1943, called for a "no more basic change" than a popularly elected governor. While Muñoz Marin supported this proposed reform, the CPI "condemned it as a 'smokescreen' to cover a colonial government."[131]

The CPI and Muñoz were again on opposite sides when, two years later, Senator Tydings introduced another independence bill (S. 277). The terms of independence were less harsh; the bill provided a 21-year transition period with special economic adjustments.[132] Hearings were held, and Tydings also requested that the U.S. Tariff Commission provide him with supplementary information. In March 1946 the commission reported on "The Economy of Puerto Rico with Special Reference to the Implications of Independence and Other Proposals to Change Its Political Status" in what was referred to as "The Dorffman Report."

Muñoz supported the Tydings-Piñero Substitute Bill (S. 1002) introduced in May. Both bills, S. 277 and S. 1002, included the alternative status of "dominion" or "commonwealth." This inclusion made the break between Muñoz and the CPI irreversable.

At first, the break was personal; a Concepción-Muñoz polemic made front-page news.[133] Concepción criticized not the Popular Party but Muñoz for being "colonial"[134] and authoritarian.[135] Muñoz countered by threatening the Populares who were still in the CPI with expulsion. Because Muñoz took the criticisms of himself as criticisms of his party,[136] by February 1946 he was accusing the CPI of sabotaging the PDP program.[137]

Thus, at a time when the majority of Popular Democratic Party political leaders were for independence, Muñoz seemed to cut the spirit and support for independence by declaring that it was incompatible to belong to the Independence Congress and the Popular Party simultaneously. His declaration of incompatibility was ratified by the PDP's Central Committee (the Arecibo Resolution), and independentista Populares were expelled.

By October 20, 1946, the expelled Populares had created a new party for independence. A provisional central directive board was set up, and just a few months after it had started its registration drive the newly organized Independence Party had qualified in enough municipal districts to be assured a place on the 1948 ballot.

## THE 1948 ELECTION

The 1948 election was noteworthy, not only because it was the first time in nearly two decades that a duly registered Independence Party competed for votes. It was an important election because Puerto Ricans were electing their own governor.

The history of the Elective Governor Act illustrates how Puerto Rican policy making seemed to fall between the cracks of the United States' separate institutional powers, and how neglectful and arbitrary was constitutional rule.[138] The bill started off in the executive branch. In October 1943 the Committee on the Revision of the Organic Act, chaired by Secretary of the Interior Harold Ickes, originally submitted to the Senate, in draft form (S. 1407), the bill that was to provide for an elected governor.[139] Tydings's watered-down version of the bill, providing only for an elective governor, was approved by the Senate in February 1944.

When the bill went to the House for approval it was held up by C.

Jasper Bell of Missouri who headed a special Puerto Rican investigating committee. Bell was not sympathetic to the cause of Puerto Rican reform. In fact, the Bell Committee did not issue its report until May 1945, and it was an indictment of the PDP program rather than a report.

Anxious for Puerto Rico to have a native governor, President Harry Truman appointed Jesus T. Piñero governor of Puerto Rico on July 21, 1946. Luckily for Puerto Rico, the next year the House Subcommittee on Territories and Insular Affairs had a new chair, Fred Crawford of Michigan. An elective governor bill (HR 3309) was again introduced in the House. It passed, and on August 4, 1947, with the successful passage of the Senate companion bill and the signature of the president, the bill became law. "The people of this congested island," the *New York Times* reported, "are excited and pleased as they prepare to go to the polls this fall to elect their own Governor for the first time."[140]

The 1948 election year was a stormy one and also included promises made by President Truman that he had no power to keep. In the beginning of the year, the FBI recovered 10,000 rounds of small arms ammunition that had been stolen from Borinquen Field. Speculation linked it to Nationalist activities.[141]

The next month, President Truman raised the expectations of Puerto Ricans by delivering a message on civil rights in which he said, "The present political status of our territories and possessions impairs the enjoyment of civil rights by their residents.... The people of Puerto Rico should be allowed to choose their form of government and their ultimate status with respect to the United States."[142] Less than two weeks later he visited the island and "President Truman told the people of Puerto Rico, who accorded him a hearty boisterous welcome... that they should have the right to determine their own destiny."[143]

> I have said to Congress several times, and I repeat it here, that Puerto Rican people should have the right to determine for themselves Puerto Rico's political relationship to the continental United States.[144]

The promises of the U.S. President fell between the cracks. The only action that was forthcoming was confrontations on the University of Puerto Rico campus.

The Nationalist president, Pedro Albizu Campos, had been released from the Atlanta penitentiary and was back on the island. In April he wanted to speak at the university, and Chancellor of the University Jaime Benitez refused to allow him to use the university auditorium. On April 16, about 1,000 students responded to this prohibition by invading a building, breaking up classes (attended by the remaining 7,000 students), and finally breaking into the chancellor's office. Extra police were stationed in the capitol where the legislature was in session, and police guards were strengthened at La Fortaleza, the governor's residence.

On May 5 violence again broke out at the university. Police, using tear gas, broke up a student demonstration that was being held at the university gates. According to Insular Police Chief Col. Salvador T. Roiz, the demonstration was inspired by Nationalist extremists.[145] Seven students were arrested for "unlawful assembly."[146]

Thus presidential promises and Nationalist-linked disruptions set the stage for the 1948 election. In the November election the newly formed Independence Party got 66,141 votes or 10.4 percent of the 638,687 votes cast.

Muñoz's Popular Democratic Party won the election with 392,033 votes or 61.3 percent. The next year Governor Muñoz visited Washington to request a Puerto Rican Constitution.

## COMMONWEALTH

The seeds of "commonwealth" were sown long before Muñoz's 1949 visit to Washington. Although commonwealth is described as a "novel status"[147] and "an original patttern of partial autonomy,"[148] the general concept of free state was not new at all, but had been considered as early as 1917.[149] However, the specific term commonwealth was used only a few years before Muñoz's visit, when, in 1943, Abe Fortas and Luis Muñoz Marín had served on the President's Committee on the Revision of the Organic Act.[150]

The term commonwealth itself was carefully chosen. It was probably imported from the Philippine Islands, which was formerly an unincorporated territory like Puerto Rico, but which was called a commonwealth during the decade before independence (1935–46).[151] The word, according to Friedrich, was used to emphasize the island's internal autonomy,[152] for "pride in their local culture," he said, "is the very core of the commonwealth."[153] It was used to emphasize a continued relationship with the United States,[154] with association, as a new dimension of federalism;[155] and it emphasized the fact that Puerto Rico would not be another state.[156]

The commonwealth concept was called a careful balance of federal deference to local initiative and local identification with federal goals.[157] "Not a brilliant formula conceived and brought about by a flash of genius,"[158] the carefully balanced name for commonwealth in Spanish is Estado Libre Asociado, Free Associated State.

By its opponents, commonwealth was assailed as "unrealistic," "colonial," and a "political device,"[159] but for its main defender, Muñoz Marín, it was "a new type of arrangement" and a "pioneering effort."[160] In fact, Muñoz was able to turn the interim status solution into a final solution, which he then helped to legitimize.[161]

Muñoz originally envisioned commonwealth as an interim solution through which economic stability could be reached, and after which an island plebiscite between statehood and independence would be held. Through a commonwealth arrangement, Muñoz argued in 1946, the U.S. Congress would accept a completely autonomous Puerto Rican government named "Pueblo Asociado de Puerto Rico"; and when Puerto Rico reached a certain economic level, the Puerto Rican people would choose between statehood and independence. Muñoz used as his precedent and source of inspiration Thomas Jefferson and the Northwest Ordinances: "articles of compact, forever to remain unalterable unless by common consent."[162] Such a procedure would ensure continued relations with the United States and economic assistance for Puerto Rican industrialization. These relations were essential, Muñoz argued, because "the economic problem which Puerto Rico confronts is the most grave problem, in its ramifications it affects all the others";[163] because jobs should be created for the dangerously rising population and the United States had an obligation to help;[164] and because cutting off the U.S. market for Puerto Rican produce before Puerto Rico had industrialized would strangle Puerto Rico's chance for industrialization.[165] The Popular Party Assembly of 1948 called on Congress to continue the economic and fiscal relations between Puerto Rico and the United States.[166]

Muñoz Marin, in his Fourth of July speech in 1948, urged congressional authorization for a plebiscite on status. His party called for the right of the Puerto Rican Legislature to judge when it should be held and also called for a Puerto Rican constitution.[167] The plebiscite Muñoz called for on July 4 was to have been a choice only between independence and statehood.

After the November PDP victory, however, Muñoz began to claim the 1948 election as a victory for the interim commonwealth idea. Actually, all the 1948 Popular Party platform had asked for was a Puerto Rican Constitution:[168] "No one even voiced the hope that the pending legislation would fundamentally change Puerto Rico's relationship with the United States...."[169] But in July 1950, as soon as Congress passed the law enabling Puerto Rico to write its own constitution, Muñoz began interpreting the law as the "foundation of a new political status for Puerto Rico."[170]

The Popular Party was referring to the election of 1948 not merely as an election but as a plebiscite on commonwealth, and the party was presenting commonwealth not merely as an interim solution but as a status alternative in its own right. By 1952, Muñoz was arguing that commonwealth was "a new alternative, equal in dignity although different in nature, to independence or federated statehood."[171] And at Harvard, in 1955, he said of "Operation Commonwealth" that "its growth is not toward turning into something else—Puerto Rico is not on the road to becoming a federated state of the Union, nor an isolated republic outside of the Union."[172] Its "growth could and should be...within the genius of the creative commonwealth itself."[173]

Puerto Ricans wrote and ratified a constitution (Public Law 600), and sent it to the United States Congress for approval. This autonomous act of writing their own constitution turned into another example of "rule by Congress," for the Senate changed the constitution and the Puerto Rican people had to go through the ratifying procedure a second time.

On April 22, 1952, Truman sent a message to Congress commending the Puerto Rican Constitution as "a proud document that embodies the best of our democratic heritage."[174] The House Committee on Interior and Insular Affairs gave it unanimous approval, but this time the Senate was less receptive.

In the Senate hearings Muñoz had to answer allegations that there was an island dictatorship, that independence was being planned, and that Public Law 600 had been misrepresented on the island. After lengthy debates on whether Congress could be legally bound to consult with the people of Puerto Rico on future changes in United States–Puerto Rican relations, the Senate changed parts of, and then passed, the Puerto Rican Constitution. The senators deleted Article II, Section 20, on basic human rights,[175] and Article II, Section 5, on compulsory school attendance,[176] and objected to the use of the word democracy when the United States Consitution required a "republican form of government" from each of the states.[177]

The most serious change proposed in Congress was the Johnston Amendment, providing that the Puerto Rican Constitution could not be amended without congressional approval. Senator Olin Johnston, according to Gordon Lewis, was the most energetic critic of the Puerto Rican Constitution. According to Lewis, this South Carolinian was motivated by a desire to revenge a business friend who had "crossed swords" with Muñoz's regime in San Juan.[178] Muñoz himself connected the attacks of Senator Johnston with difficulties between the Puerto Rican Insular government and the South Carolina contractor, Leonard D. Long.[179] A similar assertion was made by Representative Frank T. Bow.[180] The Johnson Amendment was deleted in conference committee, but the other Senate changes concerning human rights and school attendance were accepted. On July 3, Truman signed the new Public Law with its new number, 447, affixed to it; the Puerto Rican Constitutional Convention and the Puerto Rican people had to vote again to accept their changed Constitution.

## THE NATIONALIST UPRISING

As Muñoz and the PDP tried to legitimize commonwealth as a viable and dignified status alternative, the Nationalists responded with a terrorist campaign. On October 30, just days before the 1950 registration for the first referendum to take place on July 4, 1951, six Nationalists tried to shoot their way into La Fortaleza, the governor's residence. "Armed with pistols, rifles, and a machine gun, they sprinted for the palace entrance. Yelling 'Viva Puerto Rico libre,' one Nationalist got off a wild submachine-gun burst. From the arcade, from parapets, from rooftops, guards poured fire down on the attackers."[181] At the same time, there were uprisings in Penuelas, Ponce, Arecibo, Naranjito, and gun battles in barrio obrero in San Juan. By nightfall the Nationalists had seized and controlled Jayuya, 50 miles southwest of San Juan, and the neighboring town of Utuado.[182] While "fighter planes strafed the rebels," it took troops "armed with machine guns, bazookas and tanks" to recapture the towns the next morning.[183]

They were the Nationalists' "bloodiest demonstrations" and nearly 2,000 rebels were involved.[184] "A police recount of casualties said 32 persons had been killed and 40 wounded in the rebellion. The dead included 21 Nationalists, nine policemen, and one national guards-man."[185] Hundreds of independentists were taken into police custody.

The following day, two Puerto Rican residents of New York tried to kill President Truman at Blair House.[186] They succeeded in killing one policeman and seriously wounding two others; one assassin died and one was wounded.[187]

The dead assassin was identified from a Social Security card as Griselio Torresola.[188] Two cryptic letters linking him with Albizu Campos and suggesting a conspiracy were also found on his person. One of the dead man's letters said:

My Dear Griselio—If for any reason it should be necessary for you to assume the leadership of the movement in the United States, you will do so without hesitation of any kind. We are leaving you to your high sense of patriotism and sane judgment in everything regarding this matter. Cordially yours, Pedro Albizu Campos.[189]

The wounded assassin, however, denied the connection. He "denied that Pedro Albizu Campos, leader of the Puerto Rican Nationalist extremists, had anything to do with his determination to kill the President. He and Torresola, he said, acted because his native countrymen had been 'enslaved' and the United States had made 'tools' of Puerto Rican politicians."[190]

On the island, after a two-day siege of his house, Albizu was taken into custody and charged on six counts, which included subversive activities, attack with intent to kill, and four violations of a law requiring registration of firearms.[191] He was convicted and incarcerated again.

Meanwhile, the United States used this new Constitution to argue that she no longer be obliged to provide the United Nations with periodic reports on Puerto Rico. The Puerto Rican Constitution, it was argued in

November 1953, removed Puerto Rico from the non-self-governing category. Henry Cabot Lodge asserted, "Congress has agreed that Puerto Rico shall have...freedom from control or interference...in respect to internal government,"[192] and, after all, Puerto Ricans were free to choose "by an overwhelming ratifying vote" to associate themselves with their larger neighbor.[193] Puerto Rican Resident Commissioner Fernos Isern also helped defend Public Law 600 in the United Nations as a basic status change and Lodge promised the United Nations:

> I am authorized to say in behalf of the President that, if at any time, the Legislative Assembly of Puerto Rico adopts a resolution in favor of more complete, or even absolute independence, he will immediately thereafter recommend to Congress that such independence be granted.[194]

A few months later the Nationalists responded with violence.

On March 1, 1954, while the members of the U.S. House of Representatives "stood for a vote on a routine issue four Puerto Rican Nationalists in the galleries shouted 'Viva Puerto Rico' and began to shoot into the crowded well...." Five members of Congress were wounded. Seventeen Puerto Ricans were implicated and charged with conspiracy, and 13 were found guilty.[195] Albizu, who had been pardoned because of his age, ill-health, and on condition that he refrained from subversion, applauded their "sublime heroism." Five days after the incident, the Puerto Rican government revoked his pardon, "and amid another gun battle, rearrested him in a round-up that netted forty-two other Nationalists and ten Communists."[196]

The Nationalists were not alone in their opposition to commonwealth. In the 1952 election the Independence Party won 19 percent of the vote and became the second largest party. In addition, a much lower than usual number of registered voters participated in the referendums to approve the new commonwealth Constitution. This may well have been because referendums do not attract as many voters as do regular elections. But on an island where regular elections attract as many as 80 percent of the voters, the 1951 referendum resulted in a total vote of only 506,084 out of 873,085 registered in the previous election (387,016 for and 119,169 against). In percentages, only 58 percent of the registered voters voted in 1951 and even fewer, 52 percent, participated in the 1952 referendum.

But the PDP continued to win regular elections by wide margins with strong popular participation, and Luis Muñoz Marin led his party and determined the island's direction. For 16 years Muñoz was governor while his party controlled the Insular Legislature. During this period, the island was changed irreversibly with industrialization and outmigration. Both were PDP policies, the consequences of which only now are being fully experienced.

Industrialization started with the New Deal program of running island-owned factories. By 1947 the factories were sold and policy shifted to attracting private investments to build up new industry.[197] In 1951 the industrializing program was reorganized into the Economic Development Administration called Fomento, and "Operation Bootstrap" began transforming the island.[198]

## FOMENTO

By 1961, new factories were opening at an average rate of five per week,[199] and between 1948 and 1965, there were 1,027 new manufacturing plants located on the island[200] (See Table 2). In fact, in 1960, Puerto Rican brassiere and electric shaver plants supplied one-fourth of the total number of these products used in the United States.[201]

Operation Bootstrap industrialized the agricultural island as agricultural employment declined from 36.3 percent of total employment in 1948 to 17.5 percent in 1965.[202] "For the period 1948–65 ... net income from manufacturing increased from $58 million to $449 million or from ten percent to twenty percent of the value of the product ... a measure of the importance of the Fomento promotional effort...."[203]

The PDP changed slogans as quickly as visions. As already described, Muñoz had started the Popular Democratic Party with a notion of an acre of land for each jíbaro; this he expressed with the slogan, "Bread, land, liberty" and with a campaign emphasis on implementing the 500 Acre Law. Now his party goal had become a sophisticated plan of industrial develpment; this he expressed with the slogan, "Land reform, liberty and industrial development."[204] In an interview (January 4, 1978) Muñoz explained that the island-owned industries cost so much and employed so few that attracting outside industry was economically necessary.

Fomento attracted labor-intensive industry to the island with a series of inducements. The Puerto Rican government promised to train the workers in the necessary skills at no cost to the manufacturer, and the

### TABLE 2
### Growth in Number of Puerto Rican
### Factories, 1947–64

| Year | Number |
|------|--------|
| 1947 | 18 |
| 1950 | 82 |
| 1960 | 700 |
| 1964 | 900 |

*Source:* Robert W. Anderson, *Party Politics in Puerto Rico*, p. 6.

Puerto Rican Government Development Bank lent money at fair interest rates for the machinery. In addition, the American business people had ten years' exemption from Puerto Rico's corporate profit tax, which was in any case low by mainland standards—35 percent as contrasted with the federal profit tax of 52 percent. And the Puerto Rican government constructed the buildings for the American manufacturer, who rented them for ten years and then either bought them or built new ones.[205]

Puerto Rico was being visited and studied as a model of development. Little wonder that Maldonado Denis referred to Fomento as "a flashy showcase where the miracles of free enterprise would be shown to Latin American countries."[206] Yet it is clear that island as well as mainland benefited from the showcase and bootstrap program. With each new factory new jobs were created. By 1960, Fomento factories provided 41,500 jobs;[207] by 1962, 86,000 Puerto Ricans were employed in manufacturing under government-controlled conditions;[208] and the labor force increased absolutely from 663,000 in 1948 to 769,000 in 1965.[209] The greatest change by far was in the amount of money Puerto Ricans earned. The gross national product and per capita personal income rose dramatically (see Table 3).

Unemployment, however, continued to remain high. In fact, the unemployment rate remained substantially the same between 1948 and 1965.[210] *Look Magazine* reported "unemployment has not been solved at all. At least 14 percent of the labor force is still jobless. Even Muñoz's economic advisors admit it will be a long time before factories can give jobs to many of the unemployed."[211] What the factories were actually doing was giving jobs to the already employed, the "elite of the agricultural wage laborers."[212]

Based on interviews with a sample of 1,045 factory workers, half drawn from large plants of 120 or more workers and half from plants employing 25 to 120, Reynolds and Gregory concluded that while the factory workers were formerly rural workers they were the successful ex-

**TABLE 3**
**Gross National Product and Per Capita Income**

| Year | Annual Gross National Product (in millions of dollars) | Per Capita Personal Income (in dollars) |
|---|---|---|
| 1948 | 651 | 376 |
| 1965 | 2,757 | 900 |
| 1979 | 8,939 | 2,681 |

*Source: Status of Puerto Rico. Report,* p. 54, and *Statistical Profile,* Puerto Rico Economic Development Administration, Continental Operations Branch, 1979.

agriculturists. Only 15 percent left agriculture because of unemployment or irregular employment. Two-thirds left for higher wages; and over two-thirds said they had been employed throughout the year in their last farm job, a proportion two-and-one-half times greater than for the entire agricultural labor force in 1952.[213]

United States industry had raised the Puerto Rican standard of living not by employing the unemployed but by employing at a higher wage level formerly employed rural workers. Nevertheless, considering the fact that Puerto Rico's per capita income was $121 in 1940 and $900 in 1965, the highest per capita income in Latin America, and not embarrassingly low even by stateside standards (Mississippi's per capita income was $1,500 in 1965), Puerto Rico was profiting from American business.

Of course, higher per capita income on the island helped American business on the mainland. Mainland manufacturers depend on Puerto Rico as a market for their products. More Puerto Rican money meant more purhasing power. By 1959 mainland producers were shipping food and commodities worth one million dollars to Puerto Rico annually.[214] In fact, although Puerto Rico was only sixth among the world's purchasers of American goods,[215] it was highest in per capita purchases.[216] By 1964, Puerto Rico was spending $3,066,301 per day for goods and services from the continental United States; and by 1977, "Puerto Rico's imports contributed 153,000 jobs and $3.47 billion in gross income to the mainland economy...."[217] Products made in the United States were also thought to be an important stimulus encouraging outmigration. Says Rand,

> Even in the thirties many of the basic commodities were imported from the mainland. The people began to yearn first for a radio, then for an automobile, and eventually for a TV set. After the war they began seeing new types of food, even—frozen food and so forth. Their desires were aroused; cash became more and more important to them and New York was the place to get it.[218]

For Glazer and Moynihan, U.S. products enticed, "its mass media publicized them, and its merchandising techniques spread the desire."[219]

## MIGRATION

More than just a response to advertising campaigns and flashy products, the Puerto Rican migration is part of a general migration that originated in the restlessness brought on by World War II[220] and has its counterpart on the island itself as a migration from rural to urban areas[221] (see Table 4). Between 1950 and 1960, the population of San Juan increased by 21 percent;[222] by 1960 over half the people living in San

**TABLE 4**
**Puerto Rican Population Distribution**
**(percentages)**

| Year | Urban | Rural |
|------|-------|-------|
| 1940 | 30.3 | 69.7 |
| 1950 | 40.5 | 59.5 |
| 1960 | 44.2 | 55.8 |
| 1970 | 55.8 | 41.9 |

Source: Antonio J. Gonzales, "El Desarrolo Economico y la Estructura Economica," University of Puerto Rico, 1965 (paper), p. 67; and The Population, Vol. 1, Part 53, Puerto Rico. 1970 Census of Population, U.S. Department of Commerce, Social and Economic Statistics Department, Bureau of the Census, p. 53-57.

Juan were born in rural areas and 50 percent of all the persons born in rural areas had moved out.[223]

But out-migration was seen as more than just a move from the countryside to city. The mass exodus of hundreds of thousands of people was explained in terms of the "squeeze on the island" and the "pull of the mainland." Puerto Rico had an unrelentingly high unemployment rate and a density of population that was increasing (See Table 5). In 1960, for example, for every seven Puerto Ricans who died, 32 were born.[224] And those who were making predictions were alarmed.[225]

However, most studies suggest that "it is the pull of New York [the mainland] rather than the squeeze on the island that manifestly figures most prominently in the mind the migrant."[226] The Mills, Senior, Goldsen study was based on 1,115 interviews of New York Puerto Ricans from

**TABLE 5**
**Puerto Rican Population, Annual Rate of Growth and Density**

| Year | Population | Annual Rate of Growth (percentages) | Density |
|------|-----------|------------------------------------|---------|
| 1899 | 953, 243 | — | 279 |
| 1910 | 1,118,012 | 1.54 | 327 |
| 1920 | 1,299,809 | 1.56 | 380 |
| 1930 | 1,543,013 | 1.69 | 451 |
| 1940 | 1,869,255 | 1.93 | 546 |
| 1950 | 2,210,703 | 1.69 | 646 |
| 1960 | 2,349,544 | 0.61 | 687 |
| 1965 | 2,627,960 | 2.26 | 768 |
| 1970 | 2,947,293 | 2.32 | 862 |
| 1980 | 3,634,021 | 2.12 | 1,062 |

Source: Status of Puerto Rico. Report, p. 149.

Harlem and Morrisania. They found that "Two-thirds of the group who had planned before migrating to remain permanently in New York (89% [said] )...that they had looked forward to bettering their economic position."[227]

The search for economic opportunity is a major force for migration, "the old and never-ceasing movement of people who hope to better their condition."[228] Not surprisingly, the majority of Puerto Ricans who leave the island in search of work are between the ages of 14 and 44.[229] Between 1953 and 1961, for example, there was a net outflow of 385,000 people under 35 years old; and during the decade of 1950–60, the island's population of 14-to-34-year-olds declined by 21,000.[230]

Migration in search of economic improvement both to the Puerto Rican city as well as to the mainland city was related to education. On the island, during this period, those who worked in Fomento factories were, on the whole, better educated than Puerto Rican workers in general, and those who migrated to the United States were also, on the average, better educated than the island average.[231] A rise in educational level, one economist suggests, "doubtless increases responsiveness to new economic opportunities."[232] Thus rising expectations and increased responsiveness to opportunity brought tens of thousands of Puerto Ricans to the mainland in search of jobs and a better life.

Migration jumped from an average yearly total of less than 1,000 during the 1930s to 20,000 annually between 1941 and 1950 (see Table 6). During the 1950s the average emigration rate "skyrocketed to over 40,000 per year, and hit 70,000 in 1953."[233]

In addition to these migrants seeking jobs, over 40,000 Puerto Ricans served in the armed forces during the Korean conflict. (Over 90 percent were volunteers.)[234] Thus, as Gordon Lewis suggests, "it would be difficult...to find any small town on the island that does not possess its quota of younger people with stateside experience, or of veterans of American Armed Services."[235] This increases the likelihood of migration,

**TABLE 6**
**Migration Rate of Puerto Ricans to the**
**United States, 1910–60**

| Year | Rate (per thousand population) |
|---|---|
| 1910–20 | 0.8 |
| 1920–30 | 2.6 |
| 1930–40 | 0.5 |
| 1940–50 | 8.8 |
| 1950–60 | 19.9 |

Source: *Status of Puerto Rico. Report*, p. 151.

because the decision to move is usually made in response to personal influence; there is little dependence on formal media. Face-to-face contact and letters are the most important source of information about the mainland.[236] Thus the more friends and neighbors there are with stateside experience, the more friends and neighbors who will be influenced to migrate.

The airplane with its comparative low cost, quickened and cheapened Puerto Rican migration.[237] In fact, the plane revolutionized migration (see Table 7). "The airplane sets the Puerto Rican migrants apart from all other ethnic groups that have left their homes."[238] It is not unusual, not only to have half a Puerto Rican family on the island and half of the mainland, but for them casually to plan a Christmas family reunion in either place. Movement has become a natural part of the Puerto Rican experience.[239]

Words to refer to the United States have been developed to accommodate the new experience. Since the island is part of the United States, words such as stateside, continental, and mainland were needed as part of a new vocabulary to distinguish the mainland from the island.

As will be seen in Chapter 5, what made Puerto Rican migration so unique was not only the large numbers who went to the mainland (1,391,443 Puerto Ricans were living on the mainland by 1970)[240] but the "return migration," the flow back to the island. However, for this long period of PDP rule, there was a generally consistent net out-flow of Puerto Rican migrants. Maldonado Denis is quite correct when he says, "The history of our people is also the history of... those who had to leave."[241]

## 1959

For three reasons, 1959 was a pivotal year for Puerto Rico. First, in that year Congress granted statehood to Hawaii and Alaska. "From the

**TABLE 7**
**Number of Plane Passengers Coming and Going, 1950–66**

| Year | Number of Passengers |
| --- | --- |
| 1950 | 316,736 |
| 1960 | 1,416,158 |
| 1965 | 3,060,871 |
| 1966 | 3,364,457 |

Source: Earl Parker Hanson, *Puerto Rico: Ally for Progress*, p. 81; and Bill Jones, "Air Passenger Traffic Shows 10% Gain," *San Juan Star*, March 9, 1967, p. 16.

moment of Alaska's admission to statehood, status agitation in Puerto Rico increased notably," said Hunter. Alaska and Hawaii destroyed two basic arguments against Puerto Rican statehood—the noncontiguous argument, and the Anglo-Saxon argument.[242]

Fidel Castro came to power—a second important event—in 1959. Cuba quickly became a symbol for many independentists. Said one publication:

> For the first time a Latin American nation affirms completely the qualities of sovereignty, and with absolute independence from the United States, represents in the world scene a role of responding to its own will and interests.[243]

Other independentists were not as eager to latch on to Cuba as a symbol.[244] And for many Puerto Ricans who were against independence, Cuba represented a sinister presence. Others even believed that Cuba controlled Puerto Rican independentists—a belief expressed by J. Edgar Hoover, who testified that the modern independentists

> have been propagandized and indoctrinated by Cuba, the Soviet Union and Communist China. Their leaders have travelled widely in Communist countries...they are inspired by the success of Fidel Castro in Cuba and believe they can be equally successful in Puerto Rico.[245]

And third, in 1959 the Popular Democratic Party tried to improve commonwealth. They passed a law in the Insular Legislature urging Congress to approve modifications and clarifications in Public Law 600.[246] Resident Commissioner Fernos Isern introduced the bill in Congress. But the Fernos-Murray Bill was shelved in committee, shattering, for some, the idea that commonwealth was in any important sense, "in the nature of a contract."

Thus 1959 represented a turning point: Alaskan and Hawaiian statehood revved up the statehood party machine; Cuba inspired some, frightened many others, and radically changed the terms of debate around independence; and the Fernos-Murray Bill symbolized a falseness in the promise of commonwealth.

The PDP continued to try to improve commonwealth. Their attempts in the 1960s resulted in the creation of a United States-Puerto Rican commission to study the status question, STACOM, which met from 1964 to 1966.* The commission report called for a plebiscite, which was scheduled for July 1967, in which the people of Puerto Rico would choose among commonwealth, statehood, and independence. Commonwealth, as will be discussed in Chapter 6, won the plebiscite with a little

---

*See Appendix D for list of members.

over 60 percent support, but 60 percent was too small a margin to permanently settle the status issue.

## THE FINAL DECADES

The next two decades (1960–80) brought important changes to Puerto Rico. Economically, the euphoria of rapid growth was to end; internationally, the involvement of the United Nations "in the case of Puerto Rico" was to begin; and, politically, the reign of Luis Muñoz Marin was over.

The pattern of U.S. investment in Puerto Rico began to change. Old factories started closing down as the ten-year Fomento leases came to an end. Many of these labor-intensive industries relocated in other parts of the world where they could pay lower wages.[247] During 1970 and 1971 alone, over 100 factories closed down in Puerto Rico,[248] and from June 1974 to February 1975, 53 "enterprises sponsored by Fomento closed."[249] Puerto Rico's garment industry was severely hit. Garment exports from Puerto Rico to the mainland fell from "37 percent of the total United States purchases in 1961 to 16 percent in 1974."[250] It was the cost of locating in Puerto Rico that was driving the factories out. The average hourly wage in Puerto Rico had risen above the minimum wage in the United States.[251]

By 1975, to compensate for Puerto Rico's wage disadvantage, the PDP government initiated a program to lure manufacturers to the island with lower shipping rates. The commonwealth bought the three shipping lines that served the island. They hoped to take advantage of the fact that "the freighters that sail south from east and Gulf Coast ports, bringing in ninety-eight percent of all the food, raw materials, and manufactured goods consumed [in Puerto Rico] arrive full. But the freighters that sail north from the island, carrying fibers, textiles, pharmaceuticals, rum, sugar, women's clothes and other export goods leave only 35 percent full."[252] The plan was to offer industry this sixty-five percent unused space at special rates.

But the next year, even with special shipping rates, a panel headed by Professor James Tobin of Yale University, warned, "Puerto Rico is pricing itself out of the market for industries, which provide jobs and require little capital."[253] The warnings came too late. This two-decade period marked the passage for Puerto Rico from a labor-intensive U.S. investment pattern to a capital-intensive pattern. By 1979 the most valuable industries in Puerto Rico were petrochemicals, pharmaceuticals, and electronics. At the top of the list, and the best example, of course, of capital-intensive industry, is the Puerto Rican petrochemical complex.[254]

The Commonwealth Oil Refining Company (CORCO) was actually established before 1960, "attracted to Puerto Rico in the early 1950s by the lure of cheap crude oil and tax breaks...."[255] But dramatic expansion took place in the 1960s, and by the early 1970s, the Puerto Rican petrochemical industry had capital investments totalling over $1.2 billion. With 16 corporations, it is one of the largest complexes of its kind in the world. Yet, all 16 companies together employ only 6,000 workers.[256]

The pattern of capital-intensive investment would intensify into the 1970s. Says journalist Vidal, in 1976, "Factories keep coming, especially in drugs and electronics, but not as fast and they aren't the labor-intensive plants of the past." In his article Vidal specifically pointed to Allergan Pharmaceutics of Irvine, California, as an example. Induced to the island by tax exemption privileges, the Allergan plant would employ seven Puerto Ricans![257]

The cruel consequence of the shift away from labor-intensive investments is a dangerously high island unemployment rate. In 1975 alone, there was a net loss of 19,300 jobs, and estimates of Puerto Rican unemployment today go as high as 40 percent. During the best single year of labor-intensive industrializing, under Fomento, 37,000 jobs were created. But Puerto Rico would need to create 42,000 jobs every year in order to keep unemployment down to 12 percent.[258] Optimism of the 1960s gave way to the grim facts of the 1970s.

During the last 20 years, while Puerto Rico's economic situation worsened, the United Nations began to focus on Puerto Rico's political situation. As Chapter 7 more fully describes, during this period the U.N. Committee on Decolonization began hearing arguments and passing resolutions affirming Puerto Rico's right to self determination and independence. Puerto Rican independentists were prime movers for UN action. The Puerto Rican Movement for Independence was especially active.

*El Movimiento Pro Independencia* (MPI) was formally established in Ponce on September 22, 1959. Its published purpose was "to consolidate the independentist force into a totally integrated movement... by patriotism... as a non-partisan organization."[259] It was formed, according to movement literature, because "The electorial disaster of the Puerto Rican Independence Party became imminent."[260]

The Independence Party had dropped to third place in 1956, and was losing support at each election. Gilberto Concepción de Gracia continued to head the PIP until his death in 1967 when Rubén Berríos Martinez became its leader. By the end of the 1960s, under Berriós's leadership, the Independence Party platform was calling for democratic socialism and had moved somewhat closer to, but by no means was the same as, the socialist aims of the MPI.[261]

Under the leadership of Berrios, the PIP used civil disobedience to focus attention on issues. The best initial example took place on Culebra.

Culebra and Vieques are small islands off the coast of Puerto Rico where the U.S. Navy practices gunnery and amphibious training. The first PIP confrontation took place on the U.S. Navy's firing range in Culebra. On February 18, 1971, Berrios was jailed for violating a federal injunction ordering him to leave the firing range.[262] In 1975, the navy abandoned Culebra as a firing range, and Vieques became the site for intensified naval practice bombings and shellings.

The navy claims a right to be in Vieques because two-thirds of Vieques was purchased by the navy in 1943. However, by February 7, 1973, both houses of the Puerto Rican Insular Legislature had adopted a resolution demanding immediate withdrawal by the U.S. Navy from the two islands. And, by March 8, 1978, even statehood Governor Carlos Romero Barceló was asking the federal district court in San Juan for an injunction to stop navy and marine military activities on Vieques; "a protest to President Carter from Puerto Rico...forced the cancellation of a 30,000-man military exercise...set to begin on May 5."[263]

Thus getting the navy off the offshore islands had become a popular non-independentist issue. In fact, it is the indigenous population, mostly of fishers motivated by economic interests, not political independence, who led the struggle and who mainly were involved in the Vieques confrontations. And then the tide changed.

The issue of Vieques was becoming defined as an independentist issue, again. Support for the navy's right to be there was identified as a matter of U.S. patriotism, and by January 1980, "Governor Romero said he was re-evaluating his position against the navy's use of Vieques as a target range in view of the heating up of the Cold War over Iran and Afghanistan."[264]

Surprisingly, through the economic malaise of slowdown and jobless-ness and even when the isue of Culebra and Vieques autonomy were popular ones, the Independence Party did not increase its electoral support substantially. At best, the PIP gets about 4 percent of the popular vote (see Table 8 and Figure 1).

Estimates of the number of supporters of the MPI vary. In 1964 Juan Mari Bras, secretary general, claimed 5,000 active members, and many sympathizers. Two years later the MPI claimed a following of "at least ten percent of the electorate."[265] In 1967, according to the San Juan Star, "Mari Bras [had] estimated the number of people favoring independence in Puerto Rico at 400,000 of which 20,000 support the MPI";[266] and in August of that year, in an interview, Mari Bras claimed 15,000 members.[267]

Like Concepción de Gracia, Mari Bras's connectedness with the independence movement was clear. In April 1948 he was expelled from the University of Puerto Rico because he had taken part in a rally welcoming Pedro Albizu Campos back to the island. Mari Bras had been a member of the Independence Party when he helped form the MPI.

## TABLE 8
## Puerto Rican Election Returns (in thousands)

|  | 1948 | 1952 | 1956 | 1960 | 1964 | 1968 | 1972 | 1976 |
|---|---|---|---|---|---|---|---|---|
| Commonwealth | | | | | | | | |
| Popular Demo-cratic Party | 392 | 429 | 433 | 457.8 | 487.2 | 367.3 | 609.6 | 297.6 |
| People's Party | — | — | — | — | — | 384.1 | — | — |
| Statehood | | | | | | | | |
| Republican Statehood Party | 88.1 | 85.1 | 172.8 | 252.3 | 248.6 | 4.3 | — | — |
| New Progressive Party | — | — | — | — | — | 390.9 | 524 | 312 |
| Independence | | | | | | | | |
| Puerto Rican Independence Party | 66.1 | 125.7 | 86.3 | 24.1 | 22.1 | 25.3 | 52.1 | 33.1 |
| Puerto Rican Socialist Party | — | — | — | — | — | — | — | 4.6 |

Source: Comisión de Derechos de los Estados Unidos, Puertorriqueños en Los Estados Unidos Continentales: Un Futuro  Incierto, p. 17; and David Vidal, "Pro-Statehood Candidate Stages Puerto Rican Upset," New York Times, November 3, 1976, p. 1.

By 1965 the MPI had become, for Anderson, "the principal standard bearer of the independent ideal."[268] The MPI was to play an important role in the international arena. Early in 1972, El Movimiento Pro Independencia became the Puerto Rican Socialist Party. In 1976 the Puerto Rican Socialist Party participated in the island elections, but got only 4,604 votes.

At first, only the independentists sought an audience in the United Nations. For Concepción de Gracia and the Independence Party, petitioning the United Nations was a natural outgrowth of a basic belief in a legal course of action stemming, of course, from the party's initial commitment to use "all legal and peaceful means." Independence would come not only "through the expression of the people of the island," but also "through the pressure and moral forces of the world, manifested in the United Nations and other organizations."[269] Mari Bras's ideas were similar.

For Juan Mari Bras, great importance was placed on the "dozens of new nations which were once colonies."[270] The MPI had a permanent representative in New York to keep constant contact with African nations, and even a permanent delegation in Ghana. The movement hoped, with the help of the non-aligned countries, that "independence will be achieved with pressure from the United Nations."[271]

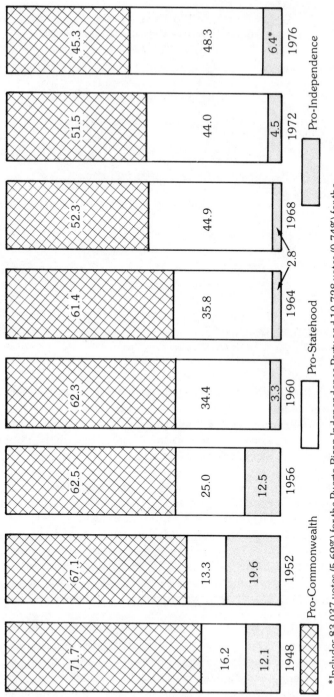

Figure 1
Trends in Percentage Distribution of Votes in Puerto Rico, 1948–76,
Classified by Political Status Preference (percent)

Pro-Commonwealth

Pro-Statehood

Pro-Independence

1948: 71.7, 16.2, 12.1
1952: 67.1, 13.3, 19.6
1956: 62.5, 25.0, 12.5
1960: 62.3, 34.4, 3.3
1964: 61.4, 35.8, 2.8
1968: 52.3, 44.9, 2.8
1972: 51.5, 44.0, 4.5
1976: 45.3, 48.3, 6.4*

*Includes 83,037 votes (5.69%) for the Puerto Rican Independence Party and 10,728 votes (0.74%) for the
Puerto Rican Socialist Party gubernatorial candidates.

Source: *Manufacturer's Ready Reference File on Puerto Rico, U.S.A.*, Puerto Rican Economic Development
Administration, Continental Operations Branch, New York, New York.

By 1967, together with the Cuban delegation, Puerto Rican indepen-dentists succeeded in getting the question of Puerto Rico placed on the UN Decolonization Committee's agenda. However, by the end of the 1970s not only the independentists but commonwealth representatives, statehooders, and members of the Puerto Rican Bar Association were making presentations for the UN Decolonization Committee.[272]

## PARTISAN POLITICS

In 1964, after 16 years in the governor's mansion (1948–64), Luis Muñoz Marin stepped down from that role. He selected Roberto Sánchez Vilella as his PDP successor and Sánchez Vilella was elected governor in 1964. But no one would really succeed a leader like Muñoz, least of all a serious, competent, but lusterless engineer. In fact, for the 1967 status plebiscite, Muñoz had to come out of retirement to campaign for commonwealth.

It was in 1968, however, that the Popular Democratic Party spell was forever broken and a new political era began for Puerto Rico. The salient feature of this new era was that no party or personality would have a hold on the voters for longer than four years. Also, Puerto Rican politics started to be played out, in earnest, in a wider arena—on the front stage of the United Nations and in the backrooms of mainland politics.

The 1968, 1972, and 1976 election results looked very much like pendulum swings as island politics moved closer to the two-party system. Each selection was unique and carried its own surprises.

In 1968 statehooder Luis Alberto Ferré became governor of Puerto Rico and the *New York Times* announced that "The 28 year old reign of the Popular Democratic Party, headed by Luis Muñoz Marin came to an end...."[273] However, two weeks before the election the *Times* was still predicting a statehood defeat,[274] and, as late as August, the *San Juan Star* was publishing articles forecasting the "death" of the statehood move-ment.[275] What happened?

As Table 8 shows, the commonwealth forces split, allowing a state-hood victory. Roberto Sánchez Vilella, PDP governor in 1964, was not supported for PDP nomination by Muñoz and the PDP leadership; however, he decided to run independently. To do this, he needed the affiliation of a duly registered party. He chose the People's Party, which had been pro-statehood but changed its goal to commonwealth with the Sánchez affiliation.

Sánchez had the support of many young PDP members including members of his cabinet and legislators. Sánchez also benefited from the fact that a "large sector of the public was sympathetic" to his accusations that "Muñoz and the 'machinery' had packed the [nominating] con-vention." He accused Muñoz of betraying democratic principles.[276]

Helping the statehood cause was the fact that Luis Ferré was the most charismatic of the candidates. The PDP candidate was the Senate majority leader, Luis Negrón López, a rural lawyer and gentleman coffee farmer. According to newspaper accounts, "In contrast to Ferré's charm, Negrón [was] a stolid and colorless figure better at manipulating votes in the Senate than in arousing popular enthusiasm."[277] Ferré, on the other hand, was the "best known and most persistent champion" of statehood. He had personal drawing power and was a very successful entrepreneur and philanthropist.[278] In every plaza, Ferré's campaign jingle sang out: "Esto tiene que cambiar" (this has got to change).[279] And the election of 1968 did represent a dramatic changing of the guard.

The election was also called a "peaceful revolution," and in some sense it was, because it broke the PDP's psychological hold over the electorate. But 1968 in no way represented a political revolution. The statehooders did not win an absolute majority; did not gain complete control of the Insular Legislature (the PDP had a majority in the Senate); and did not sustain their victory and increase their support amongst the electorate while in office. Four years later the pendulum swung back into the commonwealth camp.

The outcome of the 1972 election was met with as much surprise as that of 1968. "The Popular Democratic Party, behind its 36-year-old candidate, Rafael Hernandez Colon, swept to an overwhelming and unexpected victory ... won control of the executive mansion, both houses of the legislature, and seventy-two of the island's seventy-eight municipalities ... even leaders of the party were surprised at the magnitude of the victory."[280] Less than a month before, newspaper polls were indicating a close victory for the statehooders (44% to 40.7%).[281] What happened?

There were three possible explanations offered for the surprise PDP landslide victory—scandals in the Ferré administration, the general economic slump, and the status issue.

During the campaign, Hernandez Colon hit hard "at a series of alleged scandals" involving the Urban Renewal and Housing Corporation. The controversy involved the sale of land below market value to a relative of an executive, and a week before the election the director of the corporation resigned and then withdrew his resignation. Governor Ferré refused to take action against the parties involved until after the election, and Ferré was described as "on the defensive against the attacks on the honesty of his administration."[282]

The poor state of the Puerto Rican economy with its consistently high unemployment rate officially at 13 percent and slowed growth rate, impacted by a recession in the United States, was another explanation for the PDP victory. In fact, the prevailing state of the economy dominated Puerto Rican political discussions at the outset of the election year.

In January 1972, Governor Ferré proposed the "creation of a public venture capital fund as a novel approach toward improving the island's sagging economy," reflecting the governor's disenchantment with policies that failed to cure Puerto Rico's persistent economic problems.[283] Dispute over the state of the economy was said to be overshadowing the "volatile issue" of status. In fact, Ferré played down the statehood issue in his campaigning, and even the PDP candidate Rafael Hernandez Colon was quoted as saying, "For us, the principal issue will be the economy."[284]

But as soon as the election results were in, the massive victory of the PDP was immediately seen as a general reaffirmation of commonwealth status.[285] That was the public interpretation the PDP took. The Popular Party lost no time in using their position to try to make the commonwealth relationship more permanent and more viable.

> In July, 1973, negotiations were initiated between the President of the United States and the Governor of Puerto Rico and as a result, the Ad Hoc Advisory Group of Puerto Rico was created and its charter filed on September 20, 1973 [See Appendix E]. The Advisory Group [was given] the directive to develop the maximum of self-government and self-determination within the four pillars of association—common defense, common market, common currency, and common citizenship....[286]

Through private and public meettings, there were "considerable differences of opinion between the Puerto Rican half of the Committee and the mainland members on what commonwealth status is...."[287] And as Chapter 7 will illustrate, no concrete changes resulted from the final report.

The Advisory Group recommended "that the Compact be referred to both Houses by the President of the United States with his endorsement for Congressional action."[288] Rather than responding to the request for endorsement, however, President Gerald Ford waited a year and then issued a strong pro-statehood statement from a ski resort in Vail, Colorado, and introduced a pro-statehood bill.

This was not merely an example of a president having a different policy point of view from Congress's. What was really happening was the emergence of a new game. The Puerto Rican status issue was no longer a mere victim of institutional "checks and balances" in the U.S. federal government. The political status of Puerto Rico was becoming a political football played out in the most partisan of ways.

For decades there had been a connection between island and mainland parties. The Popular Party identified with and worked with the mainland Democrats, particularly after 1945;[289] the Statehood Party had been affiliated with the National Republican Party since 1904, participating in Republican nominating and fund-raising.[290] But starting in the 1960s the island's major parties were being described as looking like "mere appendages" of the mainland parties.[291] President Ford's endorsement of statehood can be understood in this context. Ford was merely rewarding his Puerto Rican Republican (pro-statehood) friends who faithfully supported his presidential candidacy at the 1976 Republican convention.[292]

Without formal (institutional) clout, the statehood Puerto Ricans were finding an inroad to influence—their Republican affiliation. The constant flow of Republican presidential hopefuls down to Puerto Rico in 1979 seems to verify the fact of this new and live connection.[293] In fact, Puerto Rico will be the site of "la primera primaria," the first Republican primary in 1980:

> The nation's first presidential primary next year will be held, of course, in the wintery landscape of New Hampshire, right?
>
> Wrong, amigo. The first primary votes for President will be cast in a tropical land where they're liable to be having a heat wave.
>
> Balmy Puerto Rico will replace blustery New Hampshire as the site where Americans initially make known their choices for presidential candidates.
>
> On February 11, Republicans go to the polls... in Puerto Rico's first presidential primary, an event that has suddenly thrust the island onto the national political scene.
>
> Republican candidates have already begun to hit the Caribbean campaign trail.[294]

The PDP is not immune to this kind of politicking though it seems to have been spurred on by statehood interlopers. In 1975, Franklin Delano Lopez, pro-statehooder from the South Bronx, helped found a Puerto Rican chapter of the Americans for Democratic Action (ADA) in Puerto Rico. He and his associate, Juan Manuel Garcia Passalacqua, "wrote to all the candidates for the Democratic Party presidential nomination offering the Puerto Rico ADA's support if the candidate would vow to support a party plank favoring self-determination rather than commonwealth."[295] Only one presidential aspirant, little-known candidate Jimmy Carter, responded. The connection was made, and Carter's good fortune helped legitimize Lopez's group. In 1976, Lopez still did not control the Puerto Rican Democratic Party. But he was trying. The island convention to select Democratic delegates had to be suspended because fights broke out between the regular PDP delegates who were pro–Henry Jackson and the Lopez pro–Jimmy Carter delegates.[296] By 1978, however, the Lopez group (pro-statehood) controlled the formal Democratic Party delegate selection on the island, and Carter had made good on his promise, as a 1978 San Juan editorial suggests:

President Carter went further than any previous president when he said he would support *any choice* resulting from a status referendum or plebiscite in Puerto Rico and would urge the Congress to back such a result also.[297] [emphasis added]

But partisan politicking among the Democrats did not stop. Pro-commonwealth Democrats supported Jackson in 1976 because of his status views, and in 1979 pro-commonwealth (PDP) Democrats were courting and supporting Kennedy.[298] Within the Democratic Party the status issue was deteriorating into a partisan plaything for mainland politicians.

No doubt, the lack of any concrete changes by the PDP to get a "new pact," a new commonwealth agreement, from all their public and private efforts from 1972 to 1976, helped the statehooders, not the PDP, in the next island election. The results of the 1976 election were also called a surprise, as the pendulum swung back to the New Progressives with force and clarity.

In a staggering upset, San Juan Mayor Carlos Romero Barceló of the pro-statehood New Progressive Party snatched the governorship of Puerto Rico from the incumbent Rafael Hernandez Colon.... The election was all the more surprising because the New Progressives were also on their way to assuming control of both houses of the Puerto Rican legislature as well as retaining the powerful post of mayor of San Juan."[299]

The reasons used in 1972 could be invoked again to explain the 1976 landslide victory for the statehooders—a hint of scandal, general economic malaise, and status preference. In a newspaper ad, "All the Governor's Men," run during the week of the election, the New Progressives charged the incumbent with corruption. But it was the economic situation, called "a recession imported from the mainland"[300] that seemed to be the deciding factor in the election. Inflation was even worse in Puerto Rico than in the United States, and unemployment had doubled in just a few years. Massive development projects had to be cancelled. The projects were linked to the supposed advantage of a petrochemical complex that processed cheap foreign crude oil. But the oil crisis and the skyrocketing foreign oil prices now put Puerto Rico, which used foreign oil exclusively, at a real disadvantage.

Governor Hernandez's 1975–76 budget was "one of austerity designed to bring government spending in line with the falling incomes."[301] His budget called for the dismissal of 1,600 government employees, the withholding of $100 million in scheduled pay increases from employees, and imposing $94 million in further department cuts. Austerity measures included a tax surcharge to be imposed retroactively on 1974 incomes and a 5 percent excise on all but food imports. In fact, the governor called for 25 new taxes as well as an increase in the rates of government-owned utilities.

With a rising inflation rate and the slowing down of Fomento-created jobs, it seems more than likely that the election "results reflected less a mandate for statehood than they did voter discontent with the administrative and economic problems under Mr. Hernandez Colon's leadership."[302] In fact, during the campaign statehooder Carlos Romero Barceló said that Puerto Rico's political status was not an election issue; the issue was the rebuilding of the economy. Nevertheless, after the election the new governor was vowing to educate the people about the benefits of statehood, and many were seeing the results as an expression of strong pro-statehood sentiment.

Could it be that every four years whoever is in office would get punished for the economic problems plaguing the island and the pendulum would swing endlessly? Supporting this possibility is the fact that there was an equally dramatic landslide in 1972 for commonwealth. Also suggesting the likelihood of such swings is the fact that one-quarter of the Puerto Rican electorate is between the ages of 18 and 26. This group came to political maturity during the last decade of partisan politics, not a time of continuity of leadership, or a time when loyalties could be fixed.

On the other hand, it is possible that statehood, as the New Progressives claim, now represents the status preference of more than half of the Puerto Ricans on the island and that starting from 1976 statehood will be the majority party and elections will become, and be seen, as popular mandates on the status of the island. Buttressing this claim is the fact that statehood support has steadily increased in the last two decades, as Figure 1 graphically illustrates. Also supporting the possibility that 1976 marks the advent of a new majority is the return home to Puerto Rico of tens of thousands of mainland Puerto Ricans each year; they tend to be for statehood (as Chapter 5 will describe). One would think that their presence and numbers cannot help influencing the outcome of elections.

Was 1976 a pendulum swing or a statehood mandate? The election of 1980 holds the answer.

This chapter in Puerto Rican history began with a military landing and ends with a landslide victory for annexation and statehood. An important question must be raised: Why is it that in the midst of the present dramatic economic problems, the independentists have not been able to capitalize on the island's vulnerability and worsening economic condition? As the *New York Times* described the election of 1976, the "surprise was the relatively poor showing of the Puerto Rican Independence Party [and Socialist Party] despite economic conditions—raging inflation, high taxes, an unemployment rate well over thirty percent—that had been expected to enhance its prospects."[303] Why doesn't independence have more support? Why has the movement for independence thus far failed in Puerto Rico? The next chapter tries to answer that question.

## NOTES

1. Miguel A. D'Estefano, *Puerto Rico: Analysis of a Plebiscite*, p. 16.

2. Ralph Hancock, *Puerto Rico: A Success Story*, p. 69.

3. Thomas Aitken, Jr., *Poet in the Fortress*, p. 34.

4. The Treaty of Paris passed the Senate with 46 Republicans, 34 Democrats, and 10 minor party members ratifying it—a mere one vote over the necessary two-thirds. Credited with influencing the borderline votes are William Jennings Bryan's pro-treaty statements and the outbreak of fighting between American and Filipino soldiers.

5. George W. Davis, *Industrial and Economic Conditions of Puerto Rico*, p. 26.

6. An official report to Washington stated the following:

> The coffee lands suffered worst. These trees are planted on the hill and mountain slopes, and in many places the declivities are very abrupt. The gale tore up the trees, loosened the soil and the deluge of water converted the earth into a semifluid.
>
> Then followed landslides, and thousands of acres of coffee plantations slid down into the valley; trees, soil, rocks, and every vestige of culture are piled up in the bottom of the valleys. In such cases there is no restoration possible, for where there were smiling groves are now only bald rocks which were uncovered by the avalanche.
>
> Where the soil was not disturbed the most of the coffee trees were either uprooted, broken off, or stripped of foliage and the immature berries. The larger trees of other varieties, which are habitually grown for shade to the coffee, were blown down, and their protection to the coffee trees is also gone; so where the trees are not wholly denuded, the protection of the berries from the sun's heat is absent, and the green fruit is blighted and spoiled. (Henry K. Carroll, *Report on the Island of Porto Rico*, p. 6.)

7. General Davis wrote to the secretary of war on behalf of the Committee of Coffee Producers to suspend foreclosures of mortgages. Estates representing $80,000,000 were in danger of disappearing. Davis, op. cit., p. 45.

8. Manuel Maldonado Denis, *En Las Entrañas: .Un Analisis Socio-*

historico de la Emigración Puertorriqueña (translated by Roberto Simón Crespi), p. 75.

9. An official report to Washington read, in part:

> The sugar industry has suffered much less than the others. Some cane has been uprooted and some has been buried, and many mills have been damaged or destroyed. The margin of profit at present prices to the sugar grower is small, but there is a margin of probably a half cent per pound to the manufacturer who has modern machinery; but the old "Jamaica train" mills, which are badly damaged, will probably never be reconstructed, and the growing cane for next year can not be ground on such estates unless their owners can negotiate large loans. Many will be unable to do this, so the prediction seems justified that such growing cane will next year be left to rot in the fields (Carroll, op. cit., p. 6.)

10. *Status of Puerto Rico. Report*, p. 150; Gordon K. Lewis, *Puerto Rico: Freedom and Power in the Caribbean*, pp. 96–97; Ismael Rodriguez Bou estimates that between 79 and 95 percent of the Puerto Rican population was illiterate in "Significant Factors in the Development of Education in Puerto Rico," *Status of Puerto Rico. Selected Background Studies*, p. 156.

11. See *Documents on the Constitutional History of Puerto Rico*, pp. 64–80. Originally called the Payne Bill, its legislative history is accurately outlined in Robert J. Hunter, "Historical Survey of the Puerto Rican Status Question," *Status of Puerto Rico. Selected Background Studies*, pp. 59–64.

12. Henry Wells, *The Modernization of Puerto Rico*, p. 82.

13. Though the establishment of an unincorporated territory was new, the deprivation of citizenship rights to natives was not. The U.S. treaty with Spain in 1819 acquiring Florida had almost an identically worded citizenship rights provision as the following from the treaty with France in 1803, under which the U.S. acquired Louisiana:

> The inhabitants of the ceded territory will be *incorporated* in the union of the United States and admitted as soon as possible according to the principles of the Federal Constitution, to the *enjoyment of all the rights, advantages and immunities of citizens of the United States*; and in the meantime they shall be maintained and protected in the free enjoyment of their liberty, property and religion which they profess....

However, in the treaty with Russia for Alaska,

> the inhabitants of the ceded territory... *with the exception of uncivilized native tribes*, shall be admitted to the enjoyment of all the rights, advantages, and immunities of citizens of the United States....

Although a Joint Congressional Resolution of 1898, incorporating Hawaii, provided specifically that

> the said Hawaiian Islands and their dependencies be and are hereby annexed *as a part of the territory* of the United States....

The Puerto Rican Treaty with Spain in 1898 made Puerto Rico an *unincorporated territory* where

> the civil rights and political status of the native inhabitants...shall be determined by the Congress....

And the Foraker Act provided

> that all inhabitants...who were Spanish subjects on the eleventh day of April, 1899, and their children born subject thereto, will be deemed and held to be *citizens of Puerto Rico*, and as such entitled to the protection of the United States; and that they, together with such constitute a body politic under the name of The People of Puerto Rico, with governmental powers as hereinafter conferred....

I have added the emphasis. See Edward B. Lockett, *The Puerto Rico Problem*, pp. 30–31.

14. Earl Parker Hanson, *Puerto Rico: Ally for Progress*, p. 61.

15. *De Lima v. Bidwell*, 182 U.S. 1 (1901) "held in part that while Puerto Rico was not incorporated into the United States, it was subject to United States sovereignty as a possession."

*Downes v. Bidwell*, 182 U.S. 244 (1901) "first recognized 'unincorporation' as a judicial concept."

"This situation opened the door for numerous test cases deciding that the rights to trial by jury given in the Sixth Amendment, *Balzac v. Puerto Rico*, 258 U.S. 298 (1922); indictment by grand jury, *Ocamp v. U.S.* 234 U.S. 91 (1913); and the uniformity provision of Art. 1 Sect. 8 (*Downes v. Bidwell, supra*) are not among the fundamental rights" to be given to "the citizens of Puerto Rico." Ralph Nader, "The Commnonwealth Status of Puerto Rico," *Harvard Law Record*, Vol. 23, no. 12 (December 13, 1956): p. 2.

16. Ibid., p. 3.

17. February 18 and 19, the Federalist Party met at the Olimpo Hotel (thus, the name "Olimpo Assembly") to create the Union Party. Although it consisted mainly of old Federalists there were some Republicans in its ranks and Luis Muñoz Rivera's co-organizer was a Republican leader, Rosendo Matienzo Cintrón. Between 1904 and 1930 the Union Party was the majority party.

18. A brief outline of legislation not passed illustrates this point. In 1906, Theodore Roosevelt visited Puerto Rico and afterwards endorsed legislation providing for an elective upper house, cabinet appointments by governor, and U.S. citizenship. Congress ignored the bill. In 1910, a revision of the Foraker Act, the Olmstead Act, failed to pass the Senate; in 1912, the Jones Act, a patchwork revision of the Foraker, endorsed by Taft in his annual message, met with a similar fate; in 1931, Poindexter's bill, calling for Foraker reforms, was pigeonholded; and, in 1914, a new Organic Act, drafted by Representative William Jones and Senator John F. Shafroth, and backed by President Wilson, was tabled because of World War I.

19. Joseph M. Jones, "Let's Begin with Puerto Rico," in Eugenio Fernández Méndez, ed., *Portrait of a Society*, p. 294.

20. Even the Interdepartmental Committee for the Economic Rehabilitation of Puerto Rico, which was set up in 1934 with members from the Department of Interior and Agriculture, the Federal Emergency Relief Administration, the Farm Credit Administration, and the Treasury, never had any real coordination; and departments took unilateral action without consulting the others. Lewis, op. cit., p. 132.

21. Ibid., p. 11.

22. Jones, op. cit., p. 289.

23. Rexford G. Tugwell, *The Art of Politics as Practiced by Three Great Americans: Franklin Delano Roosevelt, Luis Munoz Marin, and Fiorello H. LaGuardia*, pp. 36–37.

24. Tugwell, ibid., p. 36.

25. Earl Parker Hanson, *Puerto Rico: Land of Wonders*, p. 94; Tugwell, op. cit., 35.

26. Wells, op. cit., p. 35.

27. H. R. 9541 provided that if appropriation bills did not pass in any year, sums equal to the previous year's would be paid.

28. Chapter 5 of Thomas Aitken's *Poet in the Fortress* presents a good sampling of such statements.

29. Three years earlier, in a speech before the Puerto Rican House of Delegates, Muñoz indicated, though slightly less explicitly, these same preferences: "Our duty is to ask, to demand, to insist that the status of Puerto Rico be resolved in the manner of a state in association with the other American colonies and if, finally, we lose all hope, we exhaust the last recourse...we will ask independence for Puerto Rico." (Ibid., p. 63.)

30. On October 24, 1915, the Union Party convention met in the Miramar Theatre of San Juan and, with a party vote of 106–35, "resolved to follow a policy entirely along the lines of self-government. The party shall confine its activities to demanding home rule leaving the independence plank in its platform simply as an ideal until some future

convention shall determine the data on which the said plank shall be considered a party issue." Cable to Bureau of Insular Affairs sent through Acting Governor Travieso, October 30, 1915.

31. Included in this independence party were Zeno Gandia and Luis Lloréns Torres. They were interested not only in political and economic independence from the United States but insular reform as well. They wanted a system of proportional representation to "rescue the legislative branch from private monopoly" (Programa Economica y Politico del Partido de la Independencia de Puerto Rico, San Juan, p. 9). They also wanted a system of direct legislation and referendums; a progressive tax system; a code for the protection of workers and for manufacturing, consumption, and distribution; nationalization of public utilities; and consumer goods price-fixing. They condemned the foreign-owned "feudal" land system and emphasized agrarian reform. See Rafael Ruiz, "The Independence Movement of Puerto Rico, 1898–1964" (Master of Arts Thesis #2562, Georgetown University, 1965), Chapter 3.

32. See *Documents on the Constitution of Puerto Rico*, pp. 81–116 for the Jones Act in full.

33. Aitken, op cit., p. 67.

34. Travieso to Barceló, November 20, 1916, in Travieso Papers, quoted in Frank Ott Gatell, "The Art of the Possible: Luis Muñoz Rivera and the Puerto Rican Bill," *Americas* 17, no. 1 (July 1960): 19.

35. See, for example, Robert J. Hunter, "Historical Survey of the Puerto Rican Status Question, 1898–1965," *Status of Puerto Rico. Selected Background Studies*, pp. 81–85; Wells, op. cit., pp. 104–08; Tugwell, op. cit., p. 147.

36. See Clarence Senior, *Santiago Iglesias: Labor Crusader*.

37. "There was an intensified pre-occupation with the status issue to the detriment of any adequate formulations for the much needed economic and social programs for treating the gaping distress of the vast majority of Puerto Ricans." Nader, op. cit., p. 3.

"The leading politicians of that time devoted so much effort to debating whether Puerto Rico should be a state or independent that they neglected the basic needs of the Puerto Rican people." Luis Muñoz Marin, describing the decade of the 1930s in an address to Popular Party leaders in Caquas, February 12, 1967. Tomas Stella, "Muñoz Backs Absentee Balloting," *San Juan Star*, February 13, 1967, p. 1.

38. Earl Parker Hanson, *Puerto Rico: Ally for Progress*, p. 75.

39. Edward B. Lockett, *The Puerto Rican Problem*, p. 99.

40. Bailey W. and Justine Diffie, *Puerto Rico: A Broken Pledge*, pp. 166–67, quoted in Wells, op. cit., p. 114.

41. Quoted in Lockett, op. cit., pp. 100–01.

42. Aitken, op. cit., p. 83.

43. Over 67 percent in 1936. Miguel Guerra Mondragón, "The Legal Background of Agrarian Reform in Puerto Rico," in *Portrait of a Society*, ed. Eugenio Fernández Méndez, p. 162.

44. Wells, op. cit., 114.

45. Nathan Glazer and Daniel Patrick Moynihan, *Beyond the Melting Pot*, p. 86.

46. Hanson, *Ally for Progress*, p. 75.

47. Henry Wells says that parties were less interested in achieving a political status than in advancing their own political fortune. "Ideology and Leadership in Puerto Rican Politics," *American Political Science Review* 49, no. 1. (March, 1955): 24.

48. Daniel J. Boorstin, "Self Discovery in Puerto Rico," *Yale Review* 45 (1955–56): 239.

49. Wells, "Ideology and Leadership," p. 27.

50. "...in offering his bill (Independence Bill) to the Senate, Mr. Tydings charged that Puerto Rican elections were largely fraudulent...." *New York Times*, April 24, 1936, p. 12.

51. According to the testimony of José Coll y Cuchí at the hearings of the House Committee on Insular Affairs in Guerra Mondragón, "The Legal Background of Agrarian Reform," p. 158.

52. Wells, *The Modernization of Puerto Rico*, p. 101.

53. Ralph Hancock, *Puerto Rico: A Success Story*, p. 63.

54. Juan Antonio Corretjer, *Albizu Campos and the Ponce Massacre*, p. 13.

55. Hunter, op. cit., p. 85.

56. Harwood Hull, "Freedom Bill Splits Puerto Rico," *New York Times*, May 3, 1936, p. 6E.

57. Ruiz, op. cit., chap. 4.

58. Wells, *The Modernization of Puerto Rico*, p. 119.

59. "He shared with other Nation-makers many traits; idealism, contempt for his own life in the service of his people, contagious enthusiasm that inspired masses, utter incorruptibility." *The Minority of One* 18, no. 8 (May 29, 1965).

60. Corretjer, op. cit., p. 8. Juan Antonio Corretjer was national secretary of the Puerto Rican Nationalist Party in 1937 and went to prison with Albizu and served six years of a ten-year sentence. In 1934 he "bore arms against the Cuban dictator Machado" during the Cuban revolt. He now leads the Socialist League of Puerto Rico, a "Marxist-Leninist organization which solidarizes with Fidel Castro and predicts that the Puerto Rican struggle for independence will, to a large degree, follow the Cuban example." He edits *Pabello Newsletter* and *Quincena*. Juan Antonio is a poet of great talent. I am indebted to him for his generous assistance.

61. Lewis, op. cit., p. 136.

62. *The Nation*, May 6, 1936, p. 568.

63. *New York Times*, May 3, 1936, quoted in Frank Otto Gatell, "Independence Rejected: Puerto Rico and the Tydings Bill of 1936," *Hispanic American Historical Review* 38, no. 1 (1958): 41.

64. Hull, op. cit.

65. Hanson, *Puerto Rico: Ally for Progress*, pp. 115–17. For an account of Ines Mendoza's (Muñoz's wife) personal attempt to change the "Washington-initiated custom of doing all the teaching in English," see Hanson, *Puerto Rico: Land of Wonders*, pp. 113–14.

66. Early in 1932, the Nationalists marched on the insular capital to protest against a bill to convert the Puerto Rican flag to a colonial banner. According to Corretjer, in a mass attack on the capital building one person was killed and dozens were wounded. Op. cit., p. 6.

A few years later, Acting Governor José Padin banned the use of any other but the U.S. flag to fly over public buildings; "over the island's public buildings no one has a right to hoist any other flag but that of the United States of America." *New York Times*, May 3, 1936, p. 39.

67. See Pauline Castro's hand-written letter dated August 27, 1965, on Albizu's "political plan," in *Collection on Pedro Albizu Campos' Life*, Harvard Archives, Widener Library.

68. See Hull, op. cit.

69. "Letter of Rebel Leader's Wife to His Harvard Classmates," *Boston Daily Globe*, November 2, 1950, pp. 1, 3.

70. The seven others were Juan Antonio Corretjer, Luis F. Valasquez, Clemente Soto Velez, Erasmo Valesquez, Juan Gallordo Santiage, Pablo Rosado Ortiz, and Rafael Ortiz Pacheco.

71. Hunter, op. cit., p. 96.

72. See Corretjer, op. cit., p. 17.

73. The issue of blame has become a political issue rather than a factual one. Hunter claims a police officer was shot first. This does not necessarily mean a Nationalist shot first. As Hunter admits, "who fired the first shot is not known." Op. cit., p. 86.

74. Estimates vary. This is Corretjer's. Hanson says 15 Nationalists, one bystander, and two policemen were killed, and 55 people were wounded. *Puerto Rico: Land of Wonders*, pp. 112–13. Hunter says 19 were killed (including two policemen) and over 100 were wounded. Op. cit., p. 96.

75. Wells, *The Modernization of Puerto Rico*, p. 116.

76. The report was commissioned by the U.S. Department of Agriculture in 1934.

77. Hanson, *Ally for Progress*, pp. 32–33.

78. See Hunter, op. cit., pp. 88–90.

79. Wells, *The Modernization of Puerto Rico*, p. 117.

80. Hunter, op. cit., p. 91.

81. Ibid., p. 97.

82. For an example of the kind of opposition the 500 Acre Law Reform encountered, see the letter from the president of the Farmers Association of Puerto Rico to Governor Tugwell, dated May 29, 1941, in U.S. Congress, House, Committee on Insular Affairs, Subcommittee, *Investigation of Political, Economic and Social Conditions in Puerto Rico: Hearings persuant to H. Res. 159,* 78th Cong., 1st sess., 1943, Appendix.

*83. Wells, The Modernization of Puerto Rico, p. 116.*

84. Tugwell, op. cit., p. 79.

85. Earl Parker Hanson, *Puerto Rico: Land of Wonders*, p. 107. Tugwell emphasizes the same issue. Ickes's reports of Muñoz were unfavorable. Ickes was shocked by Nationalist attacks on Governor Winship, and the murder of Police Chief Riggs by terrorists; he suspected Muñoz of having connections with or sympathies toward the *nacionalistas.* Tugwell, op. cit., p. 146.

86. Wells, *The Modernization of Puerto Rico*, p. 117.

87. Tugwell, op. cit., p. 79.

88. Ibid.

89. Hanson, *Ally for Progress*, p. 32.

90. Wells, *The Modernization of Puerto Rico*, p. 116.

91. Hanson, *Puerto Rico: Land of Wonders*, p. 106.

92. Wells, *The Modernization of Puerto Rico*, p. 116.

93. *New York Times*, April 24, 1936, p. 1.

94. *New York Times*, February 24, 1936, p. 9.

95. *El Mundo*, April 25, 1936, p. 33.

96. *New York Times*, April 24, 1936, p. 12.

97. Ibid., p. 1.

98. *The Nation*, May 6, 1936, p. 567.

99. "The Tydings bill as interpreted here has been considered as providing for a obnoxious choice between an economically ruinous indepedece and a continuance of the present unsatisfactory colonialism." Hull, op. cit.

100. *The Nation*, May 6, 1936, p. 568.

101. Hunter, op. cit., p. 93.

102. And referring to the killing, as well as to the "ungrateful" Puerto Rican who is the recipient of millions in relief funds, *The Nation* said "Childish as it may seem, our attitude is that if the Puerto Ricans are not going to play fair, we won't play at all." May 6, 1936, p. 568.

103. "Washington's offer to free Puerto Rico is little more than window trimming for the coming Pan American conference." *Business Week*, May 2, 1936, pp. 41–42.

104. The sugar beet growers, for example, who would personally stand to gain as much from an independent Puerto Rico as from an independent Philippines because of the tariff protection. "It happens

that these groups are politically influential with the present administration." *The Nation*, May 6, 1936, p. 569.

105. *Business Week*, May 2, 1936, p. 43.

106. U.S. Congress, House Committee on Territories, *Hearings on H.R. 1934*, 74th Cong., 1st sess., 1935.

107. *The Nation*, May 6, 1936, p. 567.

108. See Hanson, *Puerto Rico: Land of Wonders*, p. 109.

109. *El Mundo*, April 25, 1936, p. 33.

110. Luis Muñoz Marin in *El Mundo*, July 21, 1940, p. 1.

111. Rivera Martinez, president of Federacion Libre de Trabajadores; Garcia Garcia Méndez, Republican speaker of the house; and Ramirez Santibáñez, Liberal Party president. Robert W. Anderson, *Party Politics in Puerto Rico*, pp. 32–42.

112. Hanson, *Puerto Rico: Land of Wonders*, pp. 127–28.

113. Robert W. Anderson, "The Puerto Rican Mainstream: The Spirit of Insular Politics," *San Juan Review* 1, no. 9 (October 1964): 18–19.

114. Charles T. Goodsell, *Administration of a Revolution*, p. 165.

115. Tugwell, op. cit., p. 78.

116. Hanson, *Puerto Rico: Land of Wonders*, p. 139.

117. See Hunter, op. cit., p. 100, and Hanson, ibid., p. 102.

118. Luis Muñoz Marin on April 12, 1941, quotd in S. L. Descartes, "Historical Account of Recent Land Reform in Puerto Rico," in *Portrait of a Society,* ed. Eugenio Fernández Méndez, p. 177.

119. See Luis Muñoz Marin, "Plight of Puerto Rico," *New Republic* 108 (January 11, 1943): 51–52.

120. Hanson, *Puerto Rico: Land of Wonders*, p. 138.

121. The manufacture of Puerto Rican rum began about 1936. When the production of liquor was cut down on the mainland because alcohol was needed for the war effort, rum production soared. The profits from the rum excise tax boosted Puerto Rico's budget from a pre-1940 $22 million to $150 million. Ibid, pp. 138–39.

122. Tugwell, op. cit., p. 150.

123. Hanson, *Puerto Rico: Land of Wonders*, p. 139.

124. Manuel Maldonado Denis, "Declinar del Movimiento Independista Puertorriqueño?" *Revista de Ciencias Sociales* 9, no. 3 (September 1965): 291–92.

125. Ironically the estimate is in an article in which Susoni argues that an independence party could prove prejudicial to the end sought. *El Mundo*, October 23, 1946, pp. 1–7; at the first CPI meeting, "Prominent *Populares*—senators, representatives, mayors and other public officials—dominated the presidential and speaker's tables." Anderson, op. cit., p. 108.

126. Hunter, op. cit., p. 108.

127. "De acuerdo con el sentimiento mayoritaria del pueblo de

Puerto Rico."Laura Albizu Campos, *Albizu Campos y la Independencia de Puerto Rico*, p. 14.

128. Anderson, op. cit., pp. 96–97.

129. Ibid., p. 98.

130. *New York Times*, March 10, 1943, p. 3.

131. Anderson, op. cit., p. 98.

132. Hunter, op. cit., p. 108.

133. See *El Mundo*, June 8, 1945, p. 1; September 7, 1945, pp. 1, 20; September 8, 1945, p. 1.

134. For example, Concepción claimed that Muñoz wanted to use a "characteristically colonial method" to decide status, a plebiscite that would include the discarded statehood alternative with no promise of U.S. congressional approval. This divides a country, he concluded, into two groups, colonialists and true citizens. *El Mundo*, September 7, 1945, pp. 1, 20.

135. Concepción suggested Muñoz was not distinguishing between his personal opinion and the opinion of the party. According to the CPI leader, Muñoz had established a personal tyranny. *El Mundo*, September 14, 1945, pp. 1, 8.

136. Muñoz claimed the two groups dividing the country were not colonialists and true citizens, but Populares and Anti-Populares. *El Mundo*, September 8, 1945, pp. 1, 13.

137. *El Mundo*, February 9, 1946, pp. 1, 22 ("El Sabataje").

138. Hunter provides documentation of the formal debates and of the bills introduced during and just after World War II. See Hunter, op. cit., pp. 102–03.

139. The Committee met daily from July 19, 1943, until August 7, 1943, and included Abe Fortas, undersecretary of Interior, Governor Tugwell, Father R. A. McGowan, Senator Celestino Iriarte, Senator Luis Muñoz Marín, Superior Court Judge Martin Travieso, and José Ramirez Santibáñez. Ibid., p. 103.

140. *New York Times*, March 25, 1948, p. 56.

141. *New York Times*, January 11, 1948, p. 19.

142. *New York Times*, February 3, 1948. "The Text of President Truman's Message on Civil Rights."

143. *New York Times*, February 22, 1948, p. 1.

144. Ibid.

145. *New York Times*, May 6, 1948, p. 9.

146. "Col. Roiz denied students' charges that half-a-dozen demonstrators had been clubbed with nightsticks. He said that the only casualty was a student who bumped his head when entering a patrol wagon." Ibid.

147. Carl J. Friedrich, *Puerto Rico: Middle Road to Freedom*, p. 213.

148. Ralph Hancock, *Puerto Rico: A Success Story*, p. 170.

149. The "free state" idea was first proposed by Representative

Howard Towner during debates on the Jones Bill in 1917. The new Irish Free State seemed to be the model for many proponents. See Hunter, op. cit., p. 80.

150. It was the same committee that originated the Elective Governor Act.

151. Jesús de Galindez, "Government and Politics in Puerto Rico, New Formulas for Self-Government," *International Affairs* 30 (1954): 337.

152. Ibid.

153. Friedrich, op. cit., p. 9.

154. Galindez, op. cit., p. 337.

155. Friedrich, op. cit., p. 9.

156. Galindez, op. cit., p. 337.

157. Jaime Benitez, *Status of Puerto Rico*, vol. 2, *Hearings*, p. 358.

158. Ibid.

159. Hunter, op. cit., pp. 113–14.

160. Luis Muñoz Marin, *New York Times*, July 26, 1962, text of letter, p. 8.

161. According to Tugwell, "In the early thirties...there was no middle ground; either you were for statehood or independence." Tugwell, op. cit., p. 53.

162. See Luis Muñoz Marin, "Nuevos Caminos Hacia Viejos Objectivos," *El Mundo*, June 29, 1946, pp. 1, 7.

163. Luis Muñoz Marin, "Alerta," *El Mundo*, February 1, 1946, p. 1.

164. Ibid.

165. Luis Muñoz Marin, "El Status Politico," *El Mundo*, February 10, 1946, p. 21.

166. *El Mundo*, August 16, 1948, pp. 4, 14.

167. Wells, *The Modernization of Puerto Rico*, pp. 228–29.

168. Ibid., p. 230.

169. Ibid.

170. Ibid., p. 231.

171. U.S., Congress, *Senate Hearings*, 82nd Cong., 2d sess., April 29, 1952, p. 19, quoted in Hunter, op. cit., p. 120.

172. "Remarks by the Honorable Luis Muñoz Marin, Governor of the Commonwealth of Puerto Rico, at Harvard University on June 16, 1955."

173. *New York Times*, text of Muñoz letter, July 26, 1962, p. 8.

174. U.S., Congress, House,*House Document No. 435*, 82nd Cong., 2d sess., April 29, 1952, p. 4, quoted in Hunter, op. cit., p. 120.

175. "The Commonwealth also recognizes the existence of the following human rights:

The right of every person to receive free elementary and secondary education.
The right of every person to obtain work.

The right of every person to a standard of living adequate for the health and well-being of himself and of his family, and especially to food, clothing, housing and medical care and necessary social services.

The right of motherhood and childhood to special care and assistance.

The rights set forth in this section are closely connected with the progressive development of the economy of the Commonwealth and require, for their full effectiveness, sufficient resources and an agricultural and industrial development not yet attained by the Puerto Rican community. In the light of their duty to achieve the full liberty of the citizen, the people and the government of Puerto Rico shall do everything in their power to promote the greatest possible expansion of the system of production, to assure the fairest distribution of economic output, and to obtain the maximum understanding between individual initiative and collective cooperation. The executive and judicial branches shall bear in mind this duty and shall construe the laws that tend to fulfill it in the most favorable manner possible. By Resolution number 34, approved by the Constitutional Convention and ratified in the Referendum held on November 4, 1952, Section 20 of Article II was eliminated."

*Documents on the Constitutional History of Puerto Rico*, pp. 172–73.

176. "Every person has the right to an education which shall be directed to the full development of the human personality and to the strengthening of respect for human rights and fundamental freedoms. There shall be a system of free and wholly non-sectarian public education. Instruction in the elementary and secondary schools shall be free and shall be compulsory in the elementary schools to the extent permitted by the facilities of the state. No public property or public funds shall be used for the support of schools or educational institutions other than those of the state. Nothing contained in this provision shall prevent the state from furnishing to any child non-educational services established by law for the protection of welfare of children.

By Resolution number 34, approved by the Constitutional Convention and ratified in the Referendum held on November 4, 1952, Section 5 of Article II was amended, adding to such section the following declaration: 'Compulsory attendance at elementary public schools to the extent permitted by the facilities of the state as herein provided shall not be construed as applicable to those who receive elementary education in schools established under non-governmental auspices.' " *Documents on the Constitutional History of Puerto Rico*, p. 169.

177. See Hunter, op. cit., pp. 120–23.

178. Gordon K. Lewis, "Puerto Rico: A New Constitution in American Government," *Journal of Politics* 15 (1953): 49.

179. U.S., Congress, Senate, *Congressional Record* (February 11, 1952) 98, no. 21: 970 ff., from *El Mundo*, May 1, 1952, and referred to in Peter J. Fliess, "Puerto Rican Political Status Under the New Constitution," *Western Political Quarterly* 5, no. 4 (December 1952): 646.

180. U.S., Congress, Senate, *Congressional Record* (June 26, 1952), 98, no. 113: 8,378, referred to in Fliess, op. cit., p. 646.

181. *Time*, November 13, 1950, p. 38.

182. *Boston Daily Globe*, November 1, 1950, p. 17.

183. Ibid.

184. *New York Times*, April 22, 1965, p. 33.

185. Ibid.

186. "We came with the express purpose of shooting the President." *Boston Herald*, November 2, 1950, p. 3.

187. Oscar Collazo's death sentence was commuted to life imprisonment by President Truman on July 24, 1950. Anthony Leviero, "Assassin Spared by Truman in Gesture to Puerto Rico," *New York Times*, July 25, 1952.

188. *Boston Herald*, November 2, 1950, p. 3.

189. Ibid.

190. *Boston Traveler*, November 2, 1950, p. 7.

191. *Boston Daily Globe*, November 15, 1950, p. 23.

192. "Puerto Rico's New Self-Governing Status Transmitted to Secretary General," *U.S. Department of State Bulletin* 28, April 20, 1953, p. 587.

193. Tugwell, op. cit., p. 226.

194. United Nations General Assembly, Off. Rec. 8th Session. Plenary at 311; see Rubén Berrios Martinez, "The Commonwealth of Puerto Rico: Its Reality in the National and World Community" (Divisional Thesis, Yale Law School, 1964), p. 179.

195. Hunter, op. cit., p. 125.

196. *New York Times*, April 22, 1965.

197. According to Corretjer, "The prospect of Taft in the White House made Muñoz sell the factories to Luis Ferré," because of fear of chastisement from a Republican president. Juan Antonio Corretjer in an interview, April 14, 1967.

198. Robert W. Anderson, *Party Politics in Puerto Rico*, pp. 6–8.

199. Hanson, *Puerto Rico: Ally for Progress*, p. 103.

200. *Status of Puerto Rico. Report*, 1966, p. 54. In 1967, construction reached a new high, which represented an increase of 20 percent over fiscal 1966, a rise of $100 million. The greatest increases were in highway construction and industrial facilities, which rose 53.8 percent. Everett H. Trop, "Island's Construction Reaches a Record High," *San Juan Star*, August 4, 1967, p. 6.

201. Hancock, op. cit., p. 164.

202. *Status of Puerto Rico. Report*, p. 54.

203. Ibid.

204. "He [Muñoz] added that his group would continue to carry forward its program of land reform, liberty and industrial movement." *New York Times*, March 25, 1948, p. 56.

205. Hanson, *Puerto Rico: Ally for Progress*, p. 102.

206. Maldonado Denis, *En las Entrañas*, p. 50.

207. Hancock, op. cit., p. 164.

208. Hanson, *Puerto Rico: Ally for Progress*, p. 103.

209. *Status of Puerto Rico. Report*, p. 54.

210. Ibid.; and Antonio J. Gonzalez, "El Desarrollo Economico y la Estructura Economica," University of Puerto Rico, 1965 (paper), pp. 48–49.

211. *Look Magazine*, January 17, 1961, quoted in Edward B. Lockett, *The Puerto Rican Problem*, p. 140.

212. Lloyd G. Reynolds and Peter Gregory, *Wages, Productivity, and Industrialization in Puerto Rico*, p. 253.

213. Ibid., pp. 253–54. The manufacturing workers were also younger than the general labor force and more highly educated. (See pp. 199–200.) In addition, Gonzalez reports that between 1950 and 1960, 81,000 *employed* rural workers left agriculture. Op. cit., p. 48.

214. Lockett., op. cit., p. 143.

215. The first five are Canada, United Kingdom, Japan, Germany, and Venezuela. Hanson, *Puerto Rico: Ally for Progress*, p. 76.

216. $290 per person was spent to purchase American goods in 1959. Ibid.

217. Commonwealth of Puerto Rico, Department of Labor, Migration Division, *Facts and Figures 1964,* 1965 edition, p. 9; "P.R. imports seen aiding U.S. economy," *San Juan Star*, December 11, 1978, p. 8.

218. Christopher Rand, *The Puerto Ricans*, p. 53.

219. Glazer and Moynihan, op. cit., p. 97.

220. Ibid., p. 52.

221. Patricia Aran Gosnell, *The Puerto Ricans in New York City* (an abridgement of a dissertation in the Department of Sociology, New York University, 1949), p. 3.

222. Hanson, *Puerto Rico: Ally for Progress*, p. 53.

223. Also, fewer than 10 percent of those living in San Juan were born in San Juan, and fewer than 5 percent of those living in rural areas were born in nonrural areas. Melvin M. Tumin and Arnold S. Feldman, *Social Class and Social Change in Puerto Rico*.

224. Hanson, *Puerto Rico: Land of Wonders*, p. 31.

225. Maldonado Denis quotes Dr. Silva Iglesias, associate secretary

of health for family planning as a recent example, see *En Las Entrañas*, Chapter 2.

226. Rand, op. cit., p 43.

227. C. Wright Mills et al., *The Puerto Rican Journey*, p. 49. In the 1880s for the same reason, economic self-improvement, the first Puerto Rican out-migration of any significance occurred. The move was to Hawaii, which needed field hands in its sugar industry. Hanson, *Puerto Rico: Ally for Progress*, p. 51.

228. Lawrence R. Chenault, *The Puerto Rican Migrant in New York City*, p. 156.

229. *Status of Puerto Rico. Report*, p. 150.

230. Reynolds, op. cit., p. 32.

231. Ibid, pp. 31, 119–200; Mills, op. cit., p. 31.

232. Reynolds, op. cit., p. 211.

233. Lockett, op. cit., p. 115.

234. Hancock, op. cit., p. 143; Commonwealth of Puerto Rico, *Facts and Figures, 1964*, 1965, p. 8.

235. Lewis, *Puerto Rico: Freedom and Power in the Caribbean*, p. 7.

236. "Fully 81 percent of the migrants referred to informal face to face contact as their single most important source of information—conversations with and letters from friends or relatives who were living in or had visited the city." Mills, op. cit., p. 54.

237. Lockett, op. cit., p. 128.

238. Hanson, *Puerto Rico: Land of Wonders*, p. 37.

239. See Oscar Lewis, *La Vida*.

240. *Subject Reports. Puerto Ricans in the United States*, 1970 Census, p. 1.

241. Maldonado Denis, *En Las Entrañas*, p. 88.

242. Hunter, op. cit., pp. 119, 126.

234. "Por primera vez una nación latinamericana affirma a plenitud los atributos de gu soberania, y con absoluta independencia de Estados Unidos, representa en el esconario mundial un papel que dicta su propria voluntad y responde a sus libérrimos intereses?" "La Hora de la Independencia, Tesis Politica del MPI," p. 47.

244. Maldonado suggested that the Cuban revolution changed the outlook of what a revolution is like and split the intelligentsia into factions that disagree over the tempo and direction in which social change is to take place. Manuel Maldonado Denis, "Ideologies and Attitudes Among the Spanish Speaking 'Intelligentsia' in the Caribbean" (Paper presented at the Annual Meeting of the American Sociological Society in Chicago, Illinois, August 30–September 2, 1965).

245. J. Edgar Hover, testimony before an appropriations subcommittee (February 16, 1967), quoted in Harry Turner "Polanco, Ferre

Disagree with Hoover on Violence," *San Juan Star*, May 18, 1967, p. 6.

246. The Fernos-Murray Bill to clarify commonwealth status would have allowed Puerto Rico to determine the limits of her debt-incurring capacity, provided for several kinds of federal laws affecting Puerto Rico to be formally accepted by Puerto Rico, and provided for Puerto Rican financial contributions to the Federal Treasury. Hanson, *Puerto Rico: Land of Wonders*, p. 314.

247. In 1972, for example, Governor Luis Ferré, explaining the closing down of factories, said, "We've had some shutdowns in industry—not because of any government policy but because we had to compete with Korea, Taiwan, and Japan in the apparel industry and Korea and Spain in the shoe industry. They can offer cheaper products due to cheaper wages." Juan M. Vasquez, "Economy Dominates Puerto Rico's Politics," *New York Times*, February 2, 1972, p. 22; also, in 1974, because the average wage in Puerto Rico was higher, even, than the minimum wage in the United States, according to a special business committee report, it took Puerto Rico out of the running compared to "the Far-Eastern, Caribbean and Latin-American nations that compete directly against Puerto Rico for labor-intensive industries." David Vidal, "Opening Troubles in Puerto Rico," *New York Times*, February 15, 1976, III, p. 4.

248. Vasquez, op. cit.

249. Michael Stern, "Puerto Rico Pays Heavily for Mainland's Recession," *New York Times*, March 22, 1975, p. 15.

250. Vidal, op. cit.

251. Ibid.

252. Stern, op. cit.; also see, "ILA Sets Criteria for OK of PR Merchant Marine," *San Juan Star*, May 28, 1974, pp. 1, 16.

253. Vidal, op. cit.

254. Alan Patureau, "Textile industry continues exodus from island," *San Juan Star*, November 4, 1979, p. B-1; for a focus on why the Caribbean is so attractive an area for building petrochemical complexes, see Aaron Segal, "Oil and the Caribbean: Who's got the Superport?" *San Juan Star*, September 27, 1973, p. 22.

255. "Tesoro's $130 million burden," *Business Week*, May 9, 1977, p. 93.

256. Henry Pelham Burn, "Two Faces of Development: Puerto Rico," *Vista* 9, no. 3 (December 1973): 32, 33.

257. Vidal, op. cit., p. 1.

258. Ibid.

259. *The Time for Independence: Political Thesis—Pro Independence Movement of Puerto Rico*, p. 11; a November 22, 1959, first meeting date is given in Jenaro Rentas, "El desarrollo del Movimiento Pro Independencia," *Nueve Lucha. Revista de discusion political del MPI*, No. 1, November 1970, pp. 8–9, 11.

260. *Time for Independence*, p. 5. "Bastante influyeron, además, en el debacle de PIP, las medidas de carácter reformista adoptadas por el régimen...." Rentas, op. cit., p. 8.

261. "Plataforma o Programa?" PIP Program, 1971, p. 1.

262. See Rubén Berríos Martínez, "From a Puerto Rican Prison," *New York Times*, April 28, 1971, p. 47.

263. See "Culebra Pullout Urged," *New York Times*, February 8, 1973; Christopher Pala, "Hearing on Navy action in Vieques ends today," *San Juan Star*, December 11, 1978, p. 10; Christopher Pala, "Fishermen block Navy exercises," *San Juan Star*, January 21, 1979, pp. 1, 18; Christopher Pala, "Fishermen reflect, reminisce—'This land is ours,'" *San Juan Star*, January 21, 1979, p. 18; Manny Suarez, "Fishermen stepping up Vieques 'cold war,'" *San Juan Star*, January 28, 1979, p. 3; Manny Suarez, "Vieques Fishermen catch Navy, Marines off guard," *San Juan Star*, February 4, 1979, pp. 1, 18; Manny Suarez, "Navy nets 21 protesters," *San Juan Star*, May 20, 1979, pp. 1, 19; "Puerto Rico Asks Injunction to Halt Military Activities on Nearby Island," *New York Times*, March 8, 1978, p. A16; and "Joint Military Exercises in Puerto Rico Canceled," *New York Times*, March 14, 1978, p. 18.

264. Manny Suarez, "Navy Flounders in Vieques," *San Juan Star*, January 20, 1980, pp. 1, 18; Harry L. Fridman, "Setback seen for U.S. if Navy loses use of Vieques," *San Juan Star*, January 20, 1980; Jane Baird, "Navy target ranges in U.S. fail to stir up 'Vieques' flap," *San Juan Star*, February 10, 1980, p. 1; "UPR student group sponsors forum on Navy Vieques issue," *San Juan Star*, February 24, 1980, p. 19.

265. *San Juan Review*, October 1964, p. 32; Marvin M. Karpatkin, "Puerto Rico. How Much Independence does it want?" *New Republic*, May 7, 1966, p. 113.

266. Ruben Arrieta, "Mari Bras Sees Independence as Final Triumph," *San Juan Star*, July 23, 1967, p. 3.

267. The estimate included high-school students. Interview, August 28, 1967.

268. Anderson, op. cit., p. 117.

269. Gilberto Concepción, "A Talk with the Candidates," *San Juan Review* 50, no. 9 (October 1964): 26.

270. Juan Mari Bras, in ibid., p. 32.

271. Juan Mari Bras, interview, August 28, 1967.

272. See, for example, Manny Suarez, "PDP slates U.N. address in commonwealth defense," *San Juan Star*, August 15, 1978, pp. 1, 14; Harold J. Liden, "Bar group asks U.N. to view Maravilla, Vieques," *San Juan Star*, August 5, 1979, p. 9; and "Repudio a la O N U 48% en contra; 30% a favor," *El Nueva Dia*, September 21, 1978, pp. 1, 2.

273. Henry Giniger, "Puerto Rico 'Peaceful Revolution,'" *New York Times*, November 10, 1968, p. 71.

274. "Puerto Rico Ruling Party Faces Its Biggest Threat in 28 Years," *New York Times*, October 20, 1968, p. 71.

275. "Statehood Death Seen in 1968 Elections," *San Juan Star*, August 10, 1968, p. 6.

276. "Puerto Rico Ruling Party Faces Its Biggest Threat in 28 Years," op. cit.

277. Giniger, op. cit.

278. Andrew T. Viglucci, "A New Era for Puerto Rico," *Look Magazine*, March 18, 1969, p. 44; for biographical information see Hancock, op. cit., pp. 171–77.

279. Giniger, op. cit.

280. "Result Surprise in Puerto Rico," *New York Times*, November 9, 1972, p. 15.

281. The poll was taken by the *San Juan Star* and designed by Professor Miguel Valencia. The results were not considered conclusive and were actually almost the reverse of an earlier poll done in August. "Record Puerto Rican Vote Foreseen in 2-Party Race," *New York Times*, October 28, 1972, p. 13.

282. Ibid.

283. Juan M. Vasquez, "Stock Fund Sought to Aid Puerto Rico," *New York Times*, January 16, 1972, p. 29.

284. Vasquez, "Economy Dominates Puerto Rico's Politics," op. cit., p. 22.

285. "Result Surprise in Puerto Rico," op. cit.

286. *Report of the Ad Hoc Advisory Group on Puerto Rico. Compact of Permanent Union Between Puerto Rico and the United States*, October 1975, pp. 3, 4.

287. Ismaro Valezquez, "P. R. Ad Hoc Group Bares Replies to Status Queries," *San Juan Star*, p. 1.

288. *Report of the Ad Hoc Advisory Group*, op. cit., p. vi; Resident Commissioner Jaime Benitez introduced the bill and Committee Co-Chair Representative Philip Burton was supposed to see a modified version of the bill through.

289. Tugwell, op. cit., p. 146.

290. Paul T. David et al., eds., *Presidential Nominating Politics in 1952*, pp. 340–55, cited in Raul Serrano Geyls, "An Introduction to the Study of the Party System of Puerto Rico" (unpublished study, May 1955), p. 27.

291. See René Marqués, "El Puertorrinqueño Docil (Literatura y realidad psycologica)" *Quadernos Americano* (Mexico) 210 (January–February 1962): 119, and *Time for Independence*, op. cit., pp. 32, 101.

292. Tom Wicker, "An American Dilemma: II," *New York Times*, August 5, 1979, and "Puerto Rican Surprises" (editorial), *New York Times*, November 5, 1976.

293. See, for example, Erin Hart, "Crane Stumps the Caguas trail pressing flesh," *San Juan Star*, June 17, 1979, p. 1; Christopher Pala, "Baker tours 2 towns, finds islanders receptive," *San Juan Star*, August 12, 1979, p. 18; Harold J. Liden, "Arrival of 4 nationalists may postpone Bush's visit," *San Juan Star*, September 9, 1979, p. 3; and Andrew Viglucci, "Carnival's Coming to Town" (editorial), *San Juan Star*, October 28, 1979, p. 6.

294. Robert Friedman, "Puerto Rico: la primera primaria," *New York Daily News*, September 9, 1979.

295. Manny Suarez, "NPP to gain 2-party power with NDP win," *San Juan Star*, October 22, 1978, p. 18.

296. David Vidal, "Fistfights Disrupt Caucuses of the Puerto Rican Democrats," *New York Times*, February 23, 1976, pp. 1, 30.

297. "Rolling status tide" (editorials), *San Juan Star*, July 26, 1978, p. 25.

298. Andrew Viglucci, "Kennedy—the PDP's Last Hope," *San Juan Star*, February 11, 1979, p. 6.

299. David Vidal, "Pro-Statehood Candidate Stages Puerto Rican Upset," *New York Times*, November 3, 1976, p. 1.

300. Stern, op. cit., pp. 1, 13.

301. Ibid, p. 1.

302. Vidal, "Pro-Statehood Candidate Stages Puerto Rican Upset," op. cit., p. 1, and Stern, op. cit.

303. "Puerto Rican Surprises," op. cit.

# *3* THE FAILURE OF INDEPENDENCE IN PUERTO RICO

Despierta, Borinqueña,
Que han dado la señal.
Despierta de ese sueñö,
Que es hora de luchar.

A ese llamar patriótico,
¿No arde tu corazón?
Ven, nos sera simpático,
El ruido del cañón.

Nosotros queremos la libertad
Y nuestro machete nos la dará.

National Anthem of Puerto Rico
Words and music by Lola Rodriquez de Tió

As South and Central America fought for and won their independence from Spain, Puerto Rico remained as loyal as the docile lamb on its
crest. As the world decolonized, Puerto Rico voted overwhelmingly in
1967, in a special plebiscite, to continue close ties with the United States.
Why did Puerto Rico remain outside the rhythm of a changing world?
Why has independence so far failed?

This chapter is a revised version of an article of the same name, originally published in
*Civilisations* 25, no. 314 (1975, Brussels).

This chapter touches on issues that are controversial and even explosive. I have tried to be objective, but I must agree with Maldonado Denis that we are only human—

> No one is perfectly impartial or perfectly objective because before anything else, the historian is [human]...living in a certain society and having a certain vision of the world, a particular social position, etc.[1]

There are many explanations offered for why Puerto Rico is not yet independent. North Americans writing about Puerto Rico generally do not spend much time on this issue. Their books usually have been attempts to show how well the once poor, neglected island is doing with the United States to help. They are self-congratulatory. Puerto Rico is our world model for peaceful development, the happy marriage of two cultures, and proof of our benevolent intentions. Sometimes the very titles themselves capture the rags to riches theme—*The Stricken Land* (Rexford C. Tugwell), *Puerto Rico: A Success Story* (Ralph Hancock), *Transformation: The Story of Modern Puerto Rico* (Earl Parker Hanson). Implicit is the assumption that independence failed on the island because continued relations with the United States proved so profitable for Puerto Rico. This notion, however, completely ignores the fact that improved economic conditions and increased literacy and self-government are often the fuel for the fire of independence.

Puerto Ricans writing about independence usually assume independence to be desirable (or inevitable).[2] For the failure of independence they have blamed independentist tactics, Muñoz Marin, imperialist acts, and a colonial system. But the failure of independence is much more complicated.

No mere error of tactics or accident of history could have prevented independence if the Puerto Rican people had been strongly committed to it. In addition, repressive acts can stimulate a national commitment; and a system of colonialism did not prevent other colonies from wanting and winning their independence. One has to go back to Puerto Rico's roots and unique historic experience to understand why the island is not independent. First, let us view how imperialist acts and a colonial system are a very real part of the Puerto Rican past and help explain the failure of independence in Puerto Rico.

Those who point to imperialism for the failure of independence either blame repression for destroying the movement or harassment for preventing a movement. Those who cite repression refer to events like the Ponce Massacre, incarceration of the Nationalist leadership, and the personalized and escalating persecution of Nationalist leader Pedro Albizu Campos. Those who blame a more subtle type of imperialism, harassment, for the failure of independence point to job discrimination, phone taps, bombings, beatings, and proven and suspected CIA and FBI surveillances.

While the imperialist explanation refers to specific acts, the colonial explanation for the failure of independence refers to a system. In general, the colonial system can be blamed for inhibiting the development of a civic culture and a national ideology. But most important, the mother country created and controlled institutions, legitimized their control as the natural order of things, and created a psychological system of colonialism, implanting a sense of inferiority and resignation and a mentality of the colonized that accepted the system.

## IMPERIALISM

Called tyranny under Spain, called imperialism under the United States, specific acts by the mother country made it difficult and often impossible for Puerto Ricans to work for their independence.

Independentists were discriminated against and harassed under U.S. rule, according to Maldonado Denis, as early as the 1920s when Governor E. Mont Reilly purged independentists from all political posts.[3] Harassment continued during the 1930s, with orders from Gruening and Winship,[4] and according to Hanson by the early 1940s FBI agents seemed to be "investigating everything." Loyalty to the United States became especially important during World War II because Puerto Rican bases were strategically close to the Panama Canal and Germany was threatening the Canal. If the candidate for a government job had been or was an independentista, the FBI advised that the person was un-American and therefore a poor risk.[5]

Muñoz himself helped discredit independentists during this period by accusing them of being disloyal to his party and of sabotaging his program. By 1946, independentista-Populares were ousted from the party, and the Popular Party in power discriminated against the independentistas when using offices as rewards (such use ensured party discipline and, just as important, party funds).[6]

Although dues-paying as a source of party funds was discontinued by the 1957 Electoral Subsidies Law, some government agencies and departments still do not hire independentistas.[7] Many departments discriminate with discretionary powers in promotion and transfers,[8] by threatening dismissals and by making jobs more difficult.[9] Known Nationalists and Communists are never hired.[10] In 1979, independentist names were being struck from lists of prospective jurors.[11]

There have been many accusations of dismissals from government jobs for independentist membership,[12] denying permits to stations that permit independence groups to broadcast on a daily basis,[13] and refusals to issue passports to independence leaders for travel in South America.[14] Independentistas have been personally threatened, bombed, or shot at— sometimes with the police standing by.[15]

With no exception, every member of FUPI (University Federation for Independence) I interviewed in 1966–67 had felt oppressed by the government. Each had an unhappy story to tell of how the police had tried to use pressure on their family or "interviews" with their neighbors to make it as difficult as possible for them to be political activists. In addition, many independentists believe their phones are tapped. I had a personal experience with the U.S. Army that makes me think their suspicions are well-founded.[16]

Perhaps the most serious government repression however, occurred in 1950 following the Nationalist movement's planned outburst of violence. As described in Chapter 2, in the early days of November 1950, just before the registration period for the referendum on the common-wealth constitution, there were a series of Nationalist uprisings. Following the violence, hundreds of Independence Party leaders were arrested or detained only because of their party membership.[17]

Independentists feel oppressed for good reason. As the Movement Pro Independence explains:

> The objective is to surround the fighters for independence, to isolate them from the rest of society. The repressive policy extends from economic pressure, press defamation, reprisals in business, professions and employment, to open and shameless police terror.[18]

This claim that independentists are oppressed seemed to be fully corroborated by FBI documents describing "an 11 year campaign in New York City and Puerto Rico to disrupt and demoralize political parties advocating Puerto Rican independence...." In fact, "Mari Bras's heart attack in 1964 was one of the 'positive results' the documents cite for the bureau's campaign against him and his party."[19]

Furthermore, because the Nationalists used violence, and because the 1970s have been dotted with nearly a hundred bombings, mostly in Chicago and New York, with FALN (Fuerzas Armada de Liberacion Nacional Puertorriqueña) claiming responsibility, the belief in indepen-dence, even of non-Nationalists, became linked with violence. That explains, for example, why the Movement Pro Independence continually disavowed the use of violence as the major tool of the movement: "Violence is not used except in extreme cases."[20] But for some, violent methods seem to be thought synonymous with independence group membership. Simplicio says, in *La Vida*, "What they [independentists] want is a republic, which means that if you're a bad governor they'll get you out without an election or anything, with bullets."[21]

The belief in independence was also linked with communism. For example, in April 1948, Chancellor Jaime Benitez blamed Communists as well as Nationalists for the student strike that closed down the university;[22] and after the November 1950 uprisings, Muñoz broadcast: "This crime confirms my conviction of the connection of these mad, grotesque and futile violence-makers in Puerto Rico with Communistic propaganda strategy all over the world...."[23] In addition, in 1967, the former Resident Commissioner Santiago Polanco Abreu claimed, "Mari Bras is only a tool of the Communist party."[24] More recently Governor Rafael Hernandez Colon said, in 1975, that "there was 'a clear tie' between the Puerto Rican Socialist Party headed by Juan Mari Bras, and Cuba, asserting that 'the officers and leaders of the party travel continuously to Cuba: they receive training in Cuba.' "[25]

It is because of this kind of accusation that the independentist groups continually assert that they are not controlled or dictated to by outside groups.[26] Nevertheless, the independentists' reliance on the Cuban delegation in the United Nations, the Puerto Rican Socialist Party's attendance of meetings in Communist countries, and their pro-Hanoi statements during the Vietnam War, further confirm for the average Puerto Rican the link between communism and belief in independence. As Simplicio expresses it, "If we become a republic now, Fidel Castro could take us over whenever he wanted to. All he'd have to do is send over a couple of Communist war planes."[27]

Tainted with notions of violence and communism the independentist is not only officially suspect, but is unofficially subject to repression.

The price of independence belief is especially high since Puerto Rican society demands a high degree of conformity. Close living is coupled with "an extreme dependency on the opinion of others,"[28] and a fear of being exposed to "what people will say."[29]

The belief in independence, particularly as it became linked with violence and communism, was not only an official liability but a personal one. *Chisme* (gossip) was often as repressive as administrative policy.

The 1959 governor's civil rights study, published in book form in 1963 by Dr. Edwin Seda Bonilla, concluded "that a high degree of ignorance, indifference, intolerance and authoritarianism existed" in Puerto Rico.[30] Sixty-four percent would deny free speech to persons with anti-religious viewpoints; 72 percent would purge public library shelves of books advocating such views; 76 percent would deny the right of an avowed atheist to teach at the university; and 30 percent would be willing to imprison communist members.[31]

Thus government repression and discrimination became more effective and more oppressive because of social pressure. That is how imperialism prevents rather than inspires independence feelings in Puerto Rico.

## COLONIALISM

You cannot accurately measure the seriousness and the consequences of others controlling your life. I am sensitive to it as a woman in a man-controlled world. I can also appreciate the effect outside control has had on Puerto Rico thanks to my experience living there, and the candor with which independentists have confided in me.

> Not so very long ago, the earth numbered two thousand million inhabitants; five hundred million men, and one thousand five hundred million natives. The former had the Word; the others had the use of it.[32]

So wrote Sartre in his preface to *The Wretched of the Earth*. And in this way the colonized were brainwashed into thinking they were wretched. Such a mentality, according to Fanon, is the natural result of colonialism.[33]

In Puerto Rico, colonial experience helped create a mentality of inferiority.

### Inferiority

Spain's rule was strict and autocratic, and the Puerto Ricans were "trained by four centuries of Spanish rule into a habit of uncomplaining submissiveness."[34] Spain treated the island as second-rate and built no great cathedrals or university. United States officials reinforced that sense, for they completely ignored Puerto Rican mores and acted as if they "believed the Island sprung from the ocean just on the eve of the landing of American troups."[35] As already described in Chapter 2, for 30 years Puerto Rican school lessons were taught in English and the island was (mis)spelled Porto Rico for the convenience of the non-Spanish colonizer.

The Puerto Rican sense of inferiority has a class[36] and a race basis.[37] Larrabee said of the Spanish American War, "in less than four months it was over; the waifs of the world deposited on our doorsteps."[38]

United States rule reinforced a sense of inferiority by making the island an unincorporated territory. The native Puerto Rican's rights were not constitutionally guaranteed but congressionally determined. For 17 years, the island citizens were called "the people of Puerto Rico" and the islander was not a citizen of any place. It was as though the "native" was not thought to be worthy of U.S. citizenship.

The slowness with which reforms were meted suggests that the native was not thought to be capable of democracy. Joseph Foraker's defense of a limited amount of island participation was described in Chapter 2. Others shared his sentiment. Senator Joseph Cannon's feelings about Puerto Rico were symptomatic of what seems like real contempt for Puerto

Ricans as "unfit for self-government." During the debates on the Jones Act, Cannon said that Caucasian civilization was not exportable to the tropics and constitutional experiments were worse than useless "if you have not the people who are competent to exercise sovereign power."[39]

Such ideas were internalized by Puerto Ricans and reflected in statements like the one from Chapter 2 made by Muñoz Rivera in 1916 asking for the Jones Act "that we may demonstrate that it is easy for us to constitute a stable republican government."

This colonial notion still seems to be prevalent. Independentist campaigner Alvarez Silva, for example, began an argument for independence in 1967: "There has been a lot of talk about the proposition that only Anglo-Saxons and the countries they dominate and govern are able to rule themselves in a stable democratic manner. This is supposed to follow from a type of national character that is suitable to democratic government."[40] Thus a popular fear that anarchy would be linked to independence must stem at least in part from U.S. rule (and its racism) and the sense of inferiority it instilled in the Puerto Ricans about their ability to govern themselves.

In addition, a sense of inferiority was communicated in the casualness with which decisions affecting the island were made. With few exceptions, shoddy, third-rate politicians, minor patronage appointees, and lame-duck congresspersons were sent to the tropics to be governor for a few years.[41] In fact, as late as 1946, soon-to-be-governor Luis Muñoz Marin said, "We hold that Puerto Rico is too mature politically to be ruled by a governor appointed out of a clear sky—or a clouded one—by influences completely alien to Puerto Rican democracy."[42] Furthermore, changes in the Organic Act governing Puerto Rico not only came slowly, after decades of petitioning false starts and disappointments, but congressional decisions were often made without regard for the island's interests (for example, the inclusion of a 500 Acre Law in the Foraker Act of 1900 to protect U.S. sugar interests). Indeed, lack of interest as well as mismanagement by the United States communicated a sense that Puerto Ricans weren't worthy of interest and attention.

A sense of inferiority (what Concepción de Gracia called "the servitude mind")[43] was buttressed by an economic dependency on the United States—first, because of the absentee-owned, one-crop status of sugar on the island. By the 1930s, "most of the best land was given over to cane and 70 percent of the island's income from exports was derived from sugar and its products—which meant that the jibaro's rice (from Louisiana and Texas), his *bacalao* (codfish, from Newfoundland) and his *machetes* (from Hartford, Connecticut) were bought with sugar money."[44] United States commentators were describing the Puerto Rican population as being in a state of virtual peonage to the "big plantation."[45]

After World War II, the island quickly became dependent on Fomento-encouraged industry, "light industry with a high percentage of labor force" which created a "dependent bourgeoisie," according to Maldonado Denis.[46] In suburb and slum alike, because of the United States, many Puerto Ricans, according to Mintz, "achieved a significantly higher standard of living."[47] This increased economic opportunity and economic prosperity are new and create an insecurity,[48] a "paranoic fear of relapsing into rural poverty,"[49] and a need to join "the American way of life."[50] As Erasmo in *La Vida* expresses it:

> Suppose the United States should decide to say, "All right, we will send no more aid to Puerto Rico." Wouldn't we be worse off even than Santo Domingo then? We would. The rice grown here and the food reserves on the island wouldn't last four months.[51]

But a sense of inferiority does not come from colonialism alone. There is also a sense of inferiority felt by those coming from a small island that has made no great contributions to the world and where nothing grand happens. As Muñoz admits:

> You cannot consider the more articulate portion of the Puerto Rican soul without getting the suggestion that it is affected with an inferiority complex. In an island where nothing grand ever happened everything happens in the grand manner...I have been called sublime for donating $2 to a worthy cause.[52]

Muñoz captures here the ambivalence between a "haunting sense of inferiority," and an exaggerated grandness.[53] Thus, the psychology of colonialism, the economics of dependency, and the smallness and poverty of the island combined to create feelings of Puerto Rican inferiority.

Yet the island's size and relative poverty is not seen as an important liability in today's decolonized world. The Movement Pro Independence, in its pamphlet, *Time for Independence*, refers to the appearance of a large group of neutralist countries "which are close to serving as a balance point in the international situation. For the first time in modern history, countries militarily weak and economically underdeveloped are playing an outstanding role in international relations."[54] Independentistas talk of Puerto Rico playing such a role.[55]

The process of decolonialization and the formation of new independent states characterizes the world after World War II.[56] The notion of the uniqueness and the value of each country gives new vision to the Puerto Rican independentist.

Paz talks about the historical alienation of dependent peoples;[57] small dependent nations have always "lived on the periphery of history," but now that there no longer is any "center of the world,"[58] there is a new appreciation for each unique "people."[59] Thus, Puerto Rico does not need a mother country to integrate the small island into the world of nations, and Concepción's lament, "We live with our windows closed to the world,"[60] is answered by a new world of experience. In such a world, independence becomes a natural state of all nationalities, and Puerto Rico, according to Juan Mari Bras, is a nationality naturally defined by her geography; she is an island.[61] Puerto Rican independentistas have tried to use the world-wide anticolonial sentiment to their advantage. The most effective arena has been the United Nations.

## Resignation

A sense of resignation was planted by a colonial system that promoted a sense of powerlessness. The Spanish reign was not only autocratic, it was unpredictable. Spanish rule created a "heritage of frustration" as political concessions from Spain would be forthcoming and then withdrawn.[62] The Puerto Rican was resigned to a life he could not completely control.

As Muñoz Marin describes it:

> When liberals got the upper hand in Spain which was rarely, they relieved their feelings by granting reforms to the colonies, reforms that, so far as Puerto Rico was concerned, were accepted gratefully and surprisedly and relinquished when the time came dumbly and humbly.[63]

United States rule created other kinds of frustration. American governors were often unpopular, like Gore and Winship, and usually uninterested in the island's welfare. In addition, congressional rule was slow and hard to predict. Committee endorsements did not insure passage of a bill and the separation of powers meant that even a President's support did not ensure congressional action. In fact, the Puerto Rican had to wade through a myriad of bills, reports, hearings, congressional committees, and executive commissions not knowing what bills would be changed and which would become law.[64] Witness, for example, the history of the Elective Governor's Act, described in the last chapter.

For the Puerto Rican petitioner, U.S. rule meant "the continuous need to anticipate what Washington will think, to court the Federal power by not asking too much or too soon, to carry on a debate the essential terms of which are set by Washington...."[65] They were conditions that did not promote "the willing feeling that the individual can command the future to serve his own ends," a "kind of ambitious focusing upon one's future and willful searching for the means of achieving it."[66] It is a legacy that made a doctor describing the Puerto Rican health program in 1950 suggest, "it is imperative that we put into the attitude of people, into their everyday conscious thinking, that illness and infirmity are to a very large measure preventable...that it is unnecessary to suffer...."[67] It is the reason that in the Fomento program "in most cases the job had to seek the worker rather than vice versa...,"[68] and it is one reason why a program of birth control never worked.[69] As Muñoz Marín candidly admits:

> We are always contemplating what we never carry out.... Visions that burst forth magnificently and take impetus as plans, cool off as calculations, and generally peter out as accomplishments.[70]

A sense of resignation comes not only from colonialism.[71] The trait that has also been described as "fatalism,"[72] "pessimism,"[73] and "hope-lessness"[74] stems in part from a class system[75] and a poverty of land that discouraged the chance for upward mobility and improvement. The "lower class became numerically dominant early in the colonial period... its relationship with the dominant group was ordered on a non-competitive basis."[76] In other words, the poor accepted their position.

On the agricultural island, the lower class were jibaros and *agregados* (squatter farmers). They had to be "satisfied with what little they could get out of the land without too much effort (if the agregado planted more productive crops he'd be obliged to share it with the owner of the land)...."[77] The poor farmer was resigned to the way things were. He did not plan; he did not save. He had no choice.[78]

The feeling of powerlessness and passivity seems also to have been a natural part of slavery, an integral part of feudalism, and a logical effect of periodic hurricanes, "periodic storms that carry all away with them and make human effort and ingenuity seem like naught...."[79] For Pedreira, "we live in constant fear, during the summer months of desolation.... This is an important element in our pessimism."[80]

A resigned acceptance of life comes also from Catholicism. "Our people have faith and hope and believe that God will provide," says a Puerto Rican woman.[81] Rural poor accept the adage, "sit down and wait for God will take care of us."[82]

So not only colonialism but Catholicism, a class system, hurricanes, and poverty have contributed to a resigned acceptance of the way things are. Maldonado Denis captures this sense of resignation. Describing the U.S. takeover he says, "The majority of the population—the peasants and workers—of course remained on the periphery, accepting the change of sovereignty with the same fatalism with which they accepted hookworm, hurricanes, and tuberculosis."[83]

Building a mass movement for independence is almost an impossible task on an island with a tradition of fatalism, of resignation. A people that blame God or fate are not quick to blame a lesser force. And if they did blame the United States, they were not quick to act. Puerto Ricans had no tradition of concerted effort or civic-style group organizing.

## Desempleo Cívico

In general, Puerto Ricans have not been "public-regarding."[84] Partly it is because of a tradition of Spanish individualism.[85] Spanish individualism emphasizes personal *dignidad*[86] with a "fighting propensity for questions of honor,"[87] and a "high premium on masculinity and virility."[88] But also *desempleo cívico* comes from Puerto Rico's colonial experience.

Under Spain, there was no opportunity for concerted economic effort. On the agricultural island, life was organized either in a hacienda fashion or isolated in jíbaro style. In addition, politically, an unresponsive autocratic rule was no incentive to civic-style group organizing. The Peninsulares ran the government and the creole (the Puerto Rican) could not participate in the administration of the island, was handicapped in business without favorable administrative influence, and had no outlet for his grievances. And under U.S. rule (as already described) petitions went unanswered and concerted effort was ignored. United States rule might have been more benevolent, but the result was the same. The effect is a lack of civic culture or desempleo civico,[89] accompanied by what Banfield calls "amoral familism."[90]

> The moral passivity of the masses, the absence of a community sense, the general indifference to every consideration save that of personal protection, all were noted with an almost obsessive exhaustiveness by Puerto Rican writers throughout the nineteenth century.[91]

The legacy remains.

In 1949, the great difficulty in organizing villages in Title V communities stemmed from a lack of community spirit. The program was to make communities of *parcelas*, a few hundred families, each with approximately one acre of land. As one knowledgeable source explained, "kin solidarity operates to the exclusion of easy identification with non-kin."[92]

Another symptom of the lack of civic culture was that power was expected to be used personally. Favoritism and nepotism are to some degree still expected to play a part in administrative decision making; according to Goodsell, the merit system was skirted for over half a century, and in 1940, "nepotism in the small island was so widespread that enforcement not only would have been impossible, but would have resulted in the government's losing vast numbers of experienced personnel, both bad and good."[93]

Lack of civic culture and the absence of a tradition of concerted effort, stemming from colonial experience, were bound to inhibit the formation of a mass independence movement. It was not lack of courage, it was that the Puerto Ricans' sense of dignity was personal, not national. So while they might be courageous for personal reasons like *machismo* (manliness) or *el nombre de la familia* (family name), Puerto Ricans "demonstrate a great incapacity to die in a group."[94] This was Spain's legacy and also the result of colonialism.

It is not surprising that Nationalist leader Albizu Campos tried to activate his countrypeople by describing the affront to the island in personal terms. Catholicism and the Spanish tradition and language were being threatened. Albizu referred to the Americanization process as a "stupid assault against our Christian social order" and "the ridiculous attempt to destroy our Spanish culture." What was even more of a macho affront was that women were being made prostitutes, "destroying the morality of a chivalrous race" under the "misleading guise of birth control."[95] These were important Nationalist arguments. They were personal.

Muñoz and the Populares were no different in this regard. *Pan, tierra, libertad* (bread, land, and liberty) were personal, not national, goals, advertised on a background of *pava*, the jibaro's hat, a personal tribute. Between 1938 and 1940 Muñoz campaigned in jibaro country, telling his countrypeople that if they didn't feel a difference in their lives, "throw us out of office." His major campaign theme was his promise to implement the 500 Acre Law so that squatter farmers and slum dwellers could acquire their own parcels of land. For the loyalty of the electorate, Muñoz was competing with the selfishness of selling votes and offering another way of making a vote personally advantageous and personally meaningful.

A tradition of resignation, a lack of civic culture, and a deep sense of personal rather than national pride made a mass independence movement highly unlikely.

## PERSONALISM

Puerto Rico has no real tradition of political ideology.[96] As a colony, there was no opportunity for political experience except as pragmatic maneuvering to win concessions from the mother country.[97] Power was on the mainland, and the great issues were decided by others. If pragmatism describes Puerto Rico's relationship with the colonizer, personalism characterizes Puerto Rican politics on the island.[98]

Partly, the roots of *personalismo* are in the centralized autocratic rule by the Spanish governor-general;[99] partly, it is rooted in the "personalistic authority of the 'patrón' in rural life,"[100] the traditional paternalistic *patrono-obrero* relationship on the sugar and coffee haciendas, which is still very much in evidence in Fomento factories, where "Puerto Rican factory workers appear to court paternalism instead of resenting it."[101]

The personalized leadership of Puerto Rican political parties is accompanied by centralized control. In 1955, Wells said of the three major parties that they were "very centralized and well-disciplined."[102] Effective control and formal leadership have traditionally been combined in the same person,[103] and the parties' general assemblies have been "primarily demonstrative, not deliberate bodies."[104] When there is meaningful debate within the party it usually means there are two leaders (Muñoz Rivera and De Diego in 1915, Muñoz Marín and Barceló in 1936, and Muñoz Marín and Concepción de Gracia in 1946). Not surprisingly, such debate can foreshadow the creation of a new party.[105]

Muñoz's following personalized his leadership. For the poor of the island, "He is our leader who has given us faith in ourselves."[106] "The common humble folk of the island worship him and many call themselves *Muñocistas*, followers of Muñoz."[107] Gordon Lewis reports a rather severe case of idolatry: at a 1956 public meeting, one voter declared, "The day that you die, Don Luis, I will hang myself."[108] Another Muñocito in Barrio Poyal, asked if he had a picture of a saint, jokingly pointed to a photo of Muñoz and reportedly said: "This is my saint; he lives in San Juan."[109]

Muñoz was a "political creator."[110] On an island with a tradition of personal leadership, his political success came from creating a personal following. "The ultimate measure of that success was that, after a decade of active leadership, his monopoly was so impregnable that it was found expedient to create an artificial opposition in the Constitution of the new Commonwealth."[111]

Muñoz's personalized power was greater than any other Puerto Rican leader's because his party had the added strength of its new support. According to Wells, the Popular Party "won the enthusiastic support of the common people who prior to 1940, had been largely indifferent to party struggles."[112] Muñoz had created a base of power for the PDP that included segments of the Puerto Rican population who had never before been active participants in the electoral process. By tapping this new source of support, Muñoz increased his party's power and therefore his own.

Although there was no plebiscite held to measure independence sentiment, a variety of sources suggest, as we have seen in Chapter 2, that independence was the preference of the majority of the Populares in the mid-1940s. Muñoz had been quite right, the "sentiment for independence" was "real enough...it only waits to be organized by a politician."[113] Aided by his party's youth, the deterioration of the opposition, a

reform-minded governor Tugwell, a 500 Acre Act ready for implementation, and the United States' growing more responsive to Puerto
Rican needs because of the island's wartime strategic location, Muñoz
quickly became undisputed leader of the island.

As leader, however, he was not organizing the "sentiment for
independence." Muñoz was against independence because it would mean
certain economic disaster, and, as will be seen in Chapter 4, he was willing
to compromise the island's autonomy for a more promising economic
relationship. Independence, he said, represented an economic tombstone, "the corpse of a free man."[114]

Thus, at a time when a majority of Popular Party members and
political leaders were for independence, Muñoz cut the spirit and support
for independence by declaring that it was incompatible to belong to the
Congress for Independence (CPI) and the Popular Party simultaneously.
His declaration of incompatibility was ratified by the party's Central
Committee (the Arecibo Resolution), and independentista Populares
were expelled.

By October 20, 1946, the expelled Populares had created a new
party for independence. A provisional central directive board was set up,
and just a few months after it had started its registration drive the newly
organized Independence Party had qualified in enough municipal districts
to be assured a place on the 1948 ballot. What had begun as a
nonpartisan movement to educate (Congress for Independence) was now
a political party (Puerto Rican Independence Party) ready to compete with
the PDP for votes in the election of 1948.

Certainly the formation of an Independence Party was a reaction to
the Popular Party over whether to postpone the independence issue. But
the new party was a reaction to the Populares in matters of organizational
style as well. The Independence Party "in its self-conscious opposition to
'one-man rule'... prided itself on its allegedly democratic internal structure and its devotion to the structural niceties of the system of separation
of powers."[115] Party rules divided decision making between the executive
commission and a board of directors.[116] The new party was reacting to
Muñoz's ironclad authority. After all, "the single most significant fact
about the Popular Party was its almost total identification with the person
of its founder and leader, Luis Muñoz Marin."[117]

Muñoz controlled his party through apparatus he created. In 1937 he
organized a central board, and he appointed a series of ad hoc electoral
committees as he traveled around the country.[118] By 1942 the party, as it
was finally developed with the establishment of a Founder's Council and
with a Central Committee (to be composed of Popular legislators),
remained completely centralized and the rule remained Muñoz's own.

In 1940, for example, Muñoz himself wrote the party platform and
the important campaign booklet, "El Catecismo del Pueblo." In fact, for

20 years the party rules were practically inaccessible to anyone but a few top leaders.[119] (Some party members even doubted that there were party *reglamentos*.)[120] In addition, the general assemblies passed all of Muñoz's resolutions by acclamation.[121]

Muñoz Marin not only ran his party, he ran the island. Even Governor Tugwell felt powerless in the face of Muñoz's influence. As president of the Senate, according to Governor Tugwell, Muñoz gave orders to Cabinet members without consulting the governor. "The bureaucrcy regarded him as its head rather than me," Tugwell complained.[122] The *New York Times*, reported in March 1948, "as things stand today, Luis Muñoz Marin is the undisputed boss of the island."[123] Power moved with Muñoz. In 1948, after President Truman signed the Elective Governor Act and Muñoz was elected governor, political power (in Puerto Rico) shifted, accordingly, from the legislative to the executive branch.[124] Muñoz not only controlled the Popular Democratic Party, he controlled the government. Formation of an Independence Party with its commitment to democratic niceties, was in part a "reaction to a highly centralized personal authority,"[125] the one-man rule of Muñoz Marin.

## 1951—PERSONALISM VERSUS IDEOLOGY

For the independence cause, the most important election of the century was held in 1952. Muñoz was promoting commonwealth as an alternative to independence, and the election was a test of his strength. The Independence Party was a legitimate, respected party, which had already participated in one island election and which offered an acceptable way to register independence preference. But it is a mistake to think of this election as a referendum between commonwealth and independence. The election pitted an ideological commitment against a personal leadership. They rested on *two different bases of support*.

Thus imperialist repression, both violent and harassing, official and unofficial, contributed to the failure of independence in Puerto Rico. So did colonialism, for it implanted on the island a colonial attitude—a feeling of inferiority, a feeling of powerlessness and, helped by Catholicism and Hispanic tradition, a sense of resignation and desempleo cívico. Furthermore, politics was characterized by personalism, and there was no tradition of national ideology. This enabled the overwhelming allegiance to Muñoz to overshadow the support for independence even though the "sentiment for independence" was there.

No one person determined more of Puerto Rico's history and future than Luis Muñoz Marin, creator and leader of the Popular Democratic Party, first elected governor, the architect of commonwealth and Operation Bootstrap. The next chapter focuses on Don Luis.

## NOTES

1. "Nadie es perfectamente 'imparcial' ni perfectamente 'objectivo,' porque antes que cada cosa el historiador es un hombre y, como tal, un ser que vive dentro de una determinada sociedad y que tiene a su vez una cierta visión del mundo, una peculiar ubicación social, etcétera." Manuel Maldonado Denis, *Puerto Rico: Una interpretacion historico-social*, p. 10.

2. Post World War II, there seems to be almost a natural law assumption that all nations should be independent.

3. Manuel Maldonado Denis, *Puerto Rico: A Socio-Historic Interpretation*, p. 114.

4. Gruening allegedly was interested in anti-American activities and at his request two special agents from the Division of Investigation of the Department of Interior were sent to Puerto Rico and FBI activities were extended. Then, under Governor Winship's instructions, the Puerto Rican Legislature set up a special investigatory commission with a similar task; and, under Gruening's orders, they checked independence infiltration in the PRRA. Juan Antonio Corretjer, *Albizu Campos and the Ponce Massacre*, pp. 6–7.

5. Earl Parker Hanson, *Puerto Rico: Land of Wonders*, p. 144.

6. After the passage in 1947 of the Personnel Act, which dropped the anti-quota provision of the 1931 Personnel Act, employees were "free to contribute" party "dues," (about 2 percent of government employees' salaries and as high as 5 percent from municipal employees). Dues were paid "semi-voluntarily, and 90 to 95 percent of the PDP's annual income came from these contributions. Henry Wells and Robert W. Anderson, "Government Financing of Political Parties in Puerto Rico," pp. 8–9; also see Robert W. Anderson, *Party Politics in Puerto Rico*, pp. 153–54.

7. Pedro Muñoz Amato, *Problemas de Derechos Civiles en la Administration de Personal de Estado Libre Associado de Puerto Rico*, 1961, in Gordon K. Lewis, *Puerto Rico: Freedom and Power in the Caribbean*, p. 132.

8. Lewis mentions the Department of Education, ibid. For example, the secretary of education ordered the transfer of 34 teachers from Escuela Superior Juan Ponce de Leon to other schools in the district because of their independence militancy. *Claridad*, No. 267, August 2, 1970, p. 3.

9. See Lewis, *Puerto Rico: Freedom and Power in the Caribbean*.

10. Lewis, ibid.

11. Juan A. Villaran, jury commissioner, testified in San Juan Superior Court, that he struck "subversives" from the juror's list.

12. Two cases are cited in Rubén Berrios Martinez. "The Commonwealth of Puerto Rico: Its Reality in the National and World Community" (Divisional Thesis, Yale Law School, 1964), p. 172.

13. *El Imparical*, June 26, 1962, p. 7, in Berrios, ibid., p. 172.

14. *El Mundo*, September 10, 1963, p. 11, in Berrios, ibid., p. 172.

15. For a list of bombings and arsons, see Gilberto Concepción Suarez, "En Blanco y Negro—El Discurso de Ferré y la Represión Posterior," *Bohemia*, No. 418 (March 29 to April 4, 1971), p. 38. See also Luis Muñiz, "NPP Accused of Post-Riot Hysteria," *San Juan Star*, March 17, 1971, p. 3; "Elementos Derechistas Atentan Contra Independentistas Bayamon," *Claridad*, No. 300, April 4, 1970, p. 7; *Claridad*, No. 269, August 16, 1971, p. 5 (PIP headquarters are shot at); *Claridad*, No. 301, April 11, 1971 (an independentist, Dr. Milton Soltero, had his pharmacy, "Domus," bombed); see Efrain Parrilla, "Independence Activists Tortugo Home Burned by Mob," *San Juan Star*, March 14, 1971 ("It was the latest in a rash of fires which have destroyed the homes of several independentists....At least three Tortugo residents who say they witnessed the attacks on Mrs. Cordero's home claimed police made little effort either time to prevent the crowd from trying to burn the house.... Four vehicles used by the activists were burned by the mob..."); also see *Claridad*, No. 298, March 21, 1971, p. 5.

16. In April 1966 I tried to call the home of Concepción de Gracia, president of the PIP, several times, to arrange an interview. I got "the army" instead, and an officer, Mike Ortiz Benitez, asked me why I was calling Concepción, arranged to meet me, and asked me questions about my work. I naively accepted his dinner invitation. I would still be thinking the wrong number was a mistake, had I not reached the army instead of Concepción so many times. Several weeks after I left the island, there was a scandal about Concepción's phone being tapped.

17. David Helfeld, "Discrimination for Political Beliefs and Associations" (unpublished report to the Puerto Rican Civil Liberties Commission, December 19, 1958), p. 25, n. 17, cited in Anderson, op. cit., p. 109.

18. *The Time for Independence: Political Thesis—Pro Independence Movement of Puerto Rico*. Translation based on the original Spanish edition published in San Juan, Puerto Rico, in 1963, p. 91.

19. Jo Thomas, "Documents Show F.B.I. Harassed Puerto Rican Separatist Parties," *New York Times*, November 22, 1977, p. 26.

20. *Time for Independence*, op. cit., p. 91.

21. Oscar Lewis, *La Vida*, p. 453.

22. *New York Times*, April 16, 1948, p. 7.

23. William H. Hackett, *The Nationalist Party*, Committee Print of the House Committee on Interior and Insular Affairs (Washington, D.C.: U.S. Government Printing Offce, 1951), p. 22.

24. Harry Turner, "Polanco Urges Big Democratic Meet," *San Juan Star*, August 25, 1967, p. 3.

25. David Binder, "Cuba said to Aid Puerto Rico Foes: Governor

Hernandez Says Castro is Training Terrorists," *New York Times*, May 20, 1976, p. 11.

26. It is why Narcisco Rabell, the MPI representative to Havana, was fired for "urging from Havana that Puerto Rican independence sympathizers go out on the streets and demonstrate against the plebiscite on July 23." It seemed like too much of a directive from "outside": "De más está subrayer que es intolerable que ningún miembro del Movimiento, menos aún un delegado en el extranjero, pretenda actuar pro encima de la dirección de nuestra organización," *Claridad*, No. 156, p. 1.

27. Oscar Lewis, op. cit., p. 454.

28. Sidney W. Mintz, "Puerto Rico: An Essay in the Definition of a National Culture" (Appendix), in *Puerto Rico Status. Selected Background Studies*, (Washington, D.C.: U.S. Government Printing Office, 1966), p. 396.

29. Gordon Lewis, op. cit., p. 289.

30. *San Juan Star*, February 4, 1967, p. 6.

31. See Edwin Seda Bonilla, *Actitud, Conocimiento y Apercepción de los Derechos Civiles en el Pueblo Puertorriqueño* (Rio Piedras: Facultad de Ciencias Sociales, Centro de Investigaciones, Sociales, mimeographed, 1959), cited in Gordon Lewis, op. cit., p. 477.

32. Jean Paul Sartre, "Preface" in Franz Fanon, *The Wretched of the Earth*, p. 7.

33. Ibid., p. 211.

34. Gordon Lewis, op. cit., p. 7.

35. Frederico Degelau, *The Political Status of Puerto Rico*, p. 3.

36. The island was mostly "lower class" and the upper class, "probably because of their colonial and feudal heritage," regarded them as inferior. Theodore Brameld, *The Remaking of a Culture*, p. 63.

37. "As the Indian and other inferior orders of the human family have ever given place to the Caucasian branch; so must, as a general law, all mixtures of that branch with these, fade before the greater intelligence of its pure blood—so certainly as the stars do before the sun." Thomas Jefferson Farnham, *Mexico: Its Geography—Its People—And Its Institutions* (New York: 1846), p. 3, quoted in Manuel P. Servin, ed., *The Mexican-Americans: An awakening minority*.

38. Harold A. Larrabee, "The Enemies of Empire," *American Heritage* 11, no. 4 (June, 1960): 76.

39. Frank Gatell, "The Art of the Possible: Luis Munoz Rivera and the Puerto Rican Jones Bill," *Americas* 17, no. 1 (July, 1960): 17–18.

40. Hector Alvarez Silva in "The Plebiscite Forum," *San Juan Star*, July 2, 1967, pp. 20, 22.

41. Rexford G. Tugwell, *The Art of Politics as Practiced by Three Great Ameicans: Franklin Delano Roosevelt, Luis Muñoz Marin, and Fiorello H. LaGuardia*, p. 36.

42. Luis Muñoz Marin, "A Plea for Puerto Rico," *The Nation*, May 11, 1946, p.572.

43. Gilberto Concepción de Gracia, Interview, April 10, 1966.

44. Ralph Hancock, *Puerto Rico: A Success Story*, p. 63.

45. See, for example, *The Nation*, May 6, 1936, p. 568.

46. Manuel Maldonado Denis, "Toward a Marxist Interpretation of the History of Puerto Rico," *The Rican* 11, no. 1 (October, 1974): 47, 48.

47. Mintz, op. cit., p. 388.

48. See Earl Parker Hanson, *Puerto Rico: Ally for.Progress*, p. 111.

49. Gordon Lewis, op. cit., p. 186.

50. Hanson, op. cit., p. 111.

51. Oscar Lewis, op. cit., p. 83.

52. Luis Muñoz Marin, "Porto Rico: The American Colony," *The Nation*, April 8, 1925, pp. 379–80.

53. Gordon Lewis talks of a "psychology of ambivalence that oscillates between an uplifted national pride and a haunting sense of inferiority." Op. cit., p. 314.

54. *Time for Independence*, p. 41.

55. See Chapter 7 for a description of the experience in international relations of the independentists themselves.

56. Milton Pabon, "La Integración Política en Puerto Rico," *Revista de Ciencias Sociales* 10, no. 2 (June, 1966): 134.

57. Octavio Paz, *The Labyrinth of Solitude: Life and Thought in Mexico*, p. 134.

58. Ibid. Alienation, he says, is a condition shared by all men, and everyone is a peripheral being.

59. "Puerto Rico is a distinctive part of the world." Gilberto Concepción de Gracia, speaking to a student audience at the well-attended foro, "La Independencia Frente Al Plebiscito," held in the Antiteatro de Estudias Generales at 8 p.m., March 4, 1967.

60. Concepción de Gracia, quoted in "A Talk with the Candidates," *San Juan Review* 50, no. 9 (October 1964).

61. Interview, August 28, 1967.

62. *Status of Puerto Rico. Report of the United States–Puerto Rico Commission on the Status of Puerto Rico*. August, 1966, p. 33.

63. Luis Muñoz Marin, "Porto Rico: The American Colony," p. 379.

64. In 1945, for example, a Tydings Independence Bill was being considered and a report on the economic consequences of independence was being prepared for him by the Commerce Department at the same time that hearings were being held on a Tydings-sponsored Elective Governor Bill.

65. Gordon Lewis, op. cit., p. 430.

66. C. Wright Mills et al., *The Puerto Rican Journey* (New York:

Harper and Brothers, 1950), p. 168. "We tried a different approach to long-run aspirations by asking each respondent, 'What kind of work would you like to be doing five years from now?'... about one quarter of the sample could not bring their minds to bear on the question..."; Lloyd G. Reynolds and Peter Gregory, *Wages, Productivity and Industrialization in Puerto Rico*, p. 276.

67. Hanson, *Puerto Rico: Land of Wonders*, p. 243.

68. In most cases the jobs had to seek the workers rather than vice versa.... In only about one quarter of the cases did the worker make active application either at the factory gate or by registering with the public employment service. Much the commonest situation was one in which a friend or relative knew of a factory vacancy, persuaded the worker to take an interest in it, and perhaps interceded with the foreman or personnel manager to secure preferential consideration." Reynolds, op. cit., p. 212.

69. "The attitude of the jíbaro in regard to children is that "God sends them." José C. Rosario, *The Development of the Puerto Rican Jíbaro and His Present Attitude Towards Society*, p. 85. But it is resignation, not religiosity, which is the reason planned families fail in Puerto Rico. J. Mayone Stycos, in "Family and Fertility in Puerto Rico," refers to Hatt's study of 13,000 Puerto Ricans (Paul K. Hatt, *Background of Human Fertility in Puerto Rico: A Sociological Survey*, p. 70), in which, of 2,125 Puerto Rican women, fewer than 5 percent mentioned religious scruples as the reason why birth control methods were not employed, in Eugenio Fernández Méndez, *Portrait of a Society: A Book of Readings on Puerto Rican Society*, pp. 70–80.

70. Muñoz Marin, "Porto Rico: The American Colony," p. 380.

71. "We are docile and passive characterized by a sense of resignation." Antonio S. Pedreira, *Insularismo Ensayos de Interpretación Puertorriqueña*, p. 33.

72. Hanson, *Puerto Rico: Land of Wonders*, p. 143; Ralph Hancock, op. cit., p. 20.

73. Pedreira, op. cit., p. 38. See also, Renė Marqués, "Pesimismo Literario y Optimismo Político: Su Coexistencia en el Puerto Rico Actual," in *Cuadernos Americanos*, 1959, pp. 43–74.

74. Brameld, op. cit., pp. 119–20.

75. Robert A. Manners and Julian H. Steward, "The Cultural Study of Contemporary Societies: Puerto Rico," in Fernández Méndez, *Portrait of a Society*, pp. 21–24.

76. Roger Rogler, "The Morality of Race Mixing in Puerto Rico," in ibid., p. 50.

77. Rosario, op. cit., pp. 28–29.

78. Ibid., p. 49.

79. "...that explains the passive helplessness of the rural community." Victor S. Clark, *Porto Rico and Its Problems*, p. 303, in Lewis, op. cit., p. 146.

80. Pedreira, op. cit., p. 38.

81. Christopher Rand, *The Puerto Ricans*, p. 71.

82. "Sentarse a esperar." Brameld, op. cit., pp. 119–120.

83. Maldonado Denis, *Puerto Rico: A Socio-Historic Interpretation*, p. 58.

84. For a definition see James Q. Wilson and Edward C. Banfield, "Public-Regardingness as a Value Premise in Voting Behavior," *American Political Science Review*, December, 1964, pp. 333–54.

85. See Hancock, op. cit., p. 159, and Hanson, *Puerto Rico: Land of Wonders*, p. 281.

86. Melvin M. Tumin and Arnold S. Feldman, *Social Class and Social Change in Puerto Rico*, p. 18.

87. Rosario, op. cit., p. 103.

88. J. Mayone Stycos, "Family and Fertility in Puerto Rico," in Fernández Méndez, *Portrait of a Society*, p. 72.

89. Gordon Lewis, op. cit., p. 254.

90. Edward C. Banfield, *The Moral Basis of a Backward Society*.

91. Gordon Lewis, op. cit., p. 60.

92. Stycos, op. cit., p. 77.

93. Charles T. Goodsell, *The Administration of a Revolution*, p. 98.

94. "...individualmente no le importa perder la vida que pone en peligro pro cualquier tonteria personal; colectivamente es lo contrario; demuestra una gran incapacidad para morir en grupo." Pedreira, op. cit., p. 33.

95. Harwood Hull, "Freedom Bill Splits Puerto Rico," *New York Times*, May 3, 1936, p. 6E.

96. This gives the island a two-dimensional quality of a society, wholly "modern," "without tradition and without ideas." Alfred Kazin, "In Puerto Rico," *Commentary* 29, no. 2 (February, 1960): 114.

97. "If the status issue has been a prison keeping Puerto Rican political thinkers from the invigorating winds of doctrine blowing outside, it has also protected them from the windiness of political metaphysics and metaphysical politicians." Daniel J. Boorstin, "Self-Discovery in Puerto Rico," *Yale Review* 45 (1955–56): 239.

98. Anderson, op. cit., p. 2.

99. "It was a highly centralized form of government. All the officers, provincial and municipal, received their positions, with few exceptions, from the Governor-General, and were removable by him." Carroll, op. cit., p. 20. Under Spain, Puerto Rico's system of government was derived from the Code of Laws of the Indies (1761) and the Revised Code of Spanish Laws (1795). Both followed the doctrine of royal absolutism. An

omnipotent governor was coupled with a high degree of governmental control over human affairs. *Status of Puerto Rico. Report*, p. 31.

100. Frederico Rupert Hernandez, "The Institutionalization of Political Parties in Developing Areas: A Case Study of the Partido Popular Democratic in Puerto Rico" (senior thesis, Harvard, April 1, 1966), p. 60.

101. Reynolds, op. cit., p. 289. They also use paternalistic dependency as an explanation for why unionization efforts were unsuccessful. Ibid., p. 287.

102. "Estos trés partidos politicos están muy centralijados y bien disciplinados." Henry Wells, "La Consecución del Govierno Propio en Puerto Rico," Editorial del Departamento de Instrucción Pública Estado Libre Asociado de Puerto Rico (San Juan, Puerto Rico: series I, MCMLV, No. LXXXI), p. 15.

103. Anderson, op. cit., p. 15.

104. Ibid., p. 134.

105. See Chapter 2.

106. Earl Parker Hanson, *Puerto Rico: Land of Wonders*, p. 280.

107. Carl J. Friedrich, *Puerto Rico: Middle Road to Freedom*, p. 15.

108. Lewis, op. cit., p. 377.

109. Henry Wells, "Ideology and Leadership in Puerto Rican Politics," *American Political Science Review* 49, no. 1 (March, 1955): 32, n. 21.

110. Goodsell, op. cit., p. 199.

111. The formula for doing this was in Article III, Section 7, of the Commonwealth Charter. Whenever in a general election a single party gained as much as two-thirds of the seats in either house, each minority party was permitted to add to its representation as many additional members as would bring its percentage of the total up to a figure about equal to the percentage of votes cast for its gubernatorial candidate in the same election. Rexford G. Tugwell, *The Art of Politics as Practiced by Three Great Americans, pp. 17–18.*

112. Wells, "Ideology and Leadership in Puerto Rican Politics," op. cit., p. 3.

113. Muñoz Marin, "Porto Rico: The American Colony."

114. Luis Muñoz Marin, "Plight of Puerto Rico," *New Republic* 108 (January 11, 1943): 51.

115. Anderson, op. cit., p. 115.

116. Of the three principal parties in Puerto Rico in 1960, only the Partido Independentista Puertorriqueño had a reglamento that clearly consigned the executive direction of the party to a statutory executive commission, which existed separately from, though theoretically subordinate to, the board of directors—the PIP counterpart of the central and territorial committees of the other two parties. The statutory distinction between the board of directors and the executive commission—a dis-

tinction not made in the other parties—meant that the formal decision-making power in the party was not the exclusive prerogative of the president and his immediate circle. Ibid., p. 140.

117. Ibid., p. 76.

118. Hernandez, op. cit., p. 67.

119. See Anderson op. cit., pp. 54, 120–21.

120. It must be noted that Popular Party rules were made more accessible a decade later. Authorized by a resolution passed at the 1956 General Assembly, Sen. Luis Negron Lopez and Secretary of State Roberto Sanchez Vilella drew up a new reglamento. The new rules were passed by acclamation at the 1960 San Juan General Assembly. Ibid., pp. 120–21.

121. "... en la forma dramática que él sólo sabe poner en escena—Muñoz hacia estas preguntas. '¿Están de acuerdo conmigo? ¿Están todos de acuerdo conmigo?' A los "siiii' clamorosos de la gente, Muñoz los cortaba en el aire con una última pregunta: ¿Los juran todos por la felicidad de Puerto Rico y por el honor de todos nosotros? Y levantaba rápidamente la mano derecha para tomar el juramento que no se hacia esperar. Los lideres también levantaban la mano. Esta es la razón por la cual ningún lider y sublider se destacó,—personal o individualmente en posición en contraria a la adaptada por Muñoz Marin en la asamblea de Ponce." Antonio Pacheco Padro, "Anotaciones de Actualidad" in *El Mundo*, December 31, 1944, pp. 4, 14.

122. Goodsell, op. cit., p. 55.

123. *New York Times*, March 25, 1948, p. 56.

124. Hernandez, op. cit., p. 73.

125. Anderson, op. cit., p. 115.

# 4 AN INTERVIEW WITH LUIS MUÑOZ MARÍN

I am the Pamphleteer of God
God's agitator
and I go with the mob of stars and hungry men
toward the great dawn.

Luis Muñoz Marin in "Pamphlet"

In May 1980, Louis Muñoz Marin died. The island mourned. Hundreds of thousands of Puerto Ricans paid their respect. They streamed past his body at the Capital where it lay in state. They attended his funeral mass in the Old San Juan Cathedral. They stood at the side of the long road to watch as his coffin moved slowly from San Juan to Barranquitas, where others waited to attend his burial.

Many of the mourners watched the proceedings on television. They watched the shower of tears as the strains of "Lamento Borincano" filled the San Juan Cathedral. They watched the shower of the rose petals fall on his coffin as the song "En Mi Viejo San Juan" filled the streets of Old San Juan. At Muñoz's grave a middle-aged Bayomon resident remarked to a newspaper reporter, "He was the first one to put shoes on my feet when I was a student." They all remembered him differently, but they all remembered him as a giant.

This chapter is a revised version of an article of the same name published by *Revista/Review Interamericana* 9, no. 2 (Summer, 1979). Reprinted with permission from *Revista/Review Interamericana*.

Luis Muñoz Marin set the political direction for Puerto Rico not just by engineering Commonwealth and creating Fomento but in ways more basic and profound. For Muñoz, the economic status of Puerto Rico was more important than any other consideration, and the liberty he considered most important was liberty from hunger. This value judgment underlay Muñoz's decisions and in fundamental ways determined the future of Puerto Rico.

I interviewed Luis Muñoz Marin on January 4, 1978. He was in good health and greeted me warmly in the study of his well-guarded complex in Trujillo Alto. We spoke for over two hours.

Muñoz was grey and old but exuded the strength and presence of a living legend. He was, as Daniel Boorstin described, "a remarkable combination of poet and pragmatist, a kind of Winston Churchill of the Caribbean."[1]

Others have called him "an artist"[2] and "a sort of liaison between two cultures";[3] his name has always been well known, recognized and respected because of his father, Luis Muñoz Rivera, who brought the Spanish Charter of Autonomy to Puerto Rico in 1897, headed the Union Party, which served and governed Puerto Rico for almost two decades, and was often referred to as the "George Washington of the island." Luis Muñoz Marin was to become as famous in his own right. It was at his father's death that 18-year-old Luis promised:

Borinquen! If someday you need my blood, count on it; it is red blood; the same that ran through his veins.[4]

His life was to make good that pledge.

Muñoz Marin's political career started when he joined the Socialist Party of Santiago Iglesias and worked for the party in 1920. He campaigned, he told me in the interview, throughout the island, but was not a Socialist candidate himself. To the question "What would your father have thought about your joining with the Socialists?" he answered that his father had spoken to him when he was 16, explaining socialism "with sympathy."

Six months after Muñoz's 1920 campaign experience, he moved to New York, where the young, brash idealist was a free-lance writer, "a poet of sorts," and in general, a Greenwich Village bohemian. He published articles in the *Baltimore Sun*, *Smart Set*, *American Mercury*, and *The Nation*, as well as an occasional book review in the *New York Herald Tribune*. He wrote the definitive Spanish translation of "Man with a Hoe" and published his own poems, of which the following is the most quoted verse:

I have drowned my dreams
in order to glut the dreams that sleep for me
in the veins

of men who sweated and wept and raged
to season my coffee?

This stanza is part of a longer poem, "Pamphlet," which ends,

I am the Pamphleteer of God,
God's agitator,
and I go with the mob of stars and hungry men
toward the great dawn.[5]

When I asked Muñoz what was "the great dawn" he was moving toward when he used that metaphor, he answered, without hesitation, "A socialist dawn." But when asked what "the great dawn" is for him today, Muñoz replied: "In a world of interdependence, to develop full autonomy for Puerto Rico under association with the United States, and to develop as much as is possible, economic and social justice." The response includes a concern for both Puerto Rico's status and its economic well-being. They have been his two life-long concerns. Which was more important seems at times to be unclear.

Muñoz was a socialist in the early 1920s. He was also an inde-pendentist. In fact, Muñoz told me that he even had a conversation with Santiago Iglesias, "trying to persuade him about independence."

As an independentist, Muñoz repudiated his father's work and ideas in a 1925 article published in The Nation when he sided with Union leader José de Diego and criticized his father's party faction for placing independence in "as innocuous position as possible."[6]

However, Muñoz was far less critical of his father when we spoke. He explained that his father also opposed U.S. citizenship, "but not very strongly," and that his father spoke against it in Congress. But U.S. citizenship, Muñoz said, was necessary to unite the Union Party, which was committed to autonomy, and at that time they "doubted that American citizenship would prevent independence."

In 1926, while still a New Yorker, Muñoz became editor of his father's own newspaper, La Democracia. It offered a forum and base even more important than party affiliation.[7]

By 1931, according to Carmelo Rosario Natal, Muñoz was defining himself as both a radical nationalist and an economic socialist. In 1932 Muñoz Marin returned to Puerto Rico and made up with the old Union Party head, Antonio Barceló. This permitted his readmission into what was now the Liberal Party and his election as a senator at large. That year, he voted for the Liberal Party and the Nationalist candidate, Pedro Albizu Campos.[8]

Muñoz Marin spent the next four years with the Liberal Party. He was the most publicized politician on the island through "statewide" connec-tions he had made during the 1920s. Two examples from this period best illustrate this point: his confrontation with Governor Gore, and his identification with the Puerto Rican Reconstruction Administration.

## MUÑOZ AND GOVERNOR GORE

Newswoman Ruby Black was a friend of Muñoz's wife, Muna Lee, and a confidant of Eleanor Roosevelt. She became Muñoz's valuable source of inside information from Washington. Black was responsible for Muñoz's successful confrontation with Puerto Rican Governor Robert H. Gore. (He had been appointed governor in July 1933.)

Ruby Black was the first to break the story that Governor Gore required undated letters of resignation from appointees to the Puerto Rican cabinet posts. The governor denied this, and Muñoz, with Black's help, wrote an English editorial in *El Mundo* headed "Governor Gore You Are a Damn Liar," in which he carefully proved his case. By the fall of 1933, again with the help of Ruby Black, Muñoz visited the White House to discuss Governor Gore "over a cup of tea with the U.S. President."[9] At this rather casual meeting with F.D.R., the president "gave his promise that Gore would resign."[10] Gore's resignation was tendered in December 1933 and accepted on January 12.

Muñoz returned to Puerto Rico on January 22. "Hailed by a wildly enthusiastic populace, heralded on the front pages of the island newspapers,"[11] and considered by all as the one responsible for getting rid of the unpopular governor, "he found thousands of people waiting to welcome him at the dock as the triumphant conqueror,"[12] a situation very much like his father's triumphant return from Spain following the 1897 Charter of Autonomy.

## MUÑOZ AND THE NEW DEAL

That same year Muñoz politically benefited from another stateside friendship, Ernest Gruening's. They were old friends. In fact, Muñoz used many of his stateside connections and played a "widely publicized role" in obtaining President Roosevelt's approval of the Chardón Plan, a plan to use the New Deal as more than a palliative relief but as an instrument of economic reform.[13] In December 1934, after three months of lobbying in Washington, Muñoz Marin returned to Puerto Rico and wrote President Roosevelt of worsening economic conditions and that "public order hangs today by a thread."[14] Roosevelt's reply authorized Muñoz to translate and broadcast the presidential message promising reconstruction for the island.

For President Roosevelt to use Muñoz was unorthodox. Muñoz was only a first-term senator of a minority party. Nonetheless, it was Muñoz who was heard in every Puerto Rican town square on December 22, 1934, reading the presidential message in Spanish:

I can and do assure you and your people of my complete goodwill and firm determination that permanent reconstruction shall be initiated at the very earliest possible moment on the basis of the Chardón Plan, the principles of which have received my approval.[15]

As we saw in Chapter 2, the New Deal was to be a great disappointment. But at this time, Muñoz "had deliberately appropriated the New Deal identification in Puerto Rico and was lifted on its powerful swell."[16]

In just two years Muñoz had become a hero with a following. In fact, by 1936, when he broke with the Liberals, Muñoz no longer needed the Liberal Party to win political office.

## MUÑOZ AND BARCELÓ

It was the independence issue that split the Liberal Party, thereby separating Antonio Barceló and Luis Muñoz Marin. The specific issue was whether to accept the 1936 Tydings Independence Bill or wait until independence was economically more feasible. In the beginning, Barceló believed that the island should be content with some form of autonomy rather than independence, keeping the latter for the ultimate goal.[17] But then he suddenly turned full circle, announcing that the Tydings proposal was acceptable "even if it meant starvation for the island."[18]

Muñoz, on the other hand, had always seemed to be an outspoken independentista, and began to define a position consistent with his past. "The supreme issue, which cannot be postponed any longer, is the termination of Puerto Rican colonial status."[19] But then he too had second thoughts and began arguing for a transitional period. He graphically compared the Tydings Bill to a Mexican *ley de fuga* (law of flight), under which the Mexican police arrested people, generously invited them to run away, and then shot them in the back.[20] Because immediate independence would have disastrous effects on the island, the United States had a responsibility, Muñoz argued, to prepare the island economically for independence. In an article published in 1953, Muñoz looks back at the Tydings Bill and the position he took:

> Because of the rigidity of our thinking, we could not disentangle the concept of love for our country from fixed ideas of separate independence.... The difficult process of clarifying these ideas began when the Tydings Bill was introduced in Congress in 1936. The Tydings Bill would have made Puerto Rico independent, but it would have shackled the people with economic misery.[21]

I asked him, in our interview, when he stopped being an independentist, he told me: "I began having doubts when the Tydings Bill was introduced in 1936...it would have killed off Puerto Rico."

Independence was the real issue, but formally the rift between Muñoz and Barceló developed over whether or not the Liberal Party should participate in the 1936 election. Muñoz, according to one historian, was afraid that a Liberal defeat might be interpreted as an anti-independence vote, and urged withdrawal from the election.[22] Barceló had agreed only to play down the Tydings issue.[23]

There was a showdown meeting on the issue of electoral participation. Muñoz's faction lost, though only by one vote. The break was permanent but, for the sake of the party, not formal until after the election. Then Muñoz was expelled. He took with him a group of proindependence liberals and formed a group called *Acción Social Independentista.*[24]

## THE POPULARES

In 1938 the Acción Social Independentista, consisting of Muñoz and his co-expellees, formed the Popular Democratic Party. With the "ablest men and women as [his] followers,"[25] Muñoz traveled in the rural areas and conducted a grassroots campaign. He emphasized economic wellbeing rather than independence because, as Muñoz told me in the interview, "I began to talk to people in the countryside, I realized the mass of people which were rural and the masses in cities feared independence and needed the doctrine that status was not an issue. Their vote was for a social and economic program."

The grassroots campaigning paid off. In the election of 1940 the Populares won control of the Senate (10 of the 19 seats) and came within a few votes of controlling the House (18 of the 39 seats). The PDP polled 214,000 votes, compared to the 224,000 of the opposition (38 percent of the total vote).

## MUÑOZ AND INDEPENDENCE

A common academic game in Puerto Rico is guessing when independence-seeking Muñoz Marin dropped the goal of independence. Of course, some claim he never really wanted independence for the island, and, like his father, only wanted autonomy or self-rule.[26] Muñoz himself says he was an independentist in the early years.

According to some, Muñoz stopped believing in independence as an ultimate solution either when he broke with Barceló (1936)[27] or when he formed the *Populares* (1938).[28] In the opinion of others, the change came when Muñoz was in power during the next decade, either because the people did not want independence for the island,[29] or because of the economic realities leadership had forced upon him.[30]In particular, the Dorffman Report, which predicted poverty and dependency for Puerto Rico, was supposed to have turned Muñoz against independence.

The Dorffman Report was supposed to have made a huge impression on Muñoz. It was a report on "The Economy of Puerto Rico" prepared by the United States Tariff Commission in March 1946; Ben Dorffman was a staff member. The major purpose of the report was to consider the "probable consequences" of implementing the Tydings Independence Bill. The major message of the report was island poverty and dependency.

> Inability of Puerto Rico to find adequate remedies for its economic problems is traceable primarily to the low ratio of its resources and productive capacity to the size of its population... unless unforeseen technolgical developments occur, the maintenance of even the present low standard of living in the island will probably be dependent on continued aid from the outside, irrespective of the political status of the island.[31]

As already described, Muñoz said he was an independentista but "began having doubts" when the 1936 Tydings Bill was introduced. In 1938, when he founded the Popular Party, most of the party leadership, he said in the interview, was for independence while the bulk of the electorate was against it. His party offered, in his own words, "no known stand on the issue." In fact, Muñoz asserted, "if I had insisted on independence, surely we would have lost the 1940 election, which was won by only a small margin."

Muñoz pointed out that he pledged, and kept his promise in the 1940 election, that votes for the Popular Party were not for a status position. He had kept this promise then, unlike the present governor and statehooder Carlos Romero Barceló, Muñoz said, who in the 1976 campaign promised that statehood was not an issue, and then switched as soon as he was in office.

By 1946, 90 percent of the Puerto Rican people were against independence, Muñoz told me in the interview. Other Popular Party leaders might have been for independence, Muñoz said, but they depended more on him than he on them and Muñoz "continued in his position."

I told Muñoz that, for me, in his internal civil war between the quest for economic and social justice, and the status issue, the former appeared to have won out as more important. Muñoz nodded in agreement. In fact, in my opinion, the pattern of Muñoz's life suggests that he was never really an independentista—by that I mean someone who believes so strongly in independence that he is willing to ignore all other considerations—for example, like Antonio Barceló, who was willing to accept independence "even if it meant starvation for the island." An honest reading of Muñoz's history suggests that the economic issue was always the most important for him. In other words, the economic status of Puerto Rico, not the island's political status, was always foremost in Muñoz's thinking.

I do not believe the economic issue was the primary issue because Muñoz lacked principles or was an opportunist politician merely reflecting his constituency. Muñoz emphasized the economic issue not because he was a pragmatist but because he was a humanist; not because he was hungry for power but because his people were hungry for food.

Consistent with the idea that the economic issue was foremost in Muñoz's mind is the fact that Muñoz's first political act was to join the Socialist Party in 1920. He joined because he was concerned about the poverty of his people.

It was this economic interest that Muñoz took with him to the United States. His concern with the island's poverty produced his poem, "Pamphlet":

> The dreams that sleep in breasts stifled by tuberculosis
>     (a little air, a little sunshine)
> The dreams that dream in stomachs strangled by hunger
>     (a bit of bread, a bit of white bread)
> The dream of bare feet
>     (fewer stones on the road, Lord, fewer broken bottles)
> The dream of calloused hands
>     (moss...clean cambric...things smooth, soft soothing)
> The dream of trampled hearts
>     (love...life...life)

Even in his articles, the core of Muñoz approach was economic. This includes his famous 1925 article, which is often quoted to prove his independence beliefs. It is the *Nation* article in which he says:

> But the sentiment for independence is real enough among young fellows and the common people, and it only waits to be organized by a politician with some poetry in his makeup.[32]

In his interview Muñoz admitted that "quite likely" he was the politician he had in mind. Nevertheless, the fact remains that basically the entire article was devoted to describing the Puerto Rican economic situation. In this 1925 *Nation* article, Muñoz really was using independence sentiment as a threat to get action, rather than as a promise of action.

In the article, Muñoz criticizes the tariff system as an "unmixed blessing." While the tariff benefits the nonresident sugar interests, it is but a "wall of protection [which] compels our poverty-stricken population to buy its staples in the same market where the American banker and bricklayer buy theirs." Muñoz argues that the economic situation cannot be corrected while Puerto Rico remains within the tariff system and warns that "only a scrupulously unselfish policy—inaugurated soon—on the part of the United States is likely to induce the Puerto Rican people, as distinguished from their politicians, to remain loyal at heart to the United States."[33] In other words, Muñoz is threatening loss of loyalty to induce a change in U.S. economic policy.

As Muñoz continued to write in English about the island, it was the description of Puerto Rican poverty that filled U.S. magazines. The following excerpt is typical:

By now the development of large, absentee-owned sugar estates, the rapid curtailment in the planting of coffee...and the concentration of cigar manufacture in the hands of the American trust, having combined to make it a land of beggars and millionaires, of flattering statistics and distressing realities. More and more it becomes a factory worked by peons, fought over by lawyers, bossed by absentee industrialists, and clerked by politicians. It is now Uncle Sam's second largest sweat-shop.[34]

Muñoz was preoccupied with Puerto Rico's poverty. "His main concern was to call attention to the social and economic distress of his homeland and to what he then regarded as its colonial bondage to the economy of the United States."[35]

Muñoz consistently viewed the problem of political status through the lens of economics. Loyal to his values, he used the *same basic argument* both to oppose statehood and to oppose the independence provided by the Tydings Bill.

During the hearings that were held on the 1935 statehood bill (HR 1394), introduced by Resident Commissioner Iglesias, Muñoz opposed the bill. Barceló also testified against the bill, but the reasons each man used were quite different, thereby foreshadowing the break between them over the Tydings Bill the following year. Barceló used ethnic reasons to argue against statehood, and, the next year, ethnic reasons to argue for independence. Muñoz, on the other hand, used economic reasons to argue against statehood, and, the next year, economic reasons to argue *against* immediate independence.

At the 1935 statehood hearings both men rejected statehood. Barceló rejected statehood because the language, customs, and culture of Puerto Rico had not changed in 37 years. Muñoz argued against statehood because he feared the loss of customs receipts and federal revenue, and that statehood would perpetuate the single-crop economy of the island. While they agreed with the general conclusion that statehood was undesirable, their 1935 testimonies set the stage for their conflict. The following year, Barceló's cultural arguments forced him to accept independence "even if it meant death," while Muñoz's emphasis on economics allowed him to reject Tydings's independence because it meant death.

Don't give us a tombstone with the inscription "Here lies the corpse of a free man."[36]

Muñoz was being perfectly consistent when he used the same reasons to reject statehood as he did to reject independence. His arguments were economic and his reasons were humanitarian. This was true for the 1936 Tydings Bill debates when Muñoz was a Liberal; this was true in the 1946 Tydings Bill debates when he was a Popular. Economic considerations were the most important considerations for Muñoz. His major concern was for his people. "The average Puerto Rican does not usually starve in the streets. Instead he is undernourished for forty-three years on the average, and then dies."[37] This was always more important for Luis Muñoz Marin, more important even than the issue of status.

But in his quest for economic improvement, Muñoz helped unleash forces—urbanization, industrialization, tourism, and out-migration—that worked to speed the Americanization process and create statehooders. Puerto Ricans increasingly wanted to be "American." While they might have toasted the jíbaro, no one wanted to remain one. The next chapter will focus on the demise of the Puerto Rican jíbaro.

## NOTES

1. Daniel J. Boorstin, "Self-Discovery in Puerto Rico," Yale Review, 45 (1955–56): 232.

2. Rexford G. Tugwell, The Art of Politics as Practiced by Three Great Americans: Franklin Delano Roosevelt, Luis Muñoz Marin, and Fiorello H. LaGuardia, p. 139.

3. Ralph Hancock, Puerto Rico: A Success Story, p. 76.

4. "Borinquenb! Si algun dia necesitas mi sangre, cuenta con ella; es sangre roja; la misma que corria por sus venas." La Democracia, December 2, 1916.

5. "Pamphlet," in Anthology of Contemporary Latin American Poetry, ed. Dudley Fitts, pp. 206–09.

6. Luis Muñoz Marin, "Porto Rico: The American Colony," The Nation, April 8, 1925, p. 281.

7. Earl Parker Hanson, Puerto Rico: Land of Wonders, p. 86; Luis Muñoz Marin, El Mundo, November 22, 1931, in Carmelo Rosario Natal, La Juventud de Luis Muñoz Marin, pp. 215, 216.

8. Ibid., p. 215.

9. Hanson says he had an appointment with the president (op. cit., p. 95), while Aitken says he first spoke to the president's wife and then was taken to the president. Thomas Aitken, Jr., Luis Muñoz Marin: Poet in the Fortress, pp. 102–03.

10. Hanson, op, cit., p. 96.

11. Aitken, op. cit., p. 103.

12. Hanson, op. cit., p. 96.

13. Henry Well, The Modernization of Puerto Rico, p. 116.

14. Robert J. Hunter, "Historical Survey of the Puerto Rico Status Question 1898–1965," in Status of Puerto Rico. Selected Background Studies, p. 94.

15. Aitken, op. cit., p. 109.

16. Tugwell, op. cit., p. 47.

17. "Autonomy Favored for the Puerto Ricans," *New York Times*, June 2, 1936, p. 10.

18. Hunter, op. cit., p. 94.

19. *El Mundo*, June 30, 1936, in Frank Otto Gatell, "Independence Rejected: Puerto Rico and the Tydings Bill of 1936," *Hispanic American Historical Review* 38 (1958): 43–44.

20. Hanson, op. cit., p. 108.

21. "Development Through Democracy," *Annals of the Academy of Politics and Social Sciences* 258 (January 1953), in Gatell, op. cit., p. 95.

22. Hunter, op. cit., p. 95.

23. Who was for what even on this issue of participation in elections seems to be unclear. Gatell cites an article from the June 18 edition of Muñoz's newspaper, *Democracia*, in which Barceló called on the leaders of all political parties to suspend the forthcoming November elections and join in a united front to fight for independence.

24. Tugwell, op. cit., p. 77.

25. Hunter, op. cit., p. 70.

26. Juan Antonio Corretjer in an interview on April 14, 1967.

27. Aitken, op. cit.

28. Wells, op. cit.

29. Rexford G. Tugwell, op. cit.

30. Robert W. Anderson, *Party Politics in Puerto Rico*.

31. U.S. Tariff Commission. *The Economy of Puerto Rico with Special Reference to the Economic Implications of Independence and Other Proposals to Change its Political Status* (Washington: U.S. Government Printing Office, 1946), p. 2.

32. Luis Muñoz Marin, "Porto Rico: The American Colony," *The Nation*, April 18, 1925.

33. Ibid., p. 282.

34. Ibid.

35. Hanson, *Puerto Rico: Ally for Progress*.

36. Wells, op. cit., p. 299.

37. Applicable here, the quote is taken from an article published ten years later. Luis Muñoz Marin, "A Plea for Puerto Rico," *The Nation* 162 (May 11, 1946): 572.

# 5 THE PUERTO RICAN JÍBARO: DEMISE OF SPIRIT AND SYMBOL

> No importa cuanto trate un jibaro de
> quitarse su mancha de plátano, esta
> siempre le acompañará.

The jibaros were rooted in the Puerto Rican earth. Their heads were protected by pavas; their hands were stained by plantains. For many, the jibaros symbolized Puerto Rico. Luis Muñoz Marin courted the jibaros and made them the foundation of the first grassroots party on the island. He spoke to their needs. But forces were at work destroying the jibaro, speeding Americanization and creating "statehooders." Puerto Ricans increasingly wanted to be American. The indigenous symbol, the jibaro and *pava* (straw hat) which was to represent the spiritual integrity of Puerto Rico, was not as strong as, for example, race and racial pride as a way of warding off the colonizer's influence. The jibaro was an old-fashioned symbol in a world that was rushing to modernize.

Two years before he died Luis Muñoz Marin argued eloquently that the jibaro is not simply a person of the past, but still very much represents the spiritual integrity of Puerto Rico. The jibaro was the person Muñoz had in mind, he told me, when he established the Popular Party in 1938; the jibaro was the person Muñoz had in mind when he delivered what he now considers one of his most important speeches, one to the Insular Legislature in March 1952 (which will be described later); and the jibaro, even in 1978 when I interviewed Muñoz, still represented for him a viable force for Puerto Rico.

---

This chapter is based on a public lecture delivered at Princeton University, November 9, 1978.

Perhaps it was Muñoz's grace, his graciousness, and his calm; but for me, at our meeting, Muñoz seemed, himself, to embody the jíbaro, the Puerto Rican, whole and intact after the jolts of the twentieth century.

## THE JÍBARO: LITERAL DESCRIPTION

The bulk of Puerto Rico, 71 percent, consists of hills and mountains. Here is where the jíbaro lived, not on the coastline or on the rich alluvial fans where Spaniards used slaves to grow sugar, but in the hills and mountains inland.

Here, there were no large sugar estates, latifundias, and generally, for all except the coffee growers, there was no cash-crop profit, no hacienda system. Instead, "The land was divided into small estates, and in the uplands there was scarcely a free man who could not own a few acres or rent them cheap." This led to a system that Muñoz described, in 1925, as "very modest but rather widespread economic semi-independence."[1] Recent research by Laird Bergad, which focuses on the rich Puerto Rican coffee area during the late nineteenth century, suggests that this highly romanticized vision of semi-independence has been exaggerated.* What is true, however, is that the jíbaros were poor. When they farmed they were generally subsistence-level farmers. But some lived on even less and used only what nature had already provided. "The plantain groves which surround their houses," said Flinter in 1833, "and the coffee trees which grow almost without cultivation, afford them a frugal subsistence."[2] Usually they lived in one-room cabins, crudely made of boards and thatch, set on poles, and void of furniture. The jíbaros wore broad-brimmed straw hats called pavas to protect them from the sun.

So poor were the jíbaros that, according to a report prepared for the U.S. government in 1899, many families ate merely one scanty meal each day, and only one-fifth of the Puerto Rican people owned a pair of shoes.[3]

The most important factor in the development of the jíbaros is that, although they were poor, they were economically independent. In fact, the jíbaros sprouted from a land of poverty arrogantly independent. All that they wanted was supplied by nature and practically within arm's reach. They did not look to the cities for luxuries and imports. They never developed a network of inland trade.

This was partially due to the lack of a system of adequate roads. Thus, insufficient transportation helped ensure the physical separateness of the jíbaros. Even if they planted for more than mere subsistence, any surplus produce had difficulty reaching the coast. By royal decree, transportation had to go over land, not sea, so it became simpler and

---

*Laird W. Bergad, "Puerto Rico, Puerto Pobre: Coffee and Growth of Agrarian Capitalism in Nineteenth Century Puerto Rico," unpublished doctoral dissertation, University of Pittsburgh, 1980.

more profitable to sell produce to smugglers while the cities went hungry.[4] This was neither legal nor reliable as a commercial endeavor. In addition, because interior communications were along dirt paths and trails, difficulty in inland transportation doubled the already high coastal price of imports. Any potential market inland was almost priced out of existence. Without a network of city–country trade, the jibaros remained isolated.

An economic self-sufficiency was accompanied by a cultural self-sufficiency. The jibaro did not depend on the city for his style of life as he had not for his food and shelter. While San Juan society danced Europeanized dances at balls, the jibaro knew only Afro-Antillean movement, as if to dramatize the cultural chasm between city and country.[5] The jibaro was content to live in what has been idealized as a "culture of leisure." He relaxed away most of his days in a hammock beneath some guava trees, playing his guitar, betting in cock fights, singing, dancing, and "thinking himself the most independent and happy being in existence."[6]

There were other qualities attributed to the jibaro—less romanticized and more controversial. One was a quality of "resignation," described by Pedreira in *Insularismo* as *docilidad*.[7] Its roots were supposed to be in poverty and in a class system that discouraged the chance of upward mobility.[8]

It is important to point out that the quality of docility has been called a colonial notion projected onto the "native" to keep the colonizer in power. This argument is best made by former president of the Movimiento Pro Independencia Youth, Juan Angel Silen.[9]

Nevertheless, there were many aspects of island life that did nurture the feeling of powerlessness and passivity. As already described in Chapter 3, a resigned acceptance of life came from Catholicism,[10] Spanish autocratic rule,[11] and U.S. rule characterized by arbitrariness and indifference. United States rule was really congressional rule, slow and hard to predict, coming from committees of ever-changing membership from a Congress that was explicitly racist during the first two decades.[12]

Another aspect of the jibaro culture was its strong individualism— questions of honor, dignity, and *machismo* (virility) were important. There seemed to be no tradition of concerted effort, group organizing, or "civic culture."

Thus the jibaro, rooted in Puerto Rican soil, was poor, independent-spirited, rural, self-sufficient, interested in questions of personal dignity, resigned because of religious belief, poverty, a class system, colonial power, and had no tradition of civic organizing.

## THE PDP AND THE JÍBARO

Luis Muñoz Marín courted the jibaro and rose to power. He broke with Antonio Barceló and the Liberal Party in 1936 and formed the Acción Social Independentista with younger independentist Liberals. In 1938 they formed the Popular Democratic Party (PDP). Muñoz lived among the country people and conducted a grassroots campaign.[13] He concentrated his efforts among the jíbaros and chose as a party symbol a jíbaro wearing a pava.

The PDP slogan was "bread, land, and liberty," inspired, Muñoz told me, by European party slogans. Muñoz emphasized the economic rather than the political status and the independence issue because, he said in our interview, he discovered that the jíbaro was not disturbed about Puerto Rico's colonial position. (But as we saw in Chapter 4, this view was also consistent with Muñoz's personal emphasis on economic well-being rather than political status.)

Muñoz pointed to this period of campaigning to answer the question, "What do you consider to be your greatest achievement?" I had expected him to answer the development of Commonwealth or Operation Bootstrap, but he did not. In the interview, Muñoz said that his greatest achievement was teaching his people "the meaning of democracy," which was the "chief emphasis," he said, of this 1940 campaign.

At the time of the campaign, many jíbaros were selling their votes. For the loyalty of the jíbaro electorate, who were poor, strongly individualistic, and who did not have a history of concerted civic effort, Muñoz was competing with vote selling; he promised another way to make voting profitable. "Throw us out of office if we don't make a difference," and his campaign ads announced *Verquenza Contra Dinero*.[14]

The jíbaro was an important part of Muñoz's vision in his campaign of 1940, in the midst of Operation Bootstrap, and even today. In 1940 his major campaign theme was his promise to implement the 500 Acre Law so that squatter farmers and slum dwellers could acquire their own parcels of land. Reminiscing with me about his goals during that period, it was clear that the simple life and the virtue of the jíbaro were what was inspiring Muñoz politically.

Muñoz told me in our interview that, first, he wanted to guarantee freedom of the home from the employer; second, to have each man able to produce all his food; third, to develop in communities easy access to school and health clinics. In fact, Muñoz boasted that Puerto Rico had invented proportional benefit farms, similar to Russian communes and Israeli kibbutzim. They were mostly in sugar cane, he said, where, in order to be productive, they needed large farms.

The jíbaro was the new source of support that gave the Popular Democratic Party a real source of legitimacy. The issues the PDP raised were those that concerned the jíbaros; the party gave them a sense of being valued and a feeling that they were being heard. A 1960 study indicated that many Puerto Ricans feel that they have a nearly personal leader, that they have access to the founts of power, that their petitions will be listened to.[15]

Also, the lack of traditional indigenous popular political institutions gave the PDP an additional source of legitimacy. According to Huntington, where the strong party is a strong source of stability, "the party is not just a supplementary organization; it is instead the source of legitimacy and authority."[16]

Thus Muñoz was lifted to power and rose on the shoulders of the jíbaros. It is, therefore, truly ironic that Muñoz himself created forces that destroyed the jíbaro and weakened his party: urbanization, industrialization, tourism, out-migration.

## ISLAND URBANIZATION AND INDUSTRIALIZATION

Fomento unleashed the forces of urbanization and industrialization on the rural island. (The name was inspired by a Chilean agency, Corporación de Fomento de la Producción; in English, Corporation for the Stimulation of Production, known as Operation Bootstrap.[17] As figures in Chapter 2 show, factories were being built at a dramatic rate in cities and towns. People in large numbers were migrating to the cities. And during this period the rural island was being transformed. It was in the growing urban areas that the support for the Statehood Party grew,[18] not only among the city's rich but among the poor as well.

In the cities, statehood support is as strong in the slums as in the suburbs. According to Mintz, Lewis, and Hanson, the Puerto Ricans who have migrated to the city are change-oriented and are enjoying increased economic opportunities but also fear relapsing into rural poverty.[19] They experienced what Hofstadter calls "status insecurity."[20] They voted Statehood Party for the security of the American way of life. Erasmo expresses it in La Vida:

> The way it is now, as a commonwealth, what is Puerto Rico anyway? Suppose the United States should decide to say, "All right, we will send no more aid to Puerto Rico." Wouldn't we be worse off even than Santo Domingo then? We would. The rice grown here and the food reserves on the island wouldn't last four months.[21]

The Puerto Ricans' fear of the impermanent status is reinforced by the presence of Cuban refugees in large numbers, "mostly middle class professional people."[22] With rare exceptions, they support Puerto Rican annexationists, or statehooders, and want the security of closer ties with the United States.[23] They are like the royalists of the nineteenth century (described in Chapter 1), who also sought security on the island. By 1965, there were 22,000 Cubans living in Puerto Rico. (They comprised .8 percent of the island population.) They reside in large cities, the majority in the San Juan area, and their effect is much greater than their numbers suggest.[24]

## TOURISM

In addition to industrialization, and with it urbanization, the PDP government also encouraged tourism and out-migration. By 1966, there were 100 times more plane passengers coming and going than there had been in 1950, and predictions were made that "the one way total of travellers in a single year [would] soon surpass the number of persons actually living in Puerto Rico."[25]

Transient passengers, that is, people who leave or visit Puerto Rico temporarily, "dominate the movement between Puerto Rico and the United States,"[26] and a large percentage of mainland transients visiting Puerto Rico are tourists. The tourist industry grew dramatically in the 1960s. With each new year, the tourist trade expanded 20 percent.[27] The number of tourists, and the money they spent in Puerto Rico, rose like magic.

The lush hotels were for some Puerto Ricans merely reminders of how poor they were. Soledad, in Oscar Lewis's La Vida, talks of "the pain one feels after being in a nice hotel and walking by the Caribe Hilton, seeing so many pretty things and then having to go back to La Esmeralda. Such terrible poverty, so much dirt, garbage scattered everywhere. They live in separate worlds, the poor and the rich."

And yet, according to Gordon Lewis, the result of two-way migration with Puerto Ricans flying north and North American tourists flying south has brought little if any widespread hatred of the Norte Americanos. Rather than resent the tourists, Puerto Ricans often see the high standard of living the tourist brings to the island as the inevitable result of being a

**TABLE 9**
**Number and Expenditures of Tourists in Puerto Rico, 1945–78**

| Year | Number of Tourists | Expenditures (millions of dollars) |
| --- | --- | --- |
| 1945 | 9,023 | 1.6 |
| 1950 | 64,023 | 6.8 |
| 1955 | 134,625 | 22.9 |
| 1960 | 347,625 | 58.1 |
| 1961 | 354,963 | 55.7 |
| 1962 | 396,675 | 67.9 |
| 1963 | 461,857 | 81.9 |
| 1964 | 552,664 | 97.5 |
| 1965 | 606,093 | 119.3 |
| 1970 | 1,088,000 | 235 |
| 1976 | 1,299,000 | 380 |
| 1977 | 1,376,000 | 411 |
| 1978 | 1,474,000 | 466 |

Source: Status of Puerto Rico. Report, p. 182; and Government Development Bank for Puerto Rico, Puerto Rico in Figures, 1979 (Economic Research Department, San Juan, Puerto Rico).

full-fledged American.[28] Thus, tourism speeds Americanization, but it does not do so as forcefully as Puerto Rican migration to the mainland.

## MIGRATION

The migration experience—of uprooting and resettling—is very much a part of Puerto Rico's political, social, and economic reality. In fact, "Puerto Rico's significance for the theory of migration lies in the fact that it ranks with Ireland in having had one of the highest rates of emigration ever to characterize an entire country."[29] No Puerto Rican remains untouched by migration, not with one out of every three Puerto Ricans residing on the mainland.[30]

As Chapter 2 describes, the migrants responded to the economic pull of the mainland, but they did not always experience it as a land of plenty. "Puerto Ricans in the United States face[d] the bitter disappointment of being relegated to poverty in the midst of glitter."[31] In 1976 the United States Commission on Civil Rights corroborated this fact.[32]

> The Commission merely had verified old news to the residents of the heavily Puerto Rican areas of the city—East Harlem, the South Bronx, Williamsburg, Bushwick—and dozens of other communities in the region, where over half of the Puerto Ricans in the United States live. After 30 years of large-scale migration by these native-born American citizens, the 1.7 million Puerto Ricans (a census figure generally regarded as an undercount) were no better off and possibly even worse....
>
> Puerto Ricans are at the bottom of the economic ladder, worse off than other Hispanics and most other ethnic groups. Their population is three times poorer than the national average. One of every four families depends on welfare, entirely or in part.... The percentage of those living in poverty rose from 29 percent in 1970 to 33 percent in 1974 and may have risen further since then.[33]

Besides poverty "in the midst of glitter," Puerto Ricans also experienced racism. One returning Puerto Rican who had lived in New York for over 30 years said, "A lot of people come [return] to Puerto Rico because of the prejudice in New York...you live there but you don't feel part of the American dream...;"[34] and another Puerto Rican said, about being in Puerto Rico after having lived 24 years in Brooklyn, "At least here I can be proud of being a Puerto Rican. In New York, the people won't even look at us."[35]

And yet, there on the mainland, in the midst of poverty, racism, and disappointment grew statehood sentiment. As one journalist, describing back-migration, put it, "For the most part, returning Puerto Ricans are ... stout statehooders, strongly pro-American, despite a deep sense of hurt over how they had been treated on the mainland."[36]

One clear example of strong mainland statehood sentiment occurred in 1967. There was a serious debate over whether Puerto Ricans residing in the United States should be allowed to vote in the Puerto Rican status plebiscite. Referring to the New York Puerto Rican, Julio E. Sabater, deputy director of an East Harlem anti-poverty program, said, "The Popular Democratic Party naturally opposes their voting because they are predominantly for statehood...."[37] Consistent with his statement is the fact that commonwealth forces had continually opposed plebiscite participation by mainland residents, while statehooders continually argued for it.[38]

Why were mainland Puerto Ricans for statehood? Statehood sentiment grew on the mainland for the same reasons it grew in the island's cities. The migrants moved for a better life, found increased economic opportunity, and wanted to keep their new lives secure. In fact, if we see migration to the mainland, as Hernandez Alvarez suggests, as just a part of a more general move from rural to urban area,[39] then it is not at all surprising that urban Puerto Ricans on the mainland are for statehood in the same way that urban Puerto Ricans on the island are for statehood. Uprooted, they have found a new loyalty.

But there is an added psychological twist for the statehooders on the mainland because the disparity between what they have and what they see around them is so great. As described in Chapter 3, dependency on the colonial power heightened and fed a sense of inferiority. The Puerto Rican mainland migrant was to feel this sense of inferiority most strongly. Thus, living on the mainland, "living in the very guts of the most powerful capitalist society cannot help but produce a group of people who want to 'pass' into the society of the metropolis even at the cost of losing their identity and national culture."[40]

Although the process was the same in mainland and island city, the mainland Puerto Ricans began to look very different from their island cousins. New terms were coined to distinguish them, like New Yoricans and Neoricans, and new labels for the island Puerto Ricans began to be used, like natives, locals, and Puerto Rico Puerto Ricans. The new terms were used with more frequency as the mainland Puerto Ricans began returning home.

## THE NEORICAN

The "new" Puerto Rican migration was back-migration. At first, it was nearly unnoticed because of the tremendous flow of people off the island. But even in the heyday of out-migration, Puerto Ricans were also

## TABLE 10
## Migration into Puerto Rico and into the Continental United States

| Year | Travel to the Continental United States | Puerto Rico | Net Migration to the Continental United States |
|------|------|------|------|
| 1920 | 19,142 | 15,003 | 4,139 |
| 1921 | 17,137 | 17,749 | −612 |
| 1922 | 13,521 | 14,154 | −633 |
| 1923 | 14,950 | 13,194 | 1,756 |
| 1924 | 17,777 | 14,057 | 3,720 |
| 1925 | 17,493 | 15,356 | 2,137 |
| 1926 | 22,010 | 16,389 | 5,621 |
| 1927 | 27,355 | 18,626 | 8,729 |
| 1928 | 27,916 | 21,772 | 6,144 |
| 1929 | 25,428 | 20,791 | 4,637 |
| 1930 | 26,010 | 20,434 | 5,576 |
| 1931 | 18,524 | 20,462 | −1,939 |
| 1932 | 16,224 | 18,932 | −2,708 |
| 1933 | 15,133 | 16,215 | −1,082 |
| 1934 | 13,721 | 16,687 | −2,966 |
| 1935 | 19,944 | 18,927 | 1,017 |
| 1936 | 24,145 | 20,697 | 3,448 |
| 1937 | 27,311 | 22,793 | 4,518 |
| 1938 | 25,884 | 23,522 | 2,362 |
| 1939 | 26,653 | 21,165 | 4,488 |
| 1940 | 24,932 | 23,924 | 1,008 |
| 1941 | 30,916 | 30,416 | 500 |
| 1942 | 29,480 | 28,552 | 928 |
| 1943 | 19,367 | 16,766 | 2,601 |
| 1944 | 27,586 | 19,498 | 8,088 |
| 1945 | 33,740 | 22,737 | 11,003 |
| 1946 | 70,618 | 45,997 | 24,621 |
| 1947 | 136,259 | 101,115 | 35,144 |
| 1948 | 132,523 | 104,492 | 28,031 |
| 1949 | 157,338 | 124,252 | 33,086 |
| 1950 | 170,727 | 136,572 | 34,155 |
| 1951 | 188,898 | 146,978 | 41,920 |
| 1952 | 258,884 | 197,226 | 61,658 |
| 1953 | 304,910 | 230,307 | 74,603 |
| 1954 | 303,007 | 258,798 | 44,209 |
| 1955 | 315,491 | 284,309 | 31,182 |
| 1956 | 380,950 | 319,303 | 61,647 |
| 1957 | 439,656 | 391,372 | 48,284 |
| 1958 | 467,987 | 442,031 | 25,956 |
| 1959 | 557,701 | 520,489 | 37,212 |
| 1960 | 666,756 | 643,014 | 23,742 |
| 1961 | 681,982 | 668,182 | 13,800 |
| 1962 | 807,549 | 796,186 | 11,363 |
| 1963 | 930,666 | 952,868 | 4,798 |

| 1964 | 1,076,403 | 1,072,037 | 4,366 |
| 1965 | 1,265,096 | 1,254,338 | 10,758 |
| 1966 | 1,475,228 | 1,445,139 | 30,089 |
| 1967 | 1,628,909 | 1,594,735 | 34,174 |
| 1968 | 1,858,151 | 1,839,470 | 18,681 |
| 1969 | 2,105,217 | 2,112,264 | −7,047 |
| 1970 | 1,495,587 | 1,479,447 | 16,140 |
| 1971 | 1,566,723 | 1,605,414 | −38,691 |
| 1972 | — | — | −19,462 |
| 1973 | 1,780,192 | 1,799,071 | −18,879 |
| 1974 | 1,622,001 | 1,630,525 | −8,524 |

Source: Un Informe de la Comision de Derechos Civilos de Los Estados Unidos, Puertorriquenos en Los Estatos Unidos Continentales, pp. 28, 29.

returning. Figures for the flights to and from the island reveal the enormity of the movement. Margaret Mead captured the movement of people: "At midnight, on a 747 between New York and Puerto Rico, you'd think that all Puerto Ricans were moving in both directions."[41]

There were always significant numbers of return migrants, as opposed to transients, visitors, or what Hernandez Alvarez calls "floaters." Between 1950 and 1960, 75,000 Puerto Ricans came home to stay; between 1960 and 1965, 70,000 returned permanently (see Table 10). But by 1977, 70,000 was the number for one year's inflow of Puerto Ricans coming home.[42]

Census bureau data show that the general flow back to Puerto Rico between 1965 and 1970 (including temporary as well as permanent moves), is mostly urban people, the majority born in Puerto Rico, with the majority of returnees having mainland residence for fewer than five years (although over 120,000 are in the "over-five-years on the mainland" category) (see Table 11).

For those who have spent most of their lives on the mainland, however, returning to Puerto Rico can represent quite a culture shock. Puerto Rico seems to some like a foreign country. There, now, even exists a Neo Rican Society in San Juan, with 1,500 members, to help in the adjustment of Puerto Ricans returning to Puerto Rico.[43]

It is not only in the barrios on the mainland that the Neoricans experienced prejudice; they do so on the island as well. Neoricans often feel marginal in both places—more Puerto Rican than "American" in East Harlem, more American than Puerto Rican on the island.[44] Natives call them pushy and aggressive, tainted by the mainland lifestyle. Their clothes and ways are criticized.[45] But it is the language barrier that creates

**TABLE 11**
**Puerto Ricans, Five Years or Older, Returning to Puerto Rico from 1965 through 1970, by Urban and Rural Residence in United States, and by Length of Stay in the United States**

| Returnees to Puerto Rico 1965–70 | Total | Urban | Rural |
|---|---|---|---|
| Born in Puerto Rico | 287,035 | 171,176 | 115,859 |
| Born in the United States or elsewhere outside | 110,599 | 87,917 | 22,682 |
| Length of stay in continental United States | | | |
| 5 years or more | 120,218 | 87,471 | 32,747 |
| under 5 years | 153,254 | 87,622 | 65,632 |

*Source:* U.S. Department of Commerce, Social and Economic Statistics Administration, Bureau of the Census, *1970 Census of Population, Puerto Rico the Population*, Vol. I, Part 53, p. 53-195.

the biggest physical separation and isolation. In an article called "The loneliness of the returning Newyorican," one young woman complained, "They call us Newyoricans and if you don't speak Spanish too well they say, 'Well, why don't you go back to where you belong?' "[46]

Levittown, a Toa Baja suburb of 10,000 families located nine miles west of San Juan, became a symbol of the Neorican. Other residential enclaves developed like San Juanita in Bayamón where, because of the numbers of Neoricans, using English in school, and in everyday activities, would not be a problem.[47]

Of course, the language issue has enormous political significance. In a colonial situation, the master's language has prestige. In Puerto Rico, where North Americans are treated with some deference because of tourism and because Americans are expected to be rich, it is to some advantage to have American qualities of style and looks, and to speak English. The Neorican may very well be happy to hold on to "This halo of prestige enveloping the master's language."[48]

The irony of the situation, however, should not be lost. During the first three decades of American rule, Puerto Ricans struggled to ensure that Spanish became the language of instruction in the island's public schools. Yet in the decades to follow, hundreds of thousands of Spanish-speaking Puerto Rican children were to be educated and half-educated and miseducated in English on the mainland.

Governor Luis Ferré may have referred to Puerto Rico as the "Jíbaro State"; Governor Carlos Romero Barceló may have addressed the United

Nations in perfect Spanish; but the fact remains that many Puerto Ricans coming home to Puerto Rico use only English, and some use both languages so poorly they are not bilingual, they are called "nonlingual." Maldonado Denis refers to the "mutilation of the language" and the "idiomatic ambivalence" as symptoms of "a reality that condemns ...Puerto Ricans to the category of cultural pariahs in the metropolis as well as in the colony."[49]

Spanish has been an important symbol for Puerto Rico since 1898. In fact, the importance of Spanish to Puerto Rico was expressed that year by a "leading native scholar and lawyer" in the official Washington *Report on the Island*:

> I love the Spanish language. I lisped it in my mother's arms; I whispered its soft words to her who became my wife; I think in it, and in it are all the beautiful prose and poetry known to me.[50]

Yet Spanish is not only being lost in the barrio on the mainland. Spanish, it seems, is becoming impoverished as a language on the island, not only because of the influence of English but perhaps, also, because of the colonial tension around the use of Spanish. As one Puerto Rican professor suggests:

> the language is not managed with comfort, agility or perfection, nor with the ease and zeal of someone for whom the language is not cause for tension...; I am speaking of the difficulties of a firm, profound, clear possession of our language, our only language, in spite of the bureaucratic lie of bilingualism.[51]

For the people of Puerto Rico, loss of language is an incalculable loss. Pedreira recognized this decades ago when he wrote: "Creo...que un niño que vive de dos idiomas no llega a ser nunca *un hombre doble*; se queda siempre *un medio hombre*."[52]

Finally, it is not only because of their English and their clothing that the returning Puerto Ricans experience hostility towards themselves. In some sense, the Neoricans have become scapegoats because they are reminders to Puerto Ricans of the personal price they pay for economic progress. They are also scapegoats, according to Maldonado Denis, "Because those who have come to be called *New Yorricans* are the reminder—this time in flesh and blood—for those who believed that they could give up one-third of our population as a necessary means so that those of us who did not have to emigrate could enjoy a high standard of living."[53]

But the experience of those who left was not so different from the experience of those who stayed, and that, too, is why the Neoricans are such an abrasive reminder. The only difference was that the mainland migrant experienced economic dependency, psychological insecurity, and a sense of inferiority more intensely. And so the mainland migrant could be Americanized that much faster.

Antonio Barceló's worst fear seems to have come true.

For we would join the Union immediately...with the personality, characteristics, and idiosyncrasies of a people whose character is already formed and who have, for centuries, had a civilization perhaps older than yours. We Puerto Ricans want to be your brethren in equality, dignity, liberty and duty....What we do not wish, what frequently disturbs our minds, is the thought of having to undergo a painful, indefinite process, during which all those characteristics will perish and which will annul our personality to such an extent that, upon the accomplishment of that solution, if it ever be accomplished, *it will not be we who share the immense benefits to be derived therefrom, but a shapeless hybrid, resembling us in nothing and differing from you also.* [emphasis added][54]

Puerto Ricans' quest to be American and Americanized was made that much easier because the Puerto Rican alternative was symbolized by the jibaro, poor, rural, with pava and plantain stains.

## MUÑOZ AND THE JÍBARO

Muñoz was very clear in our 1978 interview that he believes that the jibaro continues to be a value-promulgator even if Puerto Rico is no longer predominantly rural. He insisted on the importance and the existence, still, of the jibaro. He pointed to a large framed black-and-white photo leaning against the wall on his shelf featuring a jibaro; he also mentioned and described the jibaro statue on the road to Ponce. There are still many jibaros, he said to me, and the saying "they can't wash the stains of plantains from their hands," is not said in criticism. Muñoz's vision, he said, was that "the virtue of the jibaro would be organized." This was one of the themes of a speech he had made decades before.

Muñoz was very anxious for me to have a copy of a speech he gave to the Legislative Assembly in March 1952. In the speech, which had in it visionary statements of the future, Muñoz makes it clear that economics should not determine the culture but be a servant to it and to the spiritual energy of the people, the jibaros.

At the end of their political struggle, he said in March 1952, at the top of the mountain they were climbing, would be a simple life, with equality, fraternity, and modest well-being: people involved in honorable work with modest pay, children educated as far as they could go, the sick and old taken care of, tasks done with liberty and justice, for the good of all. He saw a culture of workers appreciating people for what they do and not for the money they accumulate, deep in their respect of God, free of vain involvement. And then he concluded, to the applause of the Insular Legislature, by saying that what he has been describing is already rooted and growing in the culture of the Puerto Rican jibaro.

He went on, in his 1952 speech, to implore that the tools of the new instruction be put in the hands of the jibaros, to claim that the jibaros are not transformed by production, that their wisdom gains from urbanization, instead of being one of its victims. This is the image Muñoz said would be projected into eveyone's heart; it is the jibaro at the summit, at the end of the hard road, the hard climb.

I would like to have been convinced by Muñoz. But of course I was not. Evidence more than suggests that the jibaro has not protected the heart of Puerto Rico from the colonizer's influence.

## NOTES

1. Luis Muñoz Marin, "Porto Rico: The American Colony," *The Nation*, April 8, 1925, p. 380.

2. Colonel Flinter, *An Account of the Present State of the Island of Puerto Rico*, pp. 77–78, quoted in José C. Rosario, *The Development of the Puerto Rican Jibaro and His Present Attitude Towards Society*, p. 76.

3. Robert J. Hunter, "Historical Survey of the Puerto Rican Status Question, 1898–1965," *Status of Puerto Rico. Selected Background Studies*, pp. 53–54; a committee of businessmen in Ponce calculated the number of shoes required for the island. According to them, of the 900,000 inhabitants, 700,000 went barefoot, 150,000 wore shoes regularly, and 50,000 wore them irregularly. See Henry K. Carroll, *Report on the Island of Puerto Rico*, p. 51.

4. Earl Parker Hanson, *Puerto Rico: Land of Wonders*, p. 85.

5. Gordon K. Lewis calls it a chasm between classes. *Puerto Rico: Freedom and Power in the Caribbean*, p. 76.

6. Ibid.

7. Antonio S. Pedreira, *Insularismo*; see also René Marqués, "El Puertorriqueño Docil (Literatura y realidad psicológica)," *Quadernos Americanos* 120 (January–February 1962): 114–95.

8. Rosario, op. cit., pp. 28–29.

9. Juan Angel Silen, *Hacia Una Visión Positiva del Puertorriqueño*.

10. Christopher Rand, *The Puerto Ricans*, p. 71; Theodore Brameld, *The Remaking of a Culture*, pp. 119–26.

11. *Status of Puerto Rico. Report of the United States–Puerto Rico Commission on the Status of Puerto Rico*, August 1966, p. 33.

12. This is illustrated in the debates on the Jones Act; see, for example, Frank Gatell, "The Art of the Possible: Luis Muñoz Rivera and the Puerto Rican Jones Bill," *Americas* 17, no. 1 (July 1960): 17, 18.

13. Henry Wells, "Ideology and Leadership in Puerto Rican Politics," *American Political Science Review* 49, no. 1 (March 1955): 27.

14. Ralph Hancock, *Puerto Rico: A Success Story*, p. 86.

15. Melvin H. Tumin and Arnold S. Feldman, *Social Class and Social Change in Puerto Rico*, p. 181.

16. Samuel Huntington, "Political Development and Decay," *World Politics*, Summer 1965, p. 425.

17. Charles T. Goodsell, *The Administration of a Revolution*, pp. 176–77.

18. Robert W. Anderson, *Party Politics in Puerto Rico*, p. 43.

19. Sidney W. Mintz, "Puerto Rico: An Essay in the Definition of a National Culture," *in Status of Puerto Rico. Selected Background Studies*, p. 388; Lewis, op. cit., p. 186; Earl Parker Hanson, *Puerto Rico: Ally for Progress*, p. 111.

20. Richard Hofstadter, "The Pseudo-Conservative Revolt," in *The Radical Right*, ed. Daniel Bell.

21. Oscar Lewis, *La Vida*, p. 83.

22. Gordon K. Lewis, op. cit., p. 506.

23. "...los exilado Cubanos, con rarismas excepciones, son los aliados naturales de los anexionistas puertorriqueños." Manuel Maldonado Denis, "Declinar del Movimiento Independentista Puertorriqueño?" *Revista de Ciencias Sociales* 9, no. 3 (September 1965): 288.

24. *Status of Puerto Rico. Report*, p. 151.

25. José Hernandez Alvarez, *Return Migration to Puerto Rico*, p. 13.

26. Ibid.

27. Marvin M. Karpatkin, "Puerto Rico: How Much Independence Does It Want?" *New Republic*, May 7, 1966, p. 14.

28. Gordon K. Lewis, op. cit., p. 7; Erasmo, in Oscar Lewis's *La Vida*, says "...there's the same poverty as always, and more crime. The only way we can progress is to become a state of the Union." Op. cit., p. 83.

29. Kingsley Davis in Hernandez, op. cit., p. vii (Foreword).

30. *U.S. News and World Report*, January 17, 1977, p. 73.

31. Hernandez, op. cit., p. 7.

32. Un Informe de la Comisión de Derechos Civiles de Los Estados Unidos, *Puertorriqueños en Los Estados Unidos Continentales: Un Futuro Incierto*, October, 1976.

33. David Vidal, "Dream Still Eludes Mainland Puerto Ricans," *New York Times*, September 11, 1977, p. 6.

34. Jon Nordheimer, "Puerto Ricans Accelerating Return to Crowded Homeland," *New York Times*, May 10, 1978, p. A18.

35. Juan M. Vasquez, "Many From Puerto Rico Flee City for Homeland," *New York Times*, February 8, 1972, p. 17.

36. Nordheimer, op. cit.

37. Bill Jones, "New York Puerto Rican Backs Mainland Plebiscite Vote," *San Juan Star*, March 8, 1967, p. 11.

38. A more recent example illustrates the pro-statehood sentiment of mainland Puerto Ricans who return to Puerto Rico. When an island Democratic primary was held in October 1978 to select delegates for the New Democratic Party, pro-statehood Puerto Ricans from the mainland were thought to be responsible. Returning Puerto Ricans wanted to be able to continue to affiliate with the Democratic Party and still be pro-statehood. (The island Democrats were traditionally for commonwealth.)
Manny Suarez, "NPP to gain 2-party power with NDP win," *San Juan Star*, October 22, 1978, p. 18.

39. Hernandez focuses on "return migration" but puts it in clear perspective by seeing it as just one of many moves from A, Birthplace, to B, Puerto Rican Residence Before Migration, to C, United States Residence, to D, Puerto Rican Place of Return. By the time they return, the mainland migrants are much more urban than the island pattern, which, in 1960, still showed over 50 percent rural residence. Op. cit., especially Chapters 1 and 2.

40. Manuel Maldonado Denis, *En Las Entrañas: Un Analisis Socio-historico de la Emigración Puertorriqueña*, p. 149.

41. "Margaret Mead on Problems of Puerto Rican Cultural Identity," (interview by Bill Thompson) in *Revista/Review InterAmericana* 5, no. 1 (Spring 1975): 7.

42. Hernandez, op. cit., pp. 16, 17, 21; and Nordheimer, op. cit.

43. The Society was set up to "educate the newcomers" about housing, financial investments, and schooling. No doubt, such a club offers psychological and social benefits to its members, as well. Nordheimer, op. cit.

44. Ibid.

45. Ibid; also see William Stockton, "Going Home: The Puerto Ricans' New Migration," *New York Times Magazine*, November 27, 1978, pp. 89, 90.

46. David Vidal, "The Loneliness of the Returning Newyorican," *San Juan Star* (Outlook Section), October 5, 1975, p. 5.

47. Ibid., see also E. Seda Bonilla, *Requiem Para Una Cultura*, pp. 276–78.

48. *The Time for Independence: Political Thesis—Pro-Independence Movement of Puerto Rico* (1964), p. 35.

49. Maldonado Denis, *En Las Entrañas*, p. 140.

50. Henry K. Carroll, *Report on the Island of Porto Rico*, p. 50.

51. Luis Rafael Sánchez, "La Generación del O Sea," in *Claridad* (San Juan), January 23, 1972, p. 22, quoted in Maldonado Denis, op. cit., p. 145.

52. He was quoting Epifanio Fernández Varga. Pedreira, op. cit., p. 102.

53. Maldonado Denis, op. cit., pp. 178, 180.

54. Quoted in Ralph Hancock, *Puerto Rico: A Success Story*, p. 49.

# 6 THE 1967 PLEBISCITE: THE PEOPLE DECIDE

Preciosa te llaman las olas del mar que te baña,
Preciosa por ser un encanto, por ser un Edén,
y tienes la noble hidalquía de la Madre España,
y el fiera cantío del Indio bravío, le tienes también.
Preciosa te llaman los bardos que cantan tu historia,
No importa el tirano que trate con negra maldad,
Preciosa serás sin bandera, sin lauros, ni gloria,
Preciosa, preciosa te llaman los hijos de la liberdad.

From the song, "Preciosa," by Rafael Hernandez

In 1967 Puerto Rico held an island-wide plebiscite. Those who voted chose, by an overwhelming majority, to affiliate with the United States. At a time when nations struggle to be independent of their mother countries, Puerto Rico voted to continue close ties with hers. This chapter will describe the 1967 plebiscite, evaluate the outcome, and explain the uniqueness of the Puerto Rican situation.

## THE ISSUE OF STATUS

In 1966 and 1967 when I asked hundreds of Puerto Ricans, including political leaders, government officials, businessmen, university

This chapter is based on an article of the same name published in *Revista/Review Interamericana* 5, no. 1 (Spring 1975). Reprinted with permission from *Revista/Review Interamericana*.

professors, and students of all political persuasions, what the most important problem facing Puerto Rico was, each one, with no exceptions, said "status."[1] The status choice for the Puerto Rican is between independence, statehood, and commonwealth (*estado libre asociado*). The commonwealth concept, first inspired by the Irish model, had been considered as early as 1917, but the term itself was probably imported from the Philippines, which was called "commonwealth" during the decade before independence (1935–46).[2]

In the mid-1940s Luis Muñoz Marin, Popular Party president and first elected governor of Puerto Rico, envisioned commonwealth as an interim solution to the problem of status. Through commonwealth economic stability could be reached, after which an island plebiscite between statehood and independence would be held.

After the election of 1948, however, in which Muñoz's party got 61.3 percent of the votes cast, Muñoz began to treat commonwealth as a more permanent alternative.

In July 1950, as soon as the U.S. Congress passed a law enabling Puerto Rico to write its own constitution (Public Law 600), Muñoz began interpreting the law as "a foundation of a new political status for Puerto Rico,"[3] and by 1952 he was arguing that commonwealth was a new alternative, equal in dignity although different in nature, to independence or federated statehood.[4]

With a Puerto Rican Constitution, Muñoz not only engineered but helped legitimize the commonwealth status. In March 1953 the United States announced during the 8th session of the UN General Assembly that its reports on Puerto Rico were no longer necessary because Puerto Rico's new political status, commonwealth, removed it from the non-self-governing category.[5]

Formal Puerto Rican support for this view was essential.[6] During the hearings held by the 4th Committee on Trusteeships, the Puerto Rican resident commissioner served as an alternate delegate and defended Public Law 600 as a basic status change. With the two-thirds rule waived in November 1953, the UN General Assembly approved the United States position.[7] Commonwealth became an acceptable alternative for the world forum.

To a non-Puerto Rican, the emphasis on the status issue seems surprising. There are so many problems of education, population density, unemployment, and poverty to be solved that to name status as the number one issue seems outrageous. Yet, status is a core issue for Puerto Ricans. When they decide which status they want, in many ways they are deciding their personal identities.

> Each of the three status positions contains an ideological dimension: each involves a concept of the identity of the people of Puerto Rico, an interpretation of history, a way of life, and an aspiration for the future.[8]

The plebiscite was an attempt to resolve the question of Puerto Rico's identity. For each Puerto Rican what the status choice represented was the choice of self-image.

Since 1898 the issue of political status was the dominant one, and yet not until 1967 was an island plebiscite held. As important as the issue might have been to each Puerto Rican, the plebiscite debates were boring, the arguments were tired, and the results were predictable.[9]

## PLEBISCITE: IMMEDIATE HISTORY

In July 1962, in an exchange of letters between Popular Governor Luis Muñoz Marín and President John F. Kennedy, Muñoz asked for a "perfecting" of commonwealth, increased autonomy for the island, and also asked for an island-wide plebiscite. Kennedy, in "full sympathy" with the aims, agreed that the time was right.[10] It was the commonwealth's tenth anniversary.

The result of the Muñoz-Kennedy letters was "an Act to Establish a United States-Puerto Rico Commission on the Status of Puerto Rico." In February 1964 the president signed it into law.*

The 13-member commission existed for two years, from June 9, 1964, to August 5, 1966, acquiring "a library of more than 800 books" and many cases of documents representing "perhaps the greatest collection of information ever accumulated...."[11]

The commission's task was to "study all factors which may have a bearing on the present and future relationship between the United States and Puerto Rico,"[12] and each of the governments appropriated $900,000 for this job. The results were published as three volumes of bilingual hearings, a fine collection of background studies, and a commission report, and were made available to the public.

> The Commission's major conclusion was that all three forms of political status—Commonwealth, Statehood, and Independence—are valid and confer upon the people of Puerto Rico equal dignity with equality of status and of national citizenship. Any choice among them is to be made by the people of Puerto Rico, and the economic, social, cultural and security arrangements which would need to be made under the three status alternatives will require the mutual agreement and full cooperation of the Government of the United States.[13]

Furthermore, the commission recommended a status plebiscite, "an expression of the will of the citizens of Puerto Rico...,"[14] and on

---

*See Appendix D for list of members.

December 23, 1966, the Puerto Rican Legislature voted to hold such a plebiscite.

The plebiscite was scheduled for July 23, 1967.[15] The ballot included the three choices of statehood, represented by a royal palm; independence, represented by a wheel; and commonwealth, represented by a mountain.

The Statehood Party and the Independence Party voted not to take part in the July plebiscite. Nevertheless, there was a proliferation of groups for statehood and independence, each submitting signatures to the board of elections (signatures representing one percent of the 1964 party vote were all that was necessary to qualify) and competing for the $385,000 allotted to each formula.[16] Capturing the absurdity, an editorial in the San Juan Star said, in part:

> It all started orderly enough. There were the Popular Democratic Party, the Statehood Republican Party and the Puerto Rican Independence Party.
>
> Then the PIP rejected the plebiscite, and the Fund for the Republic took its place. The SRP also pulled out, giving way to United Statehooders, whose members included the American Reform Party, the Popular Statehood Movement, the People's Party, the United States Moral Movement, Citizens for State 51, and the American Citizens for Plebiscite Action.
>
> It looked bad then, but it got worse. With the passing of time there have arisen such groups as Businessmen for Commonwealth, Citizens for Commonwealth, Citizens for Statehood, Inc., Men of Puerto Rican Affirmation, Independentistas for a Pro-Commonwealth Vote, Committee of Labor Leaders for Commonwealth and the Sovereigntist Anti-plebiscite Concentration.
>
> Now, let's be sensible. How can anyone be expected to go to a rally somewhere and yell, "Hooray for the Sovereigntist Anti-plebiscite Concentration?"[17]

The campaign months were filled with suspicions, accusations, and legal threats within groups as well as between groups. The conflicts had to do with who voted, who represented each status choice, and who campaigned and how. Feelings ran high, and at one point there was some talk of postponing the plebiscite[18] and even some doubt that a plebiscite would be held at all.[19]

## LEGAL CONFLICTS

Some who opposed the plebiscite tried legally to prevent it from taking place on a variety of grounds, among them, that it was a private use of public funds;[20] that Puerto Ricans living in the states were disenfranchised;[21] and that there was no place on the ballot to vote against the plebiscite.[22] In all, four legal suits were filed and dismissed.

## INDEPENDENCE INFIGHTING

Although the Independence Party voted not to participate, there were two groups working for an independence vote in the plebiscite: Workers for Independence Movement, led by Ponce Independentist Waldemiro Arroyo, and Fund for the Republic, led by Independence Party member and University of Puerto Rico Professor Héctor Alvarez Silva. The Workers for Independence Movement qualified to represent independence in the plebiscite with 511 signatures; the Fund for the Republic qualified with 266. The most vicious intra-party attacks of the campaign came from the Independence Party (PIP) and were aimed at these two groups.

The PIP accused both Arroyo's group and Alvarez Silva's group of "having committed fraud" when they collected the necessary signatures,[23] and that some people who signed were either misled or were not registered voters.[24] In addition, the president of the Independence Party, Gilberto Concepción de Gracia, called Alvarez Silva's participation "improper, undemocratic, immoral, anti-political, irresponsible, colonial, contrary to independence and unpatriotic";[25] José Antonio Ortiz, Independence Party secretary, said that Alvarez Silva's attempt to represent independence "amounts to treason";[26] and the Party's executive committee voted to oust Alvarez Silva in February.[27]

It was clear that the majority of independentistas were against participation in the plebiscite and were united, at least temporarily, by their opposition. Alvarez's Fund for the Republic seemed merely to be going through the motions of campaigning. "Repudiated by the PIP high command, the leaders of the Fund ran a low-key and rather amateurish campaign in support of the independence formula."[28] The independentists seemed almost defensive about their beliefs.[29]

## ENERGETIC STATEHOODERS

Unlike the independentists, the pro-statehood campaigners were aggressive. Officially, the Statehood Party had voted not to participate in the plebiscite; but the party members were divided on the issue, and, unlike the Independence experience, it in some ways helped their cause.

According to the plebiscite law, if the party refused to defend statehood, other groups could. Seven groups collected signatures[30] and vied for a position on the five-member pro-statehood directive committee.[31] Luis Alberto Ferré, who broke with the Statehood Party to participate in the plebiscite, headed the largest group, United State-hooders, and headed the directive committee. Ferré helped separate the issue of statehood from the old Statehood Party, and his name and charisma gave the cause a fresh orientation and vigor.

Ferré was well-known. He was a successful entrepreneur, a generous philanthropist,[32] and a graduate in engineering from the Massachusetts Institute of Technology (B.S. and M.S.). His family was wealthy. From sugar, the family business had expanded into paper, glass, ceramic, and cement plants; and by 1950 their total assets had reached ten million dollars.[33] Ferré would become governor of Puerto Rico in 1968.

## COMMONWEALTH ON TRIAL

The real fight in the plebiscite was the one between commonwealth and statehood. Ferré was likened to David, Muñoz to Goliath.[34] Ferré was battling a legend, but Muñoz was fighting for his life.[35] The common-wealth status was on trial.

Muñoz had to lead the commonwealth campaign and "bore the main burden of the speech-making"[36] because Popular Governor Roberto Sánchez Vilella could not. Sánchez was involved in an extra-marital scandal,[37] and a few months before the plebiscite he announced that he would not be the party candidate for governor in 1968.[38] Sánchez's appearance and active support for commonwealth could only hurt the cause. In addition, not everyone in the Popular Party was for a common-wealth vote, and this too hurt the campaign for commonwealth. *Van-guardia*, for example, a dissident group of Popular Party members, were against participation in the plebiscite,[39] and there were Populares who supported statehood as well as independentist Populares.[40]

As the plebiscite date neared, the campaign degenerated.[41] Com-monwealth supporters and statehooders accused each other of unfair and misleading practices,[42] and what was implied often seemed more impor-tant than what was said. Truly ironic is the fact that the major issue of the campaign became independence, although most of the independence forces refused to participate in the plebiscite. It was a fear of indepen-dence that colored the campaign.[43]

## FEAR OF INDEPENDENCE

As more fully described in Chapter 3, history and political accusa-tions seemed to link independence with anarchy, violence, and commu-nism. A popular fear that certain anarchy was tied to independence must stem at least in part from U.S. rule and the sense of inferiority it instilled in Puerto Ricans about their ability to govern themselves.[44]

The idea that Puerto Ricans were not capable of governing themselves was an argument serious and important enough to need answering,[45] at least from the perspective of Alvarez Silva, independence spokesperson. He said during the plebiscite campaign:

> There has been a lot of talk about the proposition that only Anglo Saxons and the countries they dominate and govern are able to rule themselves in a stable democratic manner. This is supposed to follow from a type of national character that is suitable to democratic government....
>
> *After very serious analysis* we found that all objective considerations pointed to the fact that the Republic of Puerto Rico will be very stable and democratic....
>
> The truth is that independence will only allow the new republic to continue its preindependence way of life....
>
> The degree of political stability and democracy that you could expect to find in a new republic is a direct reflection of the amount of democracy and self-government that you find in the dependent community prior to independence. [emphasis added][46]

That he needed to make such a statement at all is the result of a system of colonialism. According to Frantz Fanon, "The effect consciously sought by colonialism was to drive into the natives' heads the idea that if the settlers were to leave they would at once fall back into barbarism, degradation and bestiality."[47] It worked.[48]

Not only anarchy but violence was linked to belief in independence. Because the Nationalists used confrontation tactics and sometimes used violence, the belief in independence, even of non-Nationalists, became linked with violence.

The clearest example occurred in November 1950, following the Nationalist uprisings when, according to PIP President Concepción de Gracia, from 700 to 1,000 PIP leaders were arrested. The number may not have been quite that high. Nevertheless, the detention of 225 party members for no other reason than party membership is a fact verified by the Civil Liberties Commission.[49] "No PIP leaders were ever implicated in the uprising itself,"[50] and Concepción accused the government of "maliciously sowing 'alarm, fear, and panic' among the sympathizers of independence by trying to instill in the minds of the masses the idea that PIP had been implicated in the...violence."[51]

The belief in independence was also linked with communism. After the 1950 uprising, Governor Muñoz broadcast his conviction of the connection between the Nationalists and "communist propaganda strategy."[52] Such accusations continue. Governor Luis Ferré, for example, in March 1971, said that the students rioting at the university were led by communists who had been trained in Cuba; they were "a small cadre" trying to destroy Puerto Rican society.[53] And, in 1975, Governor Rafael Hernandez Colon referred to the "clear and undeniable link" between Castro and the pro-communists and Socialist forces working for Puerto Rican independence.[54]

For the public, independence was linked with anarchy, violence, and communism. For the individual, belief in independence had its personal costs. As described in Chapter 3, FUPI (University Federal for Independence) and MPI members were special targets for harassment.[55]

## THE CAMPAIGN

It was a tired campaign[56] except for the "fear factor." Fear of independence gave the plebiscite a sense of urgency,[57] but it was politics at its worst. On an island where it was a liability to be an independentista, the issues being considered put commonwealth on the defensive: (1) Was Muñoz still an independentista? (2) Could commonwealth lead to independence? (3) Was American citizenship secure with commonwealth? (4) Was Puerto Rican citizenship second class citizenship?

The Statehood Party continually hammered away at the fact that Muñoz had once been an independentista, and other Popular Party leaders were also accused of "badly suppressed pro-independence sentiment."[58] Muñoz feared the independence scare would cost him votes.[59] He tried to allay the fear by calling his former independence belief "an error of youth."[60] At a San Juan rally he said about independence, "They had to go all the way back...as far back as 1936...I made those statements when I believed in independence. And when I stopped believing in independence, I told you all."[61]

Could commonwealth lead to independence? Muñoz not only had to answer for his "past statements in which he...extolled commonwealth as a status which closes neither the door to independence nor to statehood,"[62] but for the Status Commission Report, which also said that commonwealth status "leaves doors open to independence," a fact often mentioned by Ferré.[63] As statehooders continued to warn that with commonwealth independence might come through "the back door,"[64] Muñoz would answer, "commonwealth does not close any doors save the door to the Impossible, independence."[65]

But Ferré continued to warn "that Congress may give Puerto Rico its independence without the consent of the island's residents, unless statehood receives a strong endorsement in the status plebiscite." Also, statehooders warned, U.S. citizenship could be rescinded by Congress at any time.[66] This argument, however, was countered by a timely U.S. Supreme Court decision that helped the Populares.

On May 29, "the Supreme Court ruled specifically on the case of a Polish-born man whose naturalized U.S. citizenship was taken from him because he voted in an Israeli election. In making its ruling, the high court declared unconstitutional the law under which the man was deprived of his citizenship" (a Congressional law that established that a U.S. citizen who voted in another country would lose his citizenship).[67]

Commonwealth forces lost no time in praising the decision and pointing out its relevance.[68] For Resident Commissioner Polanco Abreu, it meant that "Congress lacks the authority to strip Americans of their citizenship...."[69] Pro-commonwealth ads incorporated this message.* Next to his picture, Muñoz would be quoted:

> More than a hundred times I have said that independence is out of the question for Puerto Rico, because American citizenship cannot be taken from anyone against his will and because 97 percent of all Puerto Ricans reject the status of independence. *The Supreme Court of the United States has just proven us unequivocally right.*[70]

Spending all this energy on the issue of independence makes sense only when you understand what a liability it is to be an independentista in Puerto Rico. The fact that independence belief had been linked to anarchy, violence, and communism helps explain why the commonwealth forces were so sensitive to the independence accusation.[71]

Fear of independence was the strongest ally statehooders had. They emphasized the permanence of statehood and "the insecurity of the commonwealth status."[72] While the message of commonwealth was progress,[73] the security and permanence of "first class citizenship"[74] was the statehooders' message. "We must be honest. We must be sincere. If we want to be Americans, we should vote for statehood."[75] In a televised speech Ferré said: "Think of our children and grandchildren and wish to guarantee for them the security of freedom, democracy and equal opportunity for all."[76] And in a speech at Levittown Community Center he told the crowd, "On the July 23 Plebiscite you are going to vote for your most important candidates, your children and their future."[77]

## CONTRA EL PLEBISCITO

"Unquestionably, the most formidable foe the proponents of independence in the plebiscite have to face in this campaign is not either of the

---

*See Appendix F for examples of plebiscite ads.

other two status alternatives but the boycott movement within independentista ranks."[78] Every independence group was officially against participation in the plebiscite.

Independence organizations were making overtures for creating an anti-plebiscite front. On February 12 the Movement Pro Independence (MPI) leaders evaluated proposals to set the basis for united action of all "patriotic forces" against the plebiscite.[79] At the same time, the Independence Party (PIP) was beginning to organize a combined opposition against the plebiscite but with stipulated conditions, among them the use of only the Puerto Rican flag as the insignia for the campaign and "campaigning only for independence and not in favor of the Castro government in Cuba or against the Vietnam war."[80] In addition, the hundred delegates who attended the Nationalist convention in March also proposed a formation of a "national front."[81] They declared the plebiscite "a false expression of self-determination" designed to perpetuate "Puerto Rico's military occupation, economic exploitation and cultural obliteration."[82] And in the beginning of April, the Anti-Colonialist Congress of Puerto Rico (ACPR) had "approved a resolution repudiating the upcoming 'so-called plebiscite'... asking all Puerto Ricans to abstain from voting on July 23."[83]

By May, "representatives of all pro-independence groups on the Island and advocates of associated sovereignty [had] united in a 'militant front' against what they [called] the 'plebiscite farce' scheduled for July 23."[84] On May 17, at the Ateneo meeting in San Juan, Juan Mari Bras, leader of the MPI, said, "Tonight we have done away with the isolation and dispersion of the central nucleus of Puerto Rican forces which represent the survival of our nationality."[85] The anti-plebiscite manifesto declared, in part:

> Pressured by the United States government, the government of Puerto Rico intends to hold a false plebiscite on July 23. The Puerto Rican people are expected to ratify with their votes the present status of political inferiority. The aim is to free the United States from the accusation that it is keeping Puerto Rico within a colonial regime in open defiance of United Nations norms which the U.S. is committed to uphold....
>
> Not to vote in that plebiscite will not be an indication of indifference or neutrality regarding the problem of our status; it will be a way of expression without having to go to a false and discredited plebiscite. It will amount to voting for the defeat of that plebiscite and for a demand of sovereignty.
>
> In view of the gravity of the plebiscite farce, we the undersigned, united in this historic moment above party allegiances and above group interests, call on all Puerto Ricans who are proud of being such to be present at 10 a.m. on Sunday, July 16, at Sixto Escobar Stadium, where a great gathering of Puerto Ricans will take place to express repudiation of the false plebiscite and support of the demand for sovereignty....[86]

The anti-plebiscite group was called *Concentración Soberanista Antiplebiscitaria* (Sovereigntist Antiplebiscite Concentration). A week before the scheduled rally they were estimating that between 40,000 and 60,000 followers would attend.[87]

> Sunday, July 16, cars bearing Puerto Rican flags began arriving in San Juan as early as 8 a.m. Traffic jams were reported along Ponce de León Avenue during the late morning and early afternoon.... Even after the rally ended around 3 p.m. cars were still arriving from distant points in the island at Escobar Stadium. Despite the obvious militancy of those attending, the rally had the somewhat festive air of a family reunion.[88]

An estimated 30,000 attended.[89] They heard speeches by Juan Mari Bras of the MPI, Gilberto Concepción de Gracia of the PIP, Yamil Galib and Piri Fernández de Lewis of ACPR, Gerdo Navas of Vanguardia, and Colón Martinez, former PDP member and former president of the Puerto Rican Bar Association.

## THE PLEBISCITE

J. Edgar Hoover predicted that "independence groups will trigger a new wave of violence as the July 23 plebiscite approaches."[90] But there was no violence. What is more, everyone seemed happy with the outcome.

## THE RESULTS

The pre-plebiscite registration drive was successful. There were 60,169 new voters.[91] Nevertheless, fewer than the usual number who vote in general elections (80 percent) voted on July 23—only 65.8 percent of those eligible. The 702,512 who went to the polls voted overwhelmingly for continued relations with the United States. They cast 425,079 (60.5 percent) for commonwealth and 273,315 (38.9 percent) for statehood.

Although the plebiscite turnout was better than other non-election turnouts (the ones that approved Public Laws 600 and 447 were 65.1 and 59 percent, respectively), the independentists proclaimed victory for their boycott. They were partially right. "All evidence points to the relative 'success' of the *independentista* abstention drive. Many, if not most of the persons who in 1964 cast their vote for the Puerto Rican Independence Party seemed determined to follow their leadership into abstention."[92] Only 4,205 votes were cast for independence (.6 percent).

Commonwealth was victorious with a majority larger than the ones they polled in the 1960 and 1964 general elections (58.2 and 59.3 percent, respectively). On the other hand, statehooders celebrated because their support increased four percentage points from 1964, and they carried Ponce, San Lorenzo, Corozal, Cataño, and four of the nine precincts in San Juan.

> A jubilant Luis A. Ferré—pleased with his group's showing in the status plebiscite—said... that the results clearly indicate that the statehood ideal is firmly rooted in the Puerto Rican people....
> Ferré... shouted "We've knocked down the mountain, we've slain the Goliath," as the group's victories in several municipalities became known.[93]

Each status group celebrated the results of the plebiscite: the independentists because their boycott had been so effective;[94] commonwealth, because of their clear majority; and statehood because of their gains.

## THE PUERTO RICAN PEOPLE

"The Puerto Rican, whatever his Party allegiance, is an ardent patriot."[95] But his patriotism is not loyalty to a polity. It is based on the feeling of being part of a people, of being Puerto Rican.[96] That is not to say that the average Puerto Rican knows a great deal about the island's history. On the contrary, particularly poor Puerto Ricans "showed an abysmal ignorance of Puerto Rican historical figures. Some knew more about George Washington and Abraham Lincoln than about their own heroes."[97]

Nor is the feeling of being part of a people based on a well-defined cultural tradition. On the contrary, the island has swiftly and indiscriminately absorbed many foreign cultural patterns,[98] an example of what the Movement for Independence calls "cultural infiltration."[99] (It is for this reason that Boorstin has said that "Puerto Rico is a country with a long past and a short history.")[100]

Puerto Rican culture is a conglomerate of imports and does not in itself create the feeling of being Puerto Rican. In *La Vida*, for example, Soledad's cultural remembrances, when she talks of wanting to die in Puerto Rico, her "own country,"[101] consist of "fresh cut green bananas boiled with codfish."[102] Nor is patriotic sentiment built around a strong identification with indigenous institutions, for they, too, were imports. And yet perhaps it was the very bombardment of foreign influences that created the myth of a people, for with such a myth Puerto Ricans could live more comfortably with the reality of foreign cultures and foreign rule.

For the returning Neorican, the feeling of being part of a people is strong. As tens of thousands of Puerto Ricans began returning to Puerto Rico after spending decades, sometimes generations, on the mainland, the headlines heralded "return to homeland."[103] No one questioned the accuracy of the term homeland to describe what they were feeling in their return.

The myth of a people gives a sense of belonging and of nationhood of "common origin and destiny,"[104] even in an alien world, for "myths do not enlist the complicity of our reason but rather that of our instincts."[105] Jews and Blacks seem to feel a similar sense of being part of a people. Particularly in a foreign environment, they also have a unique sense of sharing a common experience not of their making. Their feeling is like the "romantic attachment" Tumin and Feldman discover in Puerto Rico.

> Taking up residence in Puerto Rico and beginning to sketch out the design of a study, one quickly discovers that there is running through the hearts and minds of Puerto Ricans at virtually every class level a fervent identification with their society, bordering on a mystical romantic attachment.[106]

Thus there exists a romantic attachment to the island without a political commitment to its independence. Puerto Ricans love Puerto Rico, feel Puerto Rican, but fear independence. Only at rare moments does their sentiment flavor their politics. Frequently at parties, observes Kathleen L. Wolf, the first socializing phrase is "euphoric." The men feel like brothers, they sing nationalistic songs, and independence sentiment is obvious.[107] It is probably for this reason that I have often heard it said on the island that if Puerto Rico held a plebiscite on Friday night, the awnings of the houses the next day would proclaim a republic. ("Si se celebrase un plebiscito en Puerto Rico en viernes por la noche en las marquesinas de las casas al otro dia se proclamaria la república.")

Puerto Ricans can love Puerto Rico and vote for statehood. They can feel Puerto Rican and vote to be American. They can hold what may seem like contradictory political allegiances because Puerto Rico is not a nation; it is a people.

As described in the beginning of this chapter, Puerto Ricans' political status preference is related to how they see themselves. But however they see themselves and whatever their status choices are, Puerto Ricans can always feel they are part of a people, for that is not based on cultural trappings, or language. (The dozens of mainland-born Puerto Ricans who were taking a Spanish class designed for *extranjeros* [foreigners] at the University of Puerto Rico had no doubts that they were Puerto Rican.) A sense of being part of a people (unlike a nation) does not require borders or language—that sense the individual carries with him.

In the same way that the jíbaro, it is said, can never completely wash away the stain of plantains from his hands,[108] Puerto Ricans will always be Puerto Rican. They have been accommodating for centuries, absorbing foreign influences, yet their sense of being Puerto Rican remains untouched. They sing of this accommodation in a song as well known as the Puerto Rican anthem, and probably sung more often:

No importa el tirano te trate con negra maldad
Preciosa será sin bandera sin lauros ni gloria
Preciosa, preciosa te llaman los hijos de la libertad.[109]

## NOTES

1. I asked this question of "island" Puerto Ricans living in Puerto Rico. Mainland Puerto Ricans are supposedly less concerned. In fact, "A frequent complaint among Newyoricans is that the 'locals' are obsessed with the political status of Puerto Rico...'you can have a conversation about King Kong in a restaurant and somehow the conversation with swing around to the status thing.'" David Vidal, "The loneliness of the returning Newyorican," San Juan Star (Outlook Section), October 5, 1975, p. 5.

2. Jesús de Galíndez, "Government and Politics in Puerto Rico. New Formulas for Self-Government," International Affairs 30, no. 3 (July 1954): 337.

3. Henry Wells, The Modernization of Puerto Rico, p. 231.

4. U.S., Congress, Senate, Hearings, 82nd Cong., 2d sess., April 29, 1952, p. 19, quoted in Hunter, op. cit., p. 121. See also "Remarks by the Honorable Luis Muñoz Marín, Governor of the Commonwealth of Puerto Rico, at Harvard University, on June 16, 1955" and New York Times, text of Muñoz Letter, July 26, 1962, p. 8.

5. The best history of the United Nations proceedings is in Jesús de Galíndez, op. cit., pp. 340–41. See also "Puerto Rico's New Self Governing Status Transmitted to Secretary General," U.S. Department of State Bulletin 28, April 20, 1953, p. 587.

6. See Rexford G. Tugwell, The Art of Politics as Practiced by Three Great Americans: Franklin Delano Roosevelt, Luis Muñoz Marín, and Fiorello H. LaGuardia, pp. 226–27.

7. The delegates were split into three blocs: a small majority, which included most Latin American countries, supported the United States; India, Burma, Iraq, Mexico, and Guatemala plus the Soviet bloc maintained that Puerto Rico was still a non-self-governing territory; and the colonial powers abstained. The vote was the United States' position approved: 26 for, 16 against, 18 abstentions.

8. *Status of Puerto Rico. Report*, p. 6.

9. "Commonwealth is expected to win, but it is doubtful if the victory will have settled the argument or lessened to any extent the island's divisions. Consequently, many here are wondering whether the time, effort, and money are really worth it." Henry Giniger, "Puerto Rico's Future," *New York Times*, March 22, 1967.

10. Text of the Muñoz-Kennedy Letters, *New York Times*, July 26, 1962, p. 8.

11. En. F. Meyer, "Stacom Set to Go Out of Business," *San Juan Star*, February 5, 1967, p. 12.

12. Public Law 88-271, February 20, 1964: 78 Stat. 17, quoted in *Status of Puerto Rico, Report*, p. 3.

13. Ibid., p. 6.

14. Ibid., p. 8.

15. I have relied heavily on the *San Juan Star* for coverage of the plebiscite. It is the only English newspaper on the island, and had an average daily circulation of 21,384, compared to *El Mundo*'s circulation of 69,857, *El Imparcial*'s of 51,119, and *El Dia*'s of 16,667, in 1964–65. (*Status of Puerto Rico. Report*, p. 184). A preliminary comparison of reporting convinced me that its coverage was not essentially different from *El Mundo*'s. I decided to use the *San Juan Star* because it was written in English.

16. Dimas Planas, "Election Board Faces Puzzling Problem," *San Juan Star*, February 10, 1967, p. 18.

17. "Who's for What?" *San Juan Star*, July 7, 1967, p. 31.

18.Tomas Stella, "Muñoz Backs Absentee Balloting," *San Juan Star*, February 3, 1967, pp. 1, 14.

19. *San Juan Star*, February 4, 1967, p. 6.

20. Robert Friedman, "Anticolonialists File Action on Plebiscite Funds," *San Juan Star*, June 9, 1967, pp. 1, 4.

21. Robert Friedman, "Amadeo Jousts With Plebiscite Again," *San Juan Star*, July 6, 1967, p. 3.

22. Robert Friedman, "Court Dismisses Status Vote Suit," *San Juan Star*, May 26, 1967, pp. 1, 14. "The law 'indirectly prohibits' the plaintiffs, and others, from voting against the plebiscite 'since there is no place in the plebiscite ballot where plaintiffs and the class they represent can exercise the right of dissent,....'" Robert Friedman, "Three Challenge Plebiscite Law in Court Action," *San Juan Star*, May 18, 1967, p. 3.

23. *San Juan Star*, February 4, 1967, p. 3.

24. Dimas Planas, "Status Groups Meet Deadline in Plebiscite," *San Juan Star*, February 9, 1967, pp. 1, 14. "Alvarez Silva said that the petitions he will register with the election board are 'clearly defined.' He added that voters who signed them 'were fully aware that they were asking for independence representation in the Plebiscite.'" Ruben

Arrieta, "Independence Backers Seek Signatures," *San Juan Star*, February 7, 1967, p. 6.

25. *San Juan Star*, February 17, 1967, p. 6.

26. Ruben Arrieta, "Independence Backers Seek Signatures," *San Juan Star*, February 7, 1967, p. 6.

27. *San Juan Star*, February 17, 1967, p. 6.

28. Wells, op. cit., p. 260.

29. See, for example, Hector Alvarez Silva in "The Plebiscite Forum," *San Juan Star*, July 2, 1967, pp. 20, 22.

30. United Statehooders (64,094 signatures), American Reformist Party (3,535), Popular Statehood (4,247), Peoples Party (6,800), United States Moral Movement (3,187), Citizens for State 51 (3,393), American Citizens for Plebiscite Action (3,406). See the *San Juan Star*, February 15, 1967, p. 12, and Dimas Planas, "Status Groups Meet Deadline in Plebiscite," *San Juan Star*, February 8, 1967, pp. 1, 14.

32. His most famous project was the Ponce Museum of Fine Arts, "Among the Finest South of the United States Mainland." Andrew T. Viglucci, "A New Era for Puerto Rico," *Look Magazine*, March 18, 1969, p. 44.

33. For a good biography see Ralph Hancock, *Puerto Rico: A Success Story*, pp. 171–77.

34. *San Juan Star*, July 24, 1967, p. 1.

35. "This plebiscite campaign is the most important campaign in the history of our party." Muñoz Marin, quoted in Tomas Stella, "Muñoz Assures PDP Leaders Citizenship is Not 2nd Class," *San Juan Star*, February 20, 1967, p. 1.

36. Wells, op. cit., p. 260.

37. See Frank Ramos, "Dona Conchita Vetoes Divorce for Sanchez," *San Juan Star*, March 22, 1967, pp. 1, 14; Frank Ramos, "Women Deny Role in Blast at Sanchez," *San Juan Star*, March 24, 1967, pp. 1, 14.

38. Joel Magruder, "Mayors Favor Negron for Governor," *San Juan Star*, April 3, 1967, p. 14.

39. *San Juan Star*, February 28, 1967, p. 6.

40. Dimas Planas, "Senator Muñoz Sworn to Independence, Statehooder Says," *San Juan Star*, July 10, 1967, p. 3.

41. Wells, op. cit., p. 260.

42. See Dimas Planas, "PDP Chiefs suspect New Status Group," *San Juan Star*, July 8, 1967, p. 3; Dimas Planas, "Muñoz Ridicules Statehooders," *San Juan Star*, July 9, 1967, p. 3; Dimas Planas, "Ferré Warns Against Ads for July 25th," *San Juan Star*, July 7, 1967, p. 6; Dimas Planas, "Ferré Denies Connection to Pava Handbill," *San Juan Star*, July 19, 1967, p. 3; Margo Preece, "Pro-Statehood Ad Blasted by Treasury Secretary," *San Juan Star*, July 15, 1967, p. 3; Dimas Planas, "U.S.

Playing Dirty Pool, Muñoz Says," *San Juan Star*, July 20, 1967, p. 3.

43. "At this point in Puerto Rican history, fear of independence is dominant." Charles Rosario, Independence spokesperson, in "The Plebiscite Forum," *San Juan Star*, July 9, 1967, p. 21.

44. During the debates on the Jones Act (1917) Joseph Cannon said that Caucasian civilization was not exportable to the tropics and constitutional experiments were worse than useless, "if you have not the people who are competent to exercise sovereign power." Frank Gatell, "The Art of the Possible: Luis Muñoz Rivera and the Puerto Rican Jones Bill," *Americas* 17, no. 1 (July 1960): 17–18.

45. As Chapter Three illustrated, at one time, the Puerto Rican "native" was thought not even to be worthy of U.S. citizenship. See *Documents on the Constitutional History of Puerto Rico*, pp. 64–80; Edward B. Lockett, *The Puerto Rico Problem*, pp. 30–31; Earl Parker Hanson, *Puerto Rico: Ally for Progress*, p. 61; *DeLima v. Bidwell*, 182 U.S. 1 (1901), *Downes v. Bidwell*, 182 U.S. 244 (1901), *Ocamp v. United States*, 234 U.S. 91 (1913).

46. Alvarez Silva, "The Plebiscite Forum," op. cit., pp. 20, 22.

47. Franz Fanon, *The Wretched of the Earth*, p. 211.

48. "As for independence, it would never work out for Puerto Rico. Maybe there was a time when it would have, but not now. You just have to look and see the development in other countries during the past years. There's nothing but war. That's what's happening in Santo Domingo, Venezuela, Cuba, in Argentina after Peron left. When Trujillo was in power in Santo Domingo, people had to respect him but they had plenty to eat. Now the country has had three or four different governments since he died, and everything is going from bad to worse. If Puerto Ricans were granted independence the same thing would happen. We would have a President, and maybe his brother or this or that relative would own the government, and they would hire the ones who know a lot, so then the people of Puerto Rico would be automatically dominated by two or three hundred persons. Once that happened, you wouldn't be able to say, 'This man is bad,' because they would clap you in jail or stand you up against a wall and shoot you. In the United States people say anything they want to, because in a democracy you can do and undo as you please. But, of course, that leads to hooliganism because everyone can do what he wants to." Erasmo in Oscar Lewis, *La Vida*, p. 83.

49. David Helfeld, "Discrimination for Political Beliefs and Associations," December 29, 1958, p. 25, note 17 (unpublished report to the Puerto Rican Civil Liberties Commission), cited in Robert W. Anderson, *Party Politics in Puerto Rico*, p. 109.

50. Ibid., p. 109, note.

51. Ibid., p. 109. *El Mundo*, November 6, 1950, p. 2.

52. William H. Hackett, *The Nationalist Party*, p. 22.

53. Martin Arnold, "Puerto Rico is Concerned About Image," *New York Times*, March 14, 1971, p. 59.

54. David Binder, "Cuba Said to Aid Puerto Rico Foes: Governor Hernandez Says Castro is Training Terrorists," *New York Times*, May 20, 1976, p. 11.

55. Jo Thomas, "Documents Show F.B.I. Harassed Puerto Rican Separatists Parties," *New York Times*, November 22, 1977, p. 26.

56. "...we find your plebiscite campaign totally lacking in imagination and voter appeal. In fact, it's downright boring. Everybody—your opposition included—is just rehashing arguments that were milked dry years ago...." Eddie Lopez, (*Star* city editor), "Tell It to The Mountain," *San Juan Star*, May 24, 1967, p. 24.

57. Abidam Archilla, "Fear Factor in Status Debate (A Reader's Viewpoint)" *San Juan Star*, March 23, 1967, p. 10.

58. Statehooder Jesus Hernández Sanchez reminded his audience in Juana Diaz, "A solemn oath made before God binds former Governor Muñoz to fighting for ultimate independence." Dimas Planas, "Senator Muñoz Sworn to Independence, Statehooder Says," *San Juan Star*, July 10, 1967, p. 3. Menendez Monroig (a statehooder) named as "independentistas" San Juan Mayor Felisa Rincón de Gautier, Resident Commissioner Santiage Polanco Abreu, House Speaker Arcillo Alvarado, Senate President Samuel R. Quinones, House PDP leader Benjamin Ortiz, Agriculture Secretary Miguel Hernández Agosta, and Commerce Secretary Jenaro Baquero. Dimas Planas, "Ferré to Seek Federal Help for PR Coffee," *San Juan Star*, July 3, 1967, p. 3.

59. Muñoz on WIPR-TV "Ante La Prensa," February 21, 1967 quoted in Dimas Planas, "Concepción Calls Muñoz Lackey," *San Juan Star*, February 24, 1967, p. 12.

60. (Addressing 3,000 jibaros at Barrio Nuevo). Luis Vargas, "Thousands Flock to Hear Muñoz," *San Juan Star*, June 1, 1967, p. 1.

61. Dimas Planas, "Muñoz Finishes Campaign," *San Juan Star*, July 21, 1967, p. 3.

62. Dimas Planas, "Concepción Calls Muñoz Lackey."

63. Dimas Planas, "Ferré Addresses San Juan Lions Club," *San Juan Star*, March 31, 1967, p. 21. Independentistas as well as statehooders questioned Muñoz's claim that commonwealth "shut the door to independence." Juan Mari Bras refuted the allegation at the Antiplebiscite Concentration. To demonstrate the impossibility of Muñoz's pretension he asked for a raise of hands of those who were willing to struggle for Puerto Rico's liberty. Hands, flags, handkerchiefs, and placards waved furiously. *Claridad*, No. 156, July 23, 1967, p. 1.

The president of the MPI Youth Movement "criticized Secretary of Justice Rafael Hernández Colón" for having stated that Congress could not unilaterally grant independence to the island...."The Secretary pretends to overlook the historical fact that citizenship was imposed against the express wishes of the people of Puerto Rico." *San Juan Star*, March 2, 1967, p. 18.

64. "...the persistent contention of statehood backers that Muñoz and his Popular Democratic Party are trying to 'bring in independence through the back door.'" Margot Preece, "Constitution Change Requested by Muñoz," *San Juan Star*, July 14, 1967, p. 1.

65. Dimas Planas, "Concepcion Calls Muñoz Lackey."

66. In Arecibo addressing an audience of 1000; in Ponce addressing an audience of 2000. *San Juan Star*, February 23, 1967, p. 14. See also *San Juan Star*, June 8, 1967, p. 3.

67. Harry Turner, "Citizenship Decision Praised by Polanco," *San Juan Star*, June 1, 1967, p. 1.

68. For Secretary of Justice Hernandez Colon, "it destroys certain false theories that have been preached in Puerto Rico regarding the possibility of losing our American citizenship." *San Juan Star*, June 1, 1967, p. 3. See also *San Juan Star*, June 2, 1967, p. 3.

69. Turner, op. cit.

70. *San Juan Star*, July 14, 1967, p. 9.

71. See *San Juan Star*, July 7, 1967, p. 3, and Dimas Planas, "PDP Chiefs Suspect New Status Group," *San Juan Star*, July 8, 1967, p. 3.

72. Dimas Planas, "Ferré Addresses San Juan Lions Club."

73. "The president of a newly-formed pro-commonwealth group said yesterday that the outcome of the July status plebiscite is of great importance to the workers of Puerto Rico as well as to investors and businessmen."

"Guillermo Rodriquez, president of 'Businessmen Pro-Commonwealth' said the continuation of Puerto Rico's progress is at stake... his group was convinced that Commonwealth status was essential for continuing progress and the welfare of the people." *San Juan Star*, April 13, 1967, p. 6. Employees, but particularly businessmen, were constantly being quoted in commonwealth ads. They urged a continuation of commonwealth because they owed their economic well-being to progress under commonwealth.

74. Muñoz had to answer the charge that Puerto Ricans were second-class citizens, second-class partially because they couldn't vote and partially because island citizenship seemed, to the statehooder, to be revokable. To this Muñoz answered, "there is no second-class U.S. citizenship, there are simply second-class politicians." Muñoz in a speech at Barrio Nuevo, Luis Vargas, "Thousands Flock to Hear Muñoz." See also Tomas Stella, "Muñoz Assures PDP Leaders Citizenship is Not 2nd Class,' *San Juan Star*, February 20, 1967, p. 1.

75. Dimas Planas, "Ferré Addresses San Juan Lions Club."

76. Dimas Planas, "Ferré Hits Vote 'Reprisals,'" *San Juan Star*, February 3, 1967, p. 3.

77. Pedro Roman, "Ferré Calls U.S. Movement 'Crusade,'" *San Juan Star*, April 3, 1967, p. 3.

78. Dimas Planas, "Independence Boycott," *San Juan Star*, July 11, 1967, p. 20.

79. *San Juan Star*, February 12, 1967, p. 6.

80. *San Juan Star*, February 14, 1967, p. 6.

81. Tomas Stella, "Nationalists Propose Antiplebiscite Front," *San Juan Star*, March 13, 1967, p. 3.

82. Ibid.

83. John Roman, "Anticolonialists Boycott Plebiscite," *San Juan Star*, April 3, 1967, p. 6.

84. Pepe Arana, "Groups Form Front Against Status Vote," *San Juan Star*, May 18, 1967.

85. Ibid.

86. "Text of the Antiplebiscite Manifesto," *San Juan Star*, May 22, 1967, pp. 6, 43. For Juan Mari Bras's remarks see the *San Juan Star*, July 10, 1967, p. 6.

87. Tomas Stella, "30,000 Meet to Denounce Island Status Plebiscite," *San Juan Star*, July 17, 1967, p. 1.

88. Ibid.

89. Estimates vary. *Claridad* (No. 156, July 23, 1967, p. 1) estimated over 40,000 in attendance.

90. Harry Turner, "Polanco, Ferré Disagree with Hoover on Violence," *San Juan Star*, May 18, 1967, p. 6. See also *San Juan Star*, May 18, 1967, p. 18.

91. Tomas Stella, "Pro-Plebiscite Forces Claim Major Victory," *San Juan Star*, February 27, 1967, p. 1.

92. Dimas Planas, "Independentista Boycott."

93. *San Juan Star*, July 24, 1967, p. 1.

94. Also, "Concepción said statehood's defeat and the decline in voting strength of the Popular Democrats indicated that the independence cause was 'stronger than ever' and that the status debate had gained greater significance than before the plebiscite." *San Juan Star*, August 1, 1967, p. 6.

95. Gordon K. Lewis, "Puerto Rico: A New Constitution in American Government," *Journal of Politics* 15 (Fall 1953): 66.

96. "...we are a people, a collective entity, a community with which we inevitably identify." Charles Rosario, Independence spokesman in "The Plebiscite Forum," *San Juan Star*, July 9, 1967, p. 21.

97. Oscar Lewis, *La Vida*, p. xvii.

98. René Marqués, "Noted Writer Looks at Kazin's Content," *San Juan Star*, March 8, 1960, p. 19.

99. *The Time for Independence, Political Thesis—Pro Independence Movement of Puerto Rico*, p. 36.

100. Daniel J. Boorstin, "Self Discovery in Puerto Rico," *Yale Review*, 45 (1955–56): 236.

101. "I want to die in my own country. Me buried here? Oh no!...The minute I feel even a little bit sick, I'll fly right back to Puerto Rico." Oscar Lewis, op. cit., p. 135.

102. "Why, you shameless creature! You don't deserve to live. To think, that a countrywoman from Loiza Aldea shouldn't like green bananas!" Ibid.

103. David Vidal, "The loneliness of the returning Newyorican," *San Juan Star* (Outlook Section), October 5, 1975, p. 5.

104. "Most of the Puerto Rican people feel a sense of common origin and destiny." Julian H. Steward, "Culture Patterns of Puerto Rico," in *Portrait of A Society*, ed. Eugenio Fernández Méndez, p. 114.

105. Malraux, quoted in Octavio Paz, *Labyrinth of Solitude*, p. 155.

106. Melvin M. Tumin and Arnold S. Feldman, *Social Class and Social Change in Puerto Rico*, p. 30.

107. "Growing Up and Its Price in Three Puerto Rican Subcultures," in *Portrait of A Society*, ed. Eugenio Fernández Méndez, p. 237.

108. "No importa cuanto trate un jíbaro de quitarse su mancha de plátano, ésta siempre le acompañará."

109. It isn't important that the tyrant oppresses you with evil, Preciosa, you will be without flag, without honor, without glory, Preciosa, Preciosa, you are called by the sons of liberty.

# 7 PUERTO RICO: COMMONWEALTH OR COLONY?

Se oje este lamento por doquier, en mi
   desdichada Borinquen, si,
y triste el jibarito va, pensando
   asi, diciendo asi, llorando asi
   por el camino,
Que serán de Borinquen mi Dios
   querido
Que serán de mis hijos y de mi hogar.

from the song, "Lamento Borincano,"
by Rafael Hernandez

As we have seen, Puerto Rico, part of the Greater Antilles chain of Caribbean islands, was, in a sense, removed from the Caribbean community by the United States, which integrated the people, economy, and political life of the island with that of the North American mainland. That the fate of an island was determined by a faraway colonizer was not unusual in the Caribbean. That the situation continues to be Puerto Rico's fate does make the island unusual in a decolonized world.

Because of the connection with the United States, Puerto Rico is not a free actor in the Caribbean; on the contrary, Washington determines Puerto Rico's foreign relations. The role Puerto Rico plays is that of "U.S.

---

This chapter is a revised version of the chapter, "Puerto Rico: the Unsettled Question," in *The Restless Caribbean: Changing Patterns of International Relations*, ed. Richard Millett and W. Marvin Will (New York: Praeger Publishers, 1979).

agent in the Caribbean," and it has even been called "the United States' southern most border."[1] Puerto Rico's lack of autonomy was condemned by the United Nations, starting in 1973, and has been decried by proponents of all three status positions on the island: independentists, who want full autonomy with full-fledged nationhood; commonwealthers, who want more autonomy with a new pact; and statehooders, who want at least to legitimize the lack of autonomy with increased representation and participation. The United States has so integrated Puerto Rico's people, economy, and political life with that of the North American mainland that it was not until 1972 that the first course on Caribbean politics was taught at the University of Puerto Rico.[2]

## ECONOMIC INTEGRATION

Puerto Rico's depressions and prosperity are determined by the United States. During the first part of this century most of the island's income was derived from sugar and its products. The jíbaros' rice from Louisiana and Texas, their bacalao from Newfoundland, and their machetes from Hartford, Connecticut, were bought with "sugar money"; and the Puerto Rican population was described as being in a state of virtual peonage to the "big plantation."[3] In the 1930s Depression, Puerto Rico was referred to as the United States "poorhouse." *Harper's* reported that nowhere under the U.S. flag was there such a concentration of squalor, disease, and chronic starvation, and Puerto Rican Governor Theodore Roosevelt, Jr.'s personal accounts of island suffering included descriptions of "babies like skeletons" and "pathetic little groups carrying home-made coffins." Because Puerto Rico's major products were sugar, coffee, and tobacco, Luis Muñoz Marín, the island's first elected governor, described the economy as "providing all the after-dinner benefits without the dinner." The Puerto Rican New Deal (PRRA) came late and was ineffective in solving the island's economic problems.

Operation Bootstrap started in 1951, and by the 1960s the island was referred to as a United States showcase. Tourists and industries from the United States were flying south. In the heyday of the tourism expansion, 1960, new hotel construction was adding 500 rooms each year;[4] and in the heyday of Fomento, 1961, factories were going up at the rate of five per week.[5]

But Fomento manufacturing did not make the island self-sufficient—just the opposite. Puerto Rican manufacturing became an extension and just a part of the mainland's process of production. For example, while some island textile plants are still in operation today, they are not enough to supply the needs of the Puerto Rican apparel industry. This means that the apparel industry cannot go from Puerto Rican raw to finished product but is tied into the U.S. import system. In 1978, for example, the Puerto

Rican apparel industry had to import $303.3 million in textile products to supply its needs.[6]

With a slightly ironic twist, in December 1978, a Fomento study focused on how Puerto Rican imports aid the U.S. economy, contributing to jobs (153,000) and gross income ($3.47 billion). The report even broke down the benefits state by state revealing:

The five states which benefited most from supplying the island were the following:

—New York, which earned $335 million by exporting scientific and professional instruments, drugs and clothes.

—California, which earned $304 million with food products, canned food and transportation and communications equipment.

—Texas, which profited by $205 million from petroleum products, milled rice, chemicals and miscellaneous food products.

—Illinois, which showed earnings of $188 million from fabricated metal products, cleaning and toilet goods, food products and drugs.

—Florida, which earned $186 million with fresh fruits and vegetables, canned foods, paper and card board products.[7]

All this seems to corroborate what a Cuban writer calls the "parasitic" nature of colonial investment, that "the dominant countries have long been obtaining profits that are much greater than the capital originally invested."[8]

By the early 1970s economic investments had taken another direction, tying tighter the fate of the island and mainland. Petrochemical companies moved in with a total capital investment of over $1.2 billion. They were intended to make the island more energy self-sufficient. Instead, the petrochemical complex made the island completely dependent on expensive foreign oil.[9]

Nevertheless, even with an economic recession, a soaring unemployment rate, and a shaky petrocomplex,[10] Puerto Rico is economically well off, compared to her Caribbean neighbors, and was classified as a developed economy by the World Bank in 1967, the only Latin American state to be officially given that designation.[11] In 1976 the island's per capita income was $2,328, contrasted to the other islands of the Greater Antilles: Cuba, $860; (Hispaniola) Dominican Republic, $780; Haiti, $200; Jamaica, $1,070.[12]

This increased income helped mainland business. By 1959, Puerto Rico led in per capita purchases of mainland goods.[13] Today, $3 billion of the $5 billion in Puerto Rican imports comes from the United States and 85 percent of its $2.7 billion exports goes to the United States.[14] The countries' economies are so intertwined that it is impossible for Puerto Rico to really protect itself from mainland recessions.[15]

Another kind of economic system has worked to integrate the island

and mainland—the welfare system. United States aid to Puerto Rico includes housing subsidies, grants for education, welfare, and food stamps.[16] The island "is heavily dependent upon such aid—which rose from $767 million in 1970 to $3 billion in 1976. More than a third of Puerto Rican G.N.P. derives from federal funds—welfare and others—and two-thirds of the population are eligible for food stamps."[17]

The food stamp program spends far more money in Puerto Rico than in any state. In less than five years, food stamps have become "a second currency" in Puerto Rico, "growing into an addiction economists and politicians say would cripple the economy if withdrawn."[18] Economic dependency holds the island with a strong grip.

Not only U.S. money but Puerto Rican people bind the two countries. Migration intertwined the fate of the island and the mainland and resulted in a situation in which, today, out of five million Puerto Ricans, 1.8 million live on the mainland.[19] This out-migration was encouraged by the Puerto Rican government and was economically motivated.[20] Many Puerto Ricans return to the island,[21] but there are many born in mainland cities, who have never seen Puerto Rico, for whom Spanish is their second language.

Thus, Puerto Rico was integrated into the U.S. system as the movement of money, industry, and people created and fed mutual needs.

## POLITICAL INTEGRATION

Politically, the symbol of a "freely chosen union" was Estado Libre Asociado (ELA) or commonwealth. In the 1940s its architect, Luis Muñoz Marin, envisioned commonwealth merely as an interim solution, but by 1952 he was arguing that commonwealth status was "a new alternative" to independence and statehood.

A commonwealth constitution provided by Public Law 600 was to give the island unilateral power over local matters.

As the June 19, 1950, Senate Report on this bill states:

> It is important that the nature and general scope of S. 3336 be made absolutely clear. The bill under consideration would not change Puerto Rico's fundamental political, social and economic relationship to the United States.... The sections of the Organic Act which Section 5 of the bill would repeal are the provisions of the act concerned primarily with the organization of the local branches of the government of Puerto Rico and other matters of purely local concern.[22]

The law merely was to have increased political autonomy for the island. Puerto Rico, it was argued, would be able to unilaterally amend her own constitution and legislate for herself on "local matters." *El Mundo* claimed that "once the compact is formalized, the Constitution of Puerto Rico may not be amended except in the manner provided for by the Constitution itself...."[23] And, as Hanson argues, when Puerto Ricans voted to accept their Constitution, "Congress voluntarily relinquished the powers to legislate specifically for Puerto Rico...."[24] But not all authorities agreed. The Senate chair of the Committee on Interior and Insular Affairs, Joseph O'Mahoney, said after Public Law 600 was passed, "I think it may be stated as fundamental that the Constitution of the United States gives the Congress complete control and nothing in the Puerto Rican Constitution could affect or amend or alter that right...."[25] And, in addition, Irwin Silverman, legal counsel for the Department of Interior, thought Congress still had a right to annul Puerto Rican laws. "The paramount power over our colonies," he said, "is in the Congress.... The Congress could at any time, determine what course of action it would wish to take."[26]

Although heralded as a status alternative, in fact Public Law 600, which provided Puerto Rico with a Commonwealth Constitution, produced little change in the relationship between Puerto Rico and the United States. What the law did, however, was add to the relationship the symbolic dimension of joint action. This is, in fact, one theme of an insightful essay on the Puerto Rican Commonwealth written by Ralph Nader.[27]

Public Law 600 was "in the nature of a contract." The phrase has never been clarified. The United States has not treated the commonwealth relationship as the agreement between equals that Puerto Rican commonwealthers have argued it is. In fact, three times since the 1952 commonwealth "contract" Puerto Rico tried unsuccessfully to initiate a change in the relationship—Fernos-Murray, in 1959; STACOM in 1964; and the New Pact in 1974. Perhaps Robert Anderson is correct when he writes that commonwealth merely gave Puerto Rico a "slightly longer leash."[28]

Cuba's description of commonwealth status was not so mild. In 1977, it characterized commonwealth as a "juridical monster which meant that Puerto Ricans had no citizenship of their own, no rights to decide on matters of foreign policy, no rights in matters of defense and no rights to decide on how their economy or their country should be run."[29]

## UNITED NATIONS

Regardless of how little it really changed in the relationship between Puerto Rico and the United States, the Commonwealth Constitution and the official Puerto Rican status of a freely associated state did effect an important change in the United Nations' arena. According to the UN

Charter, the United States was obliged periodically to submit information concerning economic, social, and educational conditions in its non-self-governing territories. Since 1946 this had been done for Puerto Rico. However, in March 1953 the United States announced that such reports were no longer necessary because Puerto Rico's new political status, commonwealth, removed it from the non-self-governing category.[30]

Essential Puerto Rican support for this view was provided by Resident Commissioner Fernos Isern, who, as alternate delegate, appeared in the UN on behalf of the United States, "representing a free people with a voluntary government." During the hearings held by the Fourth Committee on Trusteeships, he defended Public Law 600 as a basic status change. In November 1953, the U.S. position was approved and the United States no longer had to submit periodic reports on Puerto Rico to the United Nations. According to Tugwell, the argument would not have prevailed if Muñoz had not made an issue of it and pressed it into a U.S. victory.[31]

Thus, in 1953 the countries were officially politically bound "in the nature of a contract." With the approval of the world forum, the people of Puerto Rico continued to be cast as irreversibly American. As the island was being integrated into the mainland economy, Muñoz was engineering and legitimizing commonwealth status to insure continued close ties with the United States. The real commitment to integrate politically was symbolized, not by a Puerto Rican Commonwealth Constitution, but by the Puerto Rican effort in the United Nations to convince the world she was no longer a colony.

## THE COMMITTEE OF TWENTY-FOUR AND EL PLEBISCITO

But the United Nations changed and, as a forum, began reflecting a different world view. Hollis Barber suggests 1960 as the turning point,

> when the General Assembly passed the "Declaration on the Granting of Independence to Colonial Countries and Peoples." This resolution... stated with absolute assurance that the Charter conferred on all peoples the fundamental human right of independence, that impediments to such freedom constituted "a serious threat to world peace," that the "process of liberation is 'irresistible and irreversible.' "[32]

In 1961 the General Assembly created the Committee on Decolonization, a Committee of Seventeen (soon to expand to twenty-four) to act as a watchdog on these matters. There is no question that the very existence of this committee was, in part, responsible for the 1967 plebiscite held to settle the question of Puerto Rican status.

In 1964 the UN Committee on Decolonization got its first requests from Puerto Rican independentist groups and the Cuban delegation to consider the case of Puerto Rico. Action was delayed until April 1967 when part of the committee, a nine-member working group, considered the case of Puerto Rico in closed session. At the same time, the United States and the Puerto Rican Commonwealth Government were working to further legitimize the relationship between the two countries with a plebiscite.

Following an exchange of letters in 1962 between Governor Luis Muñoz Marín and President John F. Kennedy, a United States-Puerto Rico Commission on the Status of Puerto Rico was established. Its task was to "study all factors which may have a bearing on the present and future relationship between the United States and Puerto Rico."[33] The commission's major conclusion was that all three forms of political status—commonwealth, statehood, and independence—were valid and recommended a status plebiscite, "an expression of the will of the citizens of Puerto Rico...."[34] The Puerto Rican legislature voted to hold such a plebiscite on July 23, 1967.

The Puerto Rican organizations that brought the status issue to the United Nations claimed "the U.S. had gotten the Puerto Rican government to set up the plebiscite to forestall UN action...."[35] According to Independence Party President Concepción de Gracia, the plebiscite was "nothing but an effort to stop the negotiations in the U.N. to have the Puerto Rico case reexamined."[36] This claim was supported by the fact that UN action was forestalled until after the plebiscite.

Only 65.8 percent of those eligible, fewer than the usual number who vote in island general elections (80 percent), voted in the July 23 plebiscite. The 702,512 who went to the polls voted overwhelmingly for continued relations with the United States. They cast 425,079 (60.5 percent) for commonwealth and 273,315 (38.9 percent) for statehood. Fewer than 1 percent voted for independence.

Independentist forces on the island opposed the plebiscite and had united in an antiplebiscite group called Concentración Soberanista Anti-plebiscitaria. A rally against the plebiscite held a week before the plebiscite vote had over 30,000 in attendance. There is no doubt that independentists were responsible for the boycott of many voters (perhaps 15 percent of those eligible to vote). Nevertheless, a commonwealth spokesperson could claim with some force that "it is absolutely clear that the big majority of people of Puerto Rico want permanent association with the United States."[37] The plebiscite result seemed to legitimize in the world forum the formal ties between island and mainland and stopped a condemning statement from the Committee of Twenty-four. Once again, as with Public Law 600 in 1953, without really changing relations between the United States and Puerto Rico, the two countries managed to temporarily affect the UN view of their relationship. Then, in 1973, after hearing representatives from Puerto Rican independentist groups, the Committee of Twenty-four adopted a resolution reaffirming the Puerto Rican people's right to self-determination and independence and asking the United States to refrain from any interference with the exercise of this right.

Cuba has been a prime mover in the United Nations on behalf of Puerto Rican independence. There is some evidence, however, that the United States has been trying to link improved U.S.-Cuban relations with Cuba's stand on Puerto Rico. For example, at the Algiers conference of non-aligned nations, in September 1975, Cuba made it clear that Puerto Rican independence is "non-negotiable, especially in the context of *bilateral discussions with the United States*."[38] And two years later, in 1977, GRANMA, the Cuban weekly, linked the two issues explicitly:

> On August 17, Cuba asked the U.N. Special Committee on Decolonization to reaffirm the Puerto Rican people's inalienable right to independence and self-determination.... In presenting the draft resolution, Cuban Ambassador to the U.N. Ricard Alarcóno pointed out that it "was in keeping with the principles of Cuba's foreign policy, and those principles cannot be negotiated with anybody."
>
> The above statement had to do with speculations made before the Committee by Severo Colberg, a spokesman for the People's Democratic Party of Puerto Rico, to the effect that Cuba and the United States might make a deal over the Puerto Rican case.[39]

The 1977 Cuban resolution on Puerto Rico was tabled, but then, in 1978, the Committee on Decolonization passed a new resolution that not only reaffirmed the inalienable right of the Puerto Rican people to independence but called for a "complete transfer of powers" by the United States to Puerto Rico before the island chooses its final political status. What was also different about this 1978 resolution was what seemed to be an acceptance of "free association." According to paragraph 6 of the 1978 resolution, "any form of free association between Puerto Rico and the United States must be in terms of political equality...and must recognize the sovereignty of the people of Puerto Rico."[40]

Commonwealth spokespersons heralded the UN declaration because it recognized free association as an acceptable "final solution."[41] Statehooders were not so happy. The Committee of Twenty-four "refused to recognize the Puerto Ricans' right to choose statehood within the United States."[42] Statehood Governor Carlos Romero Barceló called the resolution " 'empty rhetoric' inspired and supported by Communists."[43]

So far, UN declarations have merely embarrassed the United States. They have fallen short of changing the official classification of Puerto Rico, which would require, once again, periodic reports from the United

States. Yet, as Anderson suggests, "Puerto Rico with or without the formal [UN] declaration, will continue to be a symbol of remaining colonialism in the Third and Socialist worlds at least."[44]

It is in that arena, in the third and Socialist worlds, that Puerto Rican independentist leaders are treated like leaders of governments in exile. Representatives are granted official status and compensated from UN funds for their expenses in attending UN meetings.[45] Unlike common-wealthers and statehooders, the independentists are involved in real international relations, petitioning the United Nations and attending conferences and meetings. In 1975, Cuba recognized the Puerto Rican Independence Movement as the sole representative of the Puerto Rican nation.[46] "Delegations of the Puerto Rican National Liberation Movement have visited Governments, mass organizations, parties and peoples in various countries of Africa, Asia, Latin America, North America and Europe."[47] Independentists are changing a commonwealth reality captured by Concepción de Gracia: "we live with our windows closed to the world."[48] Under the present commonwealth status, it is in Washington, D.C., after all, that all of Puerto Rico's foreign affairs and most of Puerto Rico's internal affairs are decided. It was this situation that the New Pact was designed to change.

## NEW PACT

On April 28, 1974, the San Juan Star, headlines announced, "Governor Proposes Plan of Near Total Autonomy." The plan was the result of the work of the Ad Hoc Advisory Group on Puerto Rico, created the year before.[49] The results of this study to improve commonwealth in the four areas (pillars) of association—common defense, common market, common currency, common citizenship—included a proposal for more island autonomy in international affairs. The Compact of Permanent Union Between Puerto Rico and the United States (HR 11200) proposed, "The Free Associated State may participate in international organizations and make educational, cultural, health, sporting, professional, industrial, agricultural, financial, commercial, scientific, or technical agreements with other countries consistent with the functions of the United States, as determined by the president of the United States and the governor of the Free Associated State on a case-by-case basis."[50]

It was a clear attempt at barter: in exchange for permanent union, Puerto Rico was asking for the freedom to have independent relationships, to be, in a limited way, a country in her own right. There were other areas in which the Ad Hoc Report asked for increased autonomy. Proposed changes in shipping and commerce, for example, would affect

Puerto Rico on the international scene. But symbolically, the proposal to open the windows to the currents of international relations was most important.

The U.S. response to the *Report* tells us more about relations between Puerto Rico and the United States than even the list of changes proposed in the *Report* itself. The Interior Department, in its written response, stated that the requested name change to "Free Associated State" might be "impermissible under the U.S. Constitution" and rejected the idea of bilateral contract between two countries asserting "Puerto Rico remains a territory of the United States...."[51] The department had "serious doubts" about Puerto Rican participation in international organizations but deferred to the Department of State; it had "serious problems" with Puerto Rico's proposal to acquire property ceded to the United States from Spain; it rejected the tariff proposal but deferred to the Department of Commerce and the Treasury; it "had a problem" with Puerto Rico controlling the flow of aliens but deferred to the Departments of State and Justice; and Puerto Rican representation in both houses of Congress, would, according to Interior, require a constitutional amendment.[52] It was a strong bureaucratic rejection of practically every committee proposal with an especially loud "no" to the idea that the Puerto Rican–U.S. agreement could be anything like a contract between sovereigns. An earnest proposal, a callous reception—it was the pattern of Puerto Rican–U.S. relations for nearly three-quarters of a century.

Luis Muñoz Marin, in an interview on January 4, 1978, insisted that the New Pact proposals had interest and support in the U.S. Congress. He specifically mentioned the interest of Senators Humphrey, Kennedy, and Jackson, and that Subcommittee Chair Representative Phillip Burton, also supported the New Pact but with amendments. Nevertheless, during the congressional hearings on these proposed New Pact changes, the banter between the co-chair of the Ad Hoc Committee, Marlowe Cook, and the chair of the House Subcommittee on Territorial and Insular Affairs, Representative Phillip Burton, seems to reveal a kind of indifference to the serious problems Puerto Rico faces.

> *Mr. Cook:* Thank you Mr. Chairman. I do not have a prepared statement.
> *Mr. Burton:* That is a blessing.
> *Mr. Cook:* Thank you.
> Having previously testified before the Senate Interior Committee on December 3, I will try my best to make it brief.
> I would like to start off by saying, the first thing this morning, I received a call at home from the Washington Star, and I thought, "Gee, somebody has found some interest in Washington in The Compact between the United States and Puerto Rico."

> I went to the telephone and found out their only interest was where I was hunting in 1973 and 1974, and I was a little disappointed in that.[53]

Disappointing is an understatement for the kind of reception given the effort to change Puerto Rican–U.S. relations.

## FORD AND STATEHOOD

Nothing shows the insensitivity of Washington to Puerto Rico's needs quite so well as President Gerald Ford's New Year's Eve Statement recommending Puerto Rican statehood. It surprised, embarrassed, and shocked Puerto Rican leaders and knowledgeable statesiders. Even the newly elected statehood governor of Puerto Rico, Carlos Romero Barceló, claimed he had no advanced knowledge of Ford's statehood proposition.[54]

The Ford statehood bill was hastily put together by the Solicitor's Office at the Interior Department. The president's press secretary, Ron Nesson, tried to explain that the President's Vail statement and bill did not come out of thin air, but were a response to the work of the New Pact Ad Hoc Committee;[55] Muñoz Marín, however, suggested that President Ford had "some kind of deal with the Republicans of Puerto Rico who voted for him at the Republican Convention"[56] (which would be consistent with the new pattern of partisan politicking described in Chapter 2).

"Radio Havana in reporting Ford's call for Puerto Rican Statehood, called the President 'a frantic annexationist.' "[57] Whatever the motivation for his statement, Ford's statehood bill does reveal two things about the United States' Puerto Rican policy: its whimsical, almost arbitrary nature, and its colonial quality. Described as "abrupt, ill-timed and harmful...,"[58] the bill provided procedures for statehood before even asking the Puerto Rican people what they wanted.[59]

Criticized for this omission, the president did amend his bill to include an early referendum[60] and transmitted a draft to Congress on January 17, 1977.[61] His bill outlined steps to statehood—a joint U.S.–Puerto Rico Commission, a Commission Report to Congress to set the terms and conditions of statehood, an island-wide referendum on statehood, constitutional convention, Puerto Rican ratification of the Constitution, selection of two senators and five representatives to serve in Congress when the president would "proclaim Puerto Rico a State." President Ford then asserted, after outlining this procedure, "After more than three-quarters of a century of discussion about Puerto Rico, it is time to act and act positively. By passage of this Act the representatives of the people of 50 States will say to the people of Puerto Rico: Join us as equals."

Ford's bill might have been merely a gesture from an outgoing president. But a former statehood resident commissioner, Jorge Cordova Diaz, was referring to it as the "Grito de Vail"; and the new statehood governor was vowing to educate the people on the advantages and desirability of statehood, believing that Ford's statements would probably improve the investment climate and tourist industry.[62]

What with the Statehood Party victory in 1976,[63] with the statehood governor's 1977 tax reform plan to whittle away commonwealth tax exemptions,[64] with the well-publicized activity of the Carter-linked pro-statehood faction in the Commonwealth Party,[65] with the increased island participation in the federal electoral process, characterized as "the front end of a train whose last coach is statehood,"[66] and with 59 percent of mainland Americans favoring statehood for Puerto Rico,[67] there may well be a 1981 plebiscite or a commission established to study the possibility of Puerto Rico becoming a state. But like the Ad Hoc New Pact Commission which studied the commonwealth status, there is no guarantee that its recommendations will be treated seriously, let alone be the basis of a change in policy. The United States and Puerto Rico are not, after all, equal partners.

It is the present blatant inequality between the partners in commonwealth that explains the appeal of independence and statehood. Independence and statehood have an ideological energy. The United States, by its inaction, is killing commonwealth. Too often, commonwealth, according to Matthews, is looked upon as a "half-way station";[68] it has lost the support of mainland liberals,[69] and, for Anderson, it is "bankrupt as an idea."[70] The "joint striving for a nobler more worthwhile relationship," which Jaime Benitez points to as an essential ingredient of commonwealth, seems to be one-sided. Puerto Rico, alone, continues to strive to eliminate the "colonial-type vestiges."

By 1977 it was not only the independentists who were petitioning the United Nations for a change in the Puerto Rican situation. Statehooders, as well as representatives of the Puerto Rican Bar Association, made statements to the Committee of Twenty-four. "For the first time," said the *Washington Post*, "virtually the whole spectrum of political opinion in Puerto Rico has appeared before a U.N. committee... criticiz[ing] the island's commonwealth status...."[71] One of the more dramatic statements was made by Juan Garcia Passalacqua, representing Americans for Democratic Action. Formerly a supporter of commonwealth, he pointed to the 1976 election in which 57 percent of the vote was statehood or independence, and argued:

> The people of Puerto Rico represented here by its new anti-colonial majority, awaits your endorsement of these simple principles for decolonization. There will then be the final decisive struggle for statehood and independence—never again a colony.[72]

## CONCLUSION

Political status continues to be the most important unsettled question for Puerto Rico. Status determines the kind of relationship the island can have with its Caribbean neighbors as well as with the other countries of the world. The status issue divides the people of the island like no other issue.

As divisive as the status issue is, there is one thing that unites all three status positions. What they share is the strong desire to rid the island of its colonial vestiges: independentists, by throwing out the colonizer; state-hooders, by merging with the colonizer; and commonwealthers, by becoming more equal to the colonizer with a New Pact. All three positions, regardless of symbols and slogans, share the common insight that Puerto Rico is still a non-self-governing territory. This is a fact, regardless of petrocomplexes, high per capita income, and food stamps. It is just a matter of time before the United Nations does more than merely embarrass the United States about the colonial way it treats some of its citizens.[73]

## NOTES

1. See Robert W. Anderson, "Puerto Rico Between the United States and the Caribbean" (Paper presented at the Conference of Contemporary Trends and Issues in Caribbean International Affairs, Port of Spain, Trinidad, May 23–27, 1977), p. 11.
2. Kenneth R. Farr, *Personalism and Party Politics*, p. 118.
3. See, for example, *The Nation*, May 6, 1936, p. 568.
4. Ralph Hancock, *Puerto Rico: A Success Story*, p. 116.
5. Earl Parker Hanson, *Puerto Rico: Ally for Progress*, p. 103.
6. Alan Patureau, "Textile industry continues exodus from island," *San Juan Star*, November 4, 1979, (Business Outlook), p. B-5.
7. "P.R. imports seen aiding U.S. economy," *San Juan Star*, December 11, 1978, p. 8.
8. Miguel A. D'Estefano, *Puerto Rico: Analysis of a Plebiscite*, p. 18.
9. "Petroleum and petrochemical companies were first attracted to the island after 1965, when a presidential proclamation allowed Puerto Rico to import larger quantities of foreign oil. In the late 1960's, foreign oil was on the average $1.25 a barrel cheaper than domestic oil.... After the oil cartel began to increase foreign prices in 1973, however, Puerto Rico's former advantage became its biggest disadvantage, raising costs not only of raw material, but also of fuel and power." Jane B. Baird, "P.R. oil firms lose money in shifting market," *San Juan Star*, December 4, 1978, p. 20.

10. "Tesoro's $130 Million Burden," *Business Week*, May 9, 1977, pp. 93–94.

11. John Barlow Martin, "A Commonwealth's Choice," *Harper's*, December 1977, p. 18.

12. By comparison, Puerto Rico's per capita income in 1940 was $121; in 1965, $900. *U.S. News and World Report*, January 17, 1977, p. 73; see also "International Bank for Reconstruction and Development," *World Bank Atlas, Population, Per Capita Product, and Growth Rates,* 1977.

13. Hanson, op. cit., p. 76.

14. *U.S. News*, op. cit. See also Henry Pelham Burn, "Two Faces of Development: Puerto Rico," *Vista* 9, no. 3 (December 1973): 31–34.

15. See *Report to the Governor: The Committee to Study Puerto Rico's Finances* (James Tobin, Chair), "Principal Findings" in the Transmitting Letter, December 11, 1975.

16. *U.S. News*, op. cit.

17. Tom Wicker, "An American Dilemma: II," *New York Times,* August 5, 1979.

18. Cynthia Vice Acosta, "Food Stamps Second Currency in Puerto Rico," *Santa Cruz Sentinel*, April 1, 1979, p. 12; Rubén Berrios, head of the Independence Party, claims 71 percent of all Puerto Rican households depend on the U.S. food stamp program. Rubén Berrios Martinez, "Independence for Puerto Rico: The Only Solution," *Foreign Affairs* 55 (April 1977): 562.

19. *U.S. News*, op. cit., p. 73.

20. Berrios, op. cit., p. 569.

21. By 1960, of all Puerto Ricans who had come to the mainland, one-fourth had returned to the island. Hancock, op. cit., p. 142.

22. U.S., Congress, Senate, Committee on Public Lands, *Providing for the Organization of a Constitutional Government by the People of Puerto Rico: Report to Accompany S. 3336*, 81st Cong., 2d sess., 19 June 1950, S. Rept. 2275, p. 3. According to the Senate committee, Public Law 600 was to provide self government; it "would not change Puerto Rico's fundamental political, social and economic relationship to the United States." Peter J. Fliess, "Puerto Rico's Political Status Under Its New Constitution," *Western Political Quarterly* 5, no. 4 (December 1952): 639. According to Ralph Nader, however, Public Law 600 "preserves some provisions of the old Organic Act which are contrary to principles of local self-government. Retained, for example, was the limitation of public indebtedness of Puerto Rico and municipalities to fixed percentages of the aggregate tax valuation of total property, 69 STAT. 319 (1950), 48 U.S.C.A. sect. 745 (1952). There also remained the qualifications for Puerto Rico citizenship, 64 STAT. 319, 48 U.S.C.A. sect. 733(a) (1952)." "The Commonwealth Status of Puerto Rico,"

Harvard Law Record 23, no. 12 (December 13, 1956): 4.

23. El Mundo, July 1, 1951, in U.S., Congress, Senate, Hearings, 82nd Cong. 2d sess., April 29, 1952, pp. 43–45, quoted in Hunter, op. cit., p. 122.

24. Hanson, Puerto Rico: Ally for Progress, p. 70.

25. U.S., Congress, Senate, Committee on Interior and Insular Affairs, Hearings on SJ Res. No. 151, 82nd Cong., 2d sess., April 29, 1952, p. 40, quoted in Hunter, op. cit., p. 121.

26. U.S., Congress, Senate, Hearings, 82nd Cong., 2d sess., April 29, 1952, pp. 43–45.

27. Ralph Nader, "The Commonwealth Status of Puerto Rico," Harvard Law Record 23, no. 12 (December 13, 1956): 2–8.

28. Anderson, op. cit., p. 8.

29. GRANMA. Weekly Review 12, no. 34 (Havana, Cuba: August 21, 1977). 10. Another Cuban author wrote of commonwealth, Estado Libre Asociado (ELA), "The ELA has never been more than a simple colonial statute; it constitutes a virtual renunciation of power, contains absolutely no ways to confront the political, economic, and social problems of Puerto Rico." D'Estefano, op. cit., p. 40.

30. The best history of the UN proceedings is in Jesús de Galindez, "Government and Politics in Puerto Rico: New Formulas for Self-Government," International Affairs 30 (1954): 340–41; see also, "Puerto Rico's New Self Governing Status Transmitted to Secretary General," U.S. Department of State Bulletin 28 (April 20, 1953): 587; United Nations, General Assembly, Official Record, Eighth Session, Plenary at 311; Rubén Berríos Martínez, "The Commonwealth of Puerto Rico: Its Reality in the National and World Community" (Divisional Thesis, Yale Law School, New Haven, Conn., 1964), p. 179.

31. Rexford G. Tugwell, The Art of Politics as Practiced by Three Great Americans: Franklin Delano Roosevelt, Luis Munoz Marin, and Fiorello H. LaGuardia, pp. 226, 227.

32. Hollis W. Barber, "Decolonization: The Committee of Twenty-four," World Affairs 38, no. 2 (Fall 1975): 129.

33. Public Law 88-271, February 20, 1964; 78 Stat. 17, quoted in Status of Puerto Rico. Report of the United States–Puerto Rico Commission on the Status of Puerto Rico, August 1966, p. 3.

34. Ibid., p. 8.

35. San Juan Star, April 8, 1967, p. 6.

36. San Juan Star, March 16, 1967, p. 6.

37. San Juan Star, April 11, 1967, p. 1.

38. Puerto Rico Libre: Bulletin of The Puerto Rican Solidarity Committee 3 no. 2 (September 15, 1975): 1.

39. GRANMA. Weekly Review 12, no. 35 (Havana, Cuba: August 28, 1977): 10.

40. "U.N. panel's resolution on Puerto Rico," *San Juan Star*, September 17, 1978, p. 4.

41. Ibid., p. 5.

42. *New York Times*, (supplementary material), September 14, 1978, p. 54.

43. Ibid.

44. Anderson, op. cit., p. 15.

45. Barber, op. cit., p. 128.

46. *Puerto Rico Libre* (September 15, 1975), op. cit.

47. Juan Mari Bras, in an article based on a speech given before the UN Special Committee on Decolonization on September 2, 1976, *Black Scholar* 8 (December 1976): 19.

48. Concepción de Gracia, quoted in "A Talk with the Candidates," *San Juan Review* 50, no. 9 (October 1964): 14.

49. U.S., Congress, Senate, Committee on Interior and Insular Affairs, *Hearings*, 94th Cong., 1st sess., December 3, 1975, pp. 41, 42.

50. U.S., Congress, House, Committee on Interior and Insular Affairs, Subcommittee on Territorial and Insular Affairs, *Hearings on HR 11200 and HR 11201*, 94th Cong., 2d sess., January 20, February 9, 1976, pp. 4, 5.

51. A territory "in a new form of political relationship—not as an independent State but linked to a broader political system in a Federal association without an independent and separate existence." Ibid., pp. 49, 50.

52. Ibid., pp. 50–53.

53. U.S. Congress, House, *Hearings*, op. cit., p. 195.

54. Manny Suarez, "CBR Disagrees with Statehood Steps Outlined in Ford Bill," *San Juan Star*, January 14, 1977, p. 1; "Romero: Accion Ford Prueba EU Daria Estadidad," *El Mundo*, January 2, 1977, p. 1.

55. "Nessen: 14-Month Study Preceded Ford Statement," *San Juan Star*, January 6, 1977, p. 1.

56. Interview with Luis Muñoz Marin, January 4, 1978, Trujillo Alto.

57. *Miami Herald*, January 2, 1977.

58. Harold J. Lidin, "Gordova, Benitez Speak Minds on Status Tizzy," *San Juan Star*, January 11, 1977, p. 11.

59. Harry Turner, "Draft Bill Sets Convention Before Plebiscite on State," *San Juan Star*, January 13, 1977, p. 13; "Ford Proposal is Senseless Says Jackson," *San Juan Star*, January 4, 1977, p. 1.

60. Harry Turner, "Ford's New Statehood Bill Gives Early Referendum," *San Juan Star*, January 15, 1977, p. 1.

61. *Communication from the President of the United States transmitting A Draft of Proposed Legislation to Enable the People of Puerto Rico to Form a Constitution and State Government, to be Admitted into the Union, and for Other Purposes*, January 17, 1977.

62. Lidin, op. cit.; see also Suarez, "Romero Vows," op. cit., p. 1.

63. The Statehood party got 48.3 percent of the vote, common-wealth, 45.4 percent; "Nessen: 14-Month Study," op. cit.

64. *Latin America: Political Report* 12, no. 8 (February 24, 1978): 63.

65. *Latin America: Political Report*, 12, no. 19 (May 19, 1978): 146.

66. Ibid., p. 148.

67. "59% On Mainland Favor State in Gallup Inc. Poll," *San Juan Star*, January 5, 1977, p. 1.

68. Thomas Matthews, "Problems and Leaders in the Caribbean," in *The Caribbean: Its Hemispheric Role*, ed. A. Curtis Wilgus, vol. 17, series 1, p. 29.

69. Martin, op. cit., p. 19.

70. Anderson, op. cit., pp. 6, 7.

71. *Washington Post*, August 19, 1977.

72. *Puerto Rico Libre: Bulletin of The Puerto Rican Solidarity Committee* 5, no. 6 (October/November, 1977): 12.

73. It is also possible that the United Nations Committee on Decolo-nization will not press further on the issue of Puerto Rican independence. Their 1978 resolution did seem to accept the association as a legitimate alternative for Puerto Rico.

# APPENDIX A:

## TEXT OF PROCLAMATION BY MAJOR GENERAL NELSON A. MILES, UPON OCCUPATION OF PUERTO RICO IN 1898

To the Inhabitants of Puerto Rico:

In the prosecution of a war against the Spanish Crown, the people of the United States, inspired by the cause of liberty, justice, and humanity, have sent their armed forces to occupy the island of Puerto Rico. We have come to this country wrapped in the flag of liberty, spurred by the honorable purpose of pursuing the enemies of our country and of yours, and to destroy or capture all those who present armed resistance. We offer you the protecting arm of a nation of free citizens, whose power rests fundamentally in the sovereignty of justice and humanitarian principles. Therefore, the first effects of this occupation will be to liberate the Puerto Ricans from the political relationshps which had previously been imposed upon them and to receive, we trust, Puerto Rico's enthusiastic acceptance of the government of the United States. The principal objective of the American military forces will be to put an end to the armed authority of Spain and give to the people of this beautiful island the greatest measure of liberty that may be compatible with military occupation. We have not come to do battle with the people of this country, who for centuries have been victims of oppression, but to offer you protection of your persons and your possessions, to stimulate prosperity and grant you the rights and benefits offered by the liberal institutions of our system of government.... This is not a war of destruction. Our purpose is to grant all those who may come under the control of our military and naval forces the advantages and benefits of civilization.

Nelson A. Miles

Major General,
Commander of the Military Forces
of the United States of America

# APPENDIX B:

## APPOINTED PUERTO RICAN GOVERNORS (1940–48)

**NAME** | **PERIOD**
--- | ---
Charles Hubert Allen | May 1, 1900–September 14, 1901
William H. Hunt | September 15, 1901–July 3, 1904
Beeckman Winthrop | July 4, 1904–April 17, 1907
Regis H. Post | April 18, 1907–November 5, 1909
George R. Colton | November 6, 1909–November 5, 1913
Arthur Yager | November 6, 1913–May 16, 1921
Emmet Montgomery Reily | May 16, 1921–April 1, 1923
Horace M. Towner | April 2, 1923–October 6, 1929
Theodore Roosevelt, Jr. | October 7, 1929–January 18, 1932
James Rumsey Beverly | January 25, 1932–June 30, 1933
Robert H. Gore | July 1, 1933–January 19, 1934
Blanton Winship | February 5, 1934–August 31, 1939
William D. Leahy | September 11, 1939–December 5, 1940
Guy J. Swope | February 3, 1941–September 18, 1941
Rexford G. Tugwell | September 19, 1941–September 2, 1946
Jesus T. Piñero | September 3, 1946–January 2, 1949

# APPENDIX C:

## LETTER OF REBEL LEADER'S WIFE TO HIS HARVARD CLASSMATES

Rebel leader Albizu, who surrendered in Puerto Rico today, is a graduate of Harvard and the Harvard Law School, and served in World War I as first lieutenant of infantry in the United States Army, for which he volunteered.

When his Harvard class of 1916 was having its 25th reunion he was serving a seven-year sentence in Atlanta for inciting rebellion against the United States—so that he couldn't very well attend his Harvard reunion.

But his wife, a Radcliffe graduate student, sent to class secretary Laurence Curtis, presently running for lieutenant governor, a biography of her husband for the class report.

It was too long to use in the Class Report and it was filed in the Harvard archives. Today it becomes a document of great interest.

### The Letter of Albizu's Wife Follows

Upon my husband's return to Puerto Rico, he entered the practice of his profession as a lawyer and in his daily relations with the people, he had occasion to measure to perfection the hopeless tragedy of his country-men's life, turned alarmingly acute during the years in which he was absent.

He devoted the greatest part of his time to the study of this problem and arrived to the undisputable conviction that the whole problem was only an unavoidable consequence of the system of exploitation to which Puerto Rico had been submitted by the corporative interests, directly and indirectly protected by the United States Government.

From that very moment, he launched an active campaign of national orientation, with a view to the people's liberation from imperialist oppression, closely tied by strong ligaments to the colonial system put in force in the country through American intervention.

To that purpose, he entered the Nationalist party of Puerto Rico, which had recently been organized by other men seeking the same ends, men who like him, had correctly viewed and faced the problem and were disposed to fight on for their people's rights with the greatest unselfishness and patriotism as their motive forces. He was immediately

Reprinted from the Boston Daily Globe, Thursday, November 2, 1950 (copyright 1950, Globe Newspaper Company).

exalted to the party's vice presidency (1925) and five years later (January 1930) to the presidency of the liberating movement.

## Efforts Made to Check Patriotic Propaganda

The corporative interests brought into play every means at hand, supported by native leaders at their service, to check the patriotic propaganda. But inasmuch as the people's awakening took on unsuspected proportions, they took recourse to official support in order to put it down.

In the year 1936, Police Col. Francis E. Riggs addressed a circular to the local quarters of his force, in which the police officers were ordered to "shoot to kill" the Nationalists in every case. Consequent to these instructions, on Oct. 24 of the same year there took place the Rio Piedras massacre, in which the police force shot several members of the Nationalist party who traveled in their own automobile.

The only excuse given by the government to justify that crime consisted in pretended proof to the effect that the Nationalists were bent on bombing a students' convention, which was taking place in the university center situated in the neighborhood of the above-mentioned city (Rio Piedras).

The truth is that at the time the massacre occurred, the students' convention had already been closed, due to a majority of the students being themselves Nationalists who opposed the convention—a fact which contradicts the government's version of the affair, since it would not be reasonable to think that the Nationalists should want to shoot their own comrades. Besides, the automobile shot at by the police was at the time going in a direction contrary to that where stands the university.

## Survivor of Massacre Indicted for Murder

Only one man of those inside the automobile remained alive after the criminal assault and, his wounds still unhealed, he was taken to court to answer to an indictment for murder against his own dead comrades.

Three months afterwards, on February 23, 1937, two young Nationalists, close friends to those murdered at Rio Piedras, took justice in their own hands and shot down Police Col. Francis E. Riggs. They were shot to death at Police Headquarters within the hour, while they were being kept under custody of the police for investigation.

The people's protest against this unprecedented crime was unanimous and the government was forced to turn the case over to the Grand Jury for due process of law.

The Grand Jury found cause for an indictment of murder against the police, but notwithstanding, the police officers involved were all exonerated and lately they were promoted as recognition of their participation in the massacre.

The Grand Jury was finally and definitely dissolved by the Governor, as this American official obtained the elimination of that organism from the colonial judiciary system.

Outright arrest of the president of the Nationalist party, Don Pedro Albizu Campos, and seven of the party's direction keymen was decreed and an indictment brought against them for alleged "conspiracy to overthrow by force the government of the United States established in Puerto Rico."

The whole people of the country, regardless of political or religious creed, was deeply moved by this action. Strong nuclei of protest were organized all over the country and these devoted themselves to the collection of funds for the defense of the indicted men.

Collection of funds was speedily stopped by the government and numerous persons jailed, 27 women were among these. A jury made up of eight American citizens and four Puerto Ricans failed to agree upon a conviction and was dissolved by Federal Judge Robert A. Cooper, who presided over the court.

A second jury, composed of 10 Americans and two Puerto Ricans, these two closely bound to imperialist interests, brought in then the conviction for the alleged crime, and Dr. Albizu Campos was sentenced (along with his seven comrades) to 10 years' prison in the Federal Penitentiary at Atlanta.

## Rockwell Kent Charged Jury Was Hand-Picked

Upon the picking of this jury, the great American artist has publicly said that he was present in the Fortaleza (the Governor's palace at San Juan) when it was "hand-picked" and that the then Governor, Gen. Blanton Winship, as well as Federal Prosecutor Cecyl A. Snyder, both present there, agreed that it was "a good jury" which "could be trusted upon to bring in a conviction notwithstanding the nature of the proof presented."

This declaration of the artist has been ratified by Elmer Ellsworth, one of the American members of the jury. They addressed a joint declaration to the President of the United States, Franklin Delano Roosevelt, without this denunciation of fact having so far received the least consideration.

It should be noted that a special prosecutor was sent to Puerto Rico by the United States Department of Justice to help in the trial.

After these jailings, there have taken place in Puerto Rico other acts of flagrant and unprecedented official terrorism against those men who with due courage and frankness defend the country's right to independence, acts which it would be too long to enumerate.

Among these, the Ponce Massacre on Palm Sunday, 1937, has been the object of a serious investigation by the Union of Civil Liberties, and was cited by Dr. Arthur Garfield Hayes, who presided over the investigation, as "the greatest crime in history."

## 18 Members of Party Indicted in Federal Court

There have been just indicted before the Federal Court (the United States' Government District Court for Puerto Rico) 18 members of the Nationalist party, among them the party's temporary president and secretary.

These men have been indicted for failing to register under the Selective Service law and 17 of them have already been sentenced to 13 months in jail. Three of them are already serving their terms in the Federal Penitentiary at Talahassee, Fla.

They have made public protests to the effect that they are fervent defenders of democracy and claim as their privilege the right to fight for it, taking their places in the most dangerous spot, which is now said to be Puerto Rico, as the advance post of defense in the Western Hemisphere.

But they hold that democracy implies Liberty and Equality for all peoples, as well as for all men and they therefore refuse to serve under any strange government.

And so they demand, as an express condition to their participation in that defense, the immediate recognition of that right to the Puerto Rican Nation.

It is of interest to note that among the 17 men indicted and sentenced there is one blind youth, which shows, without any place for doubt, that it is not a question of an ordinary case of a "slacker" trying to evade military service, but that a high point of transcendental morals is involved therein, which entirely escapes the understanding of the United States Government.

The temporary president of the Nationalist party remains at freedom under bail, but we must suppose that a more severe penalty will be imposed upon him, when the fact is taken in consideration that in this case the alleged responsibility is that of "conspiracy to thwart the functioning of the Selective Service law."

Up to this date, the burying yards and jails have been filled with Puerto Rican patriots and unjust indictments against them are daily occurrences. Nevertheless, as it is not my purpose to relate herein happenings which do not directly affect my husband's life and liberty, in which that Institution is primarily interested, I will give up the description of these facts, which are of a criminal nature and repugnant to every good American's conscience.

Laura de Albizu Campos
(Mrs. Pedro Albizu Campos)
from Universidad Inay or de San Marcos, Lima, Peru,
and Radcliffe College, Cambridge, Mass.

# APPENDIX D:

## UNITED STATES–PUERTO RICO COMMISSION ON THE STATUS OF PUERTO RICO

### MEMBERS OF THE COMMISSION

Appointed by the president of the United States:

James H. Rowe, Jr., Chairman

Ambassador Patricia Roberts Harris

Professor Brewster C. Denny

Appointed by the governor of the Commonwealth of Puerto Rico as certified by—

The Popular Democratic Party:
Senator Luis Muñoz Marin[1]
Teodoro Moscoso
Senator Luis A. Negrón López
José Trias Monge (Alternate)

The Statehood Republican Party:
Senator Miguel A. Garcia Méndez
Luis A. Ferré
Raymond Acosta (Alternate)
Ramiro Colón (Alternate)

The Puerto Rican Independence Party:
Dr. Gilberto Concepción de Gracia[2]

Appointed by the president of the Senate of the United States:
Senator Henry M. Jackson,[3] Washington
Senator Jacob K. Javits,[4] New York
Senator George A. Smathers, Florida (Alternate)
Senator Thomas A. Kuchel, California (Alternate)

Appointed by the speaker of the House of Representatives of the United States:
Representative Leo W. O'Brien, New York
Representative Rogers C. B. Morton,[5] Maryland

1. Replaced Governor Roberto Sánchez Vilella on January 12, 1965.

2. Resigned May 3, 1966.

3. Replaced Senator Clinton P. Anderson of New Mexico on March 30, 1965.

4. Replaced Senator Kenneth B. Keating of New York on January 12, 1965.

5. Replaced Representative Jack Westland of Washington on January 12, 1965.

# APPENDIX E:

## AD HOC ADVISORY GROUP ON PUERTO RICO

**Delegation appointed by the president of the United States**

**Marlow W. Cook**
Co-Chairman

Senator **James L. Buckley**
New York

Representative **Don H. Clausen**
California

Representative **Thomas S. Foley***
Washington

**Paul N. Howell**, Chairman and Chief Executive Officer, Howell Corporation, Houston, Texas

Senator **J. Bennett Johnston**
Louisiana

**Richard B. Ogilvie**, Esq.
Chicago, Illinois

**Delegation appointed by the governor of Puerto Rico**

**Luis Muñoz Marin**
Co-Chairman

**Jaime Benítez**, Resident Commissioner from the Commonwealth of Puerto Rico to the United States

**Juan Cancel Ríos**, President of the Senate of the Commonwealth of Puerto Rico

Senator **Justo A. Méndez**
Legislature of the Commonwealth of Puerto Rico

**Víctor M. Pons, Jr.**, Esq.
San Juan, Puerto Rico

**Luis Ernesto Ramos Yordán**
Speaker of the House of Representatives of the Commonwealth of Puerto Rico

**Angel M. Rivera,** President, Banco Crédito y Ahorro Ponceño

---

*Resigned May 26, 1975.

# APPENDIX F:
## PLEBISCITE CAMPAIGN ADVERTISEMENTS

*Luis Muñoz Marín speaks out:*

# "The United States Supreme Court has just proven us unequivocally right: No one can be deprived of his American citizenship against his will."

"More than a hundred times I have said that independence is out of the question for Puerto Rico, because American citizenship cannot be taken from anyone against his will, and because 97 percent of all Puerto Ricans reject the status of independence. **The Supreme Court of the United States has just proven us unequivocally right.**

"On May 29, the Court declared that American citizenship cannot be taken from any person against his will. Thus, independence, which would be just as harmful economically to Puerto Rico as statehood, furthermore is without question impossible. The Supreme Court has given the last word. **All propaganda to the contrary has been, is and always will be, false.**"

*[signature: Luis Muñoz Marín]*

"The Supreme Court has just proven us unequivocably right,"
*San Juan Star,* July 14, 1967, p. 9.

# "I will vote Commonwealth, for the progress of every family in Puerto Rico."

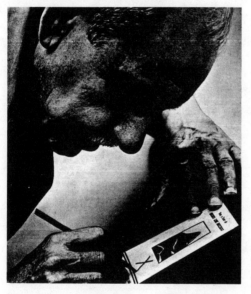

"I will vote 'under **the Mountain**' which is to vote for the acceleration of the great progress we have attained in Puerto Rico under the Commonwealth status... in permanent union with the United States and on the unalterable foundation of our common American citizenship."

*Luis Muñoz Marín*

LUIS MUÑOZ MARIN

**"I Will Vote Commonwealth for the Progress of Every Family in Puerto Rico,"** *San Juan Star,* **July 22, 1967, p. 25.**

Because... you represent the progress of tomorrow's Puerto Rico and your destiny is in our hands today.

Because... we now have the opportunity to ensure your right to inherit peace and security.

Because... your democratic right to the free choice of your destiny will be strengthened and never threatened.

Because... we think of you with the foresight and judgement of one

who is guided by love and with your best interests at heart.

We will vote... to irrevocably join Puerto Rico and your destiny to that of the most progressive nation in the world.

For your future security and happiness and that of all of Puerto Rico's children, so that tomorrow they can remember their parents with pride... we will vote - thinking of you - for Statehood!

# We will vote! Thinking of you...

This Message is sponsored by Citizens for Statehood

"We Will Vote Thinking of You," *San Juan Star*, July 19, 1967, p. 9.

"You Should be There," *San Juan Star*, April 14, 1967, p. 27.

# BIBLIOGRAPHY

## PUBLIC DOCUMENTS

Carroll, Henry K. *Report on the Island of Porto Rico*. Washington: U.S. Government Printing Office, 1899.

Commonwealth of Puerto Rico, Migration Division, Department of Labor. *A Summary of Facts and Figures*, 1964, 1965 edition.

Commonwealth of Puerto Rico, Migration Division, Department of Labor. *A Summary in Facts and Figures*, January 1959 edition.

*Communication from the President of the United States Transmitting a Draft of Proposed Legislation to Enable the People of Puerto Rico to Form a Constitution and State Government, to be Admitted into the Union, and for Other Purposes*. Washington, D.C.: U.S. Government Printing Office, January 17, 1977.

*Compact of Permanent Union Between Puerto Rico and the United States: Report of the Ad Hoc Advisory Group on Puerto Rico*, October, 1975.

*Cuatro Años Del Estado Libre Asociado por Arturo Morales Carrion, Subsecretario de Estado de Puerto Rico*. (Discurso telefundido por la televisora WAPA-TV en el programa "Actualidad Insular" el dia de Julio de 1956) July 29, 1956.

Davis, George W. *Industrial and Economic Conditions of Puerto Rico. Report*. War Department, Division of Insular Affairs, 1899. Washington: Government Printing Office, 1900.

*Documents on the Constitutional History of Puerto Rico*, U.S., Office of the Commonwealth of Puerto Rico. Washington, D.C., June 1964.

Government of Puerto Rico, Department of Labor, San Juan, P.R. *List of Labor Laws in Force in Puerto Rico by No. and Title*. Office of Industrial and Labor Relations, September 1958.

Hackett, William H. *The Nationalist Party*. Committee Print of the House Committee on Interior and Insular Affairs. Washington: U.S. Government Printing Office, 1951.

Ledru, Andres Pedro. *Viage a La Isla de Puerto Rico en El Año 1797 Ejecudado Por Una Comision de Sabios Franceses De Orden de Su Cobierno y Bajo La*

*Direccion del Capitan N. Baudin.* Puerto Rico: Imprenta Militar de J. Gonzalez, 1863.

*Statement by Dr. Arturo Morales Carrión, Under Secretary of State of the Commonwealth of Puerto Rico before the House Committee on Interior and Insular Affairs.* San Juan, Puerto Rico, December 5, 1959. Mimeographed.

*Status of Puerto Rico. Report of the United States–Puerto Rico Commission on the Status of Puerto Rico,* August 1966.

*Status of Puerto Rico. Selected Background Studies. Prepared for the United States–Puerto Rico Commission on the Status of Puerto Rico,* 1966.

Tobin, James (Chair). *Report to the Governor: The Committee to Study Puerto Rico's Finances.* December 11, 1975.

U.S., Commission on Civil Rights. *Puertorriqueños en los Estados Unidos Continentales: Un Futuro Incierto.* Un Informe de la Comisión de Derechos de los Estados Unidos. October 1976.

U.S., Congress, House. *Approving the Constitution of the Commonwealth of Puerto Rico which was adopted by the People of Puerto Rico on March 3, 1952: Report to accompany H. Res. 430.* 82d Cong., 2d sess., April 30, 1952, Rep. No. 1832.

U.S., Congress, House, Committee on Insular Affairs, Subcommittee. *Investigation of Political, Economic, and Social Conditions in Puerto Rico. Hearings pursuant to H. Res. 159,* 78th Cong., 1st sess., San Juan, Puerto Rico, June 1943.

U.S., Congress, House, Committee on Interior and Insular Affairs, Subcommittee on Territorial and Insular Affairs. *Hearings on HR 11200 and HR 11201.* 94th Cong., 2d sess., January 20, February 9, 1976.

U.S., Congress, Senate, Committee on Interior and Insular Affairs. *Hearings.* 94th Cong., 1st sess., December 3, 1975.

U.S., Congress, House, Committee on Internal and Insular Affairs. *Puerto Rico Constitution. Hearings on H.R. Res. 430,* 82d Cong., 2d sess., April 25, 1952.

U.S., Congress, Senate, Committee on Territories and Insular Affairs, Subcommittee. *A Bill to Amend the Organic Act of Puerto Rico. Hearings on S. 1407,* 78th Cong., 1st sess., November 16, 17, 18, 25, 26; December 1, 1943.

U.S., Congress, Senate. *Providing for the Organization of a Constitutional Government by the People of Puerto Rico to accompany S. 3336,* 81st Cong., 2d sess., June 19, 1950. Rep. No. 2275.

U.S., Congress, *Status of Puerto Rico. Hearings before the United States–Puerto Rico Commission on the Status of Puerto Rico.* 89th Cong., 2d sess., Document No. 108. Vol. 1, *Legal-Constitutional Factors in Relation to the Status of Puerto Rico*, San Juan, Puerto Rico, May 14, 15, 17, 18, 1965; Vol. 2, *Social-Cultural Factors in Relation to the Status of Puerto Rico*, San Juan, Puerto Rico, July 28, 29, 31, and August 2, 1965; Vol. 3, *Economic Factors in Relation to the Status of Puerto Rico*, November 27, 29, 30, and December 1, 1965.

U.S. Tariff Commission. *The Economy of Puerto Rico with Special Reference to the Economic Implications of Independence and other Proposals to Change its Political Status.* Washington, U.S. Government Printing Office, 1946.

## BOOKS

Aitken, Thomas, Jr. *Luis Muñoz Marin: Poet in the Fortress.* New York: Signet Books (New American Library), 1965.

Albizu Campos, Laura. *Albizu Campos y la Independencia de Puerto Rico.* San Juan, 1961.

Anderson, Robert W. *Party Politics in Puerto Rico.* Stanford: Stanford University Press, 1965.

Bell, Daniel, ed. *The Radical Right.* New York: Anchor Books, Doubleday and Company, 1963.

Benitez, Jose A. *Puerto Rico and the Political Destiny of America.* Southern University Press, 1958.

Bou, Ismael Rodriguez. *Esbozo de Un Fema: Las Nuevas generaciones en Puerto Rico.* Barcelona: Imprime M. Pareja Montana 16, 1965.

Brameld, Theodore. *The Remaking of a Culture.* New York: John Wiley and Sons, Inc., 1966.

Brau, Salvador. *Disquisiciones Sociologicas y Otros Ensayos.* San Juan: Ediciones del Instituto de Literatura Universidad de Puerto Rico, 1956.

Chenault, Lawrence R. *The Puerto Rican Migrant in New York City.* New York: Columbia University Press, 1938.

Coll y Cuchi, José. *A Mi Pais.* San Juan: Correo Domincal, 1929.

Colon, Jesus. *A Puerto Rican in New York and Other Sketches.* New York: Mainstream Publishers, 1961.

Corretjer, Juan Antonio. *Albizu Campos and the Ponce Massacre*. New York: World View Publishers, 1965.

_____. *La Lucha Por La Independencia de Puerto Rico*. San Juan: Publicaciones de Union del Pueblo Pro Constituyente, 1950.

Cripps, L. L. *Puerto Rico: The Case for Independence*. Cambridge, Mass.: Schenkman Publishing Company, 1974.

Cruz Monclava, Lidio, *Historia de Puerto Rico*. 3 vols. Rio Piedras, P.R.: Editorial Universitaria, 1957–62.

de Diego, José. *Plebiscito Puertorriqueño*. San Juan: Tip, Boletin Mercantil, 1917 [?].

Degeleau, Frederico. *The Political Status of Puerto Rico*. Washington: Globe Printing Company, 1902.

D'Estefano, Miguel A. *Puerto Rico: Analysis of a Plebiscite*. Translated by Ana Romeo. Tricontinental Unidad Productora 08/Berjumeda 407/La Habana, 1968.

Diffie, Bailey W., and Diffie, Justine W. *Porto Rico: A Broken Pledge*. New York: Vanguard Press, 1931.

Fanon, Franz. *The Wretched of the Earth*. New York: Grove Press, 1968.

Farr, Kenneth R. *Personalism and Party Politics*. Hato Rey, P.R.: InterAmerican University Press, 1978.

Fernández Méndez, Eugenio. *Historial Cultural de Puerto Rico 1493–1968*. San Juan: Ediciones El Cemi, 1970.

_____. *La Identitad y La Cultura*. San Juan: Ediciones El Cemi, 1959.

_____. *Portrait of a Society: A Book of Readings on Puerto Rican Society*. Rio Piedras, P.R.: University of Puerto Rico Press, 1956.

_____, ed. *Antologia de Autores Puertorriqueños*. San Juan: Ediciones Del Gobierno Estado Libre Asociado de Puerto Rico, 1957.

Friedrich, Carl J. *Puerto Rico: Middle Road to Freedom*. New York: Rinehart & Company, Inc., 1959.

Geigel Polanco, Vicente. *El Grito de Lares*. Rio Piedras, P.R.: Editorial Antillana, 1976.

_____. *La independencia de Puerto Rico: sus bases historicas, economicas y culturales*. Rio Piedras, P.R.: Imprenta Falcon, 1943.

Glazer, Nathan, and Moynihan, Daniel Patrick. *Beyond the Melting Pot*. Cambridge, Mass.: MIT Press and Harvard University Press, 1964.

Goodsell, Charles T. *Administration of a Revolution*. Cambridge, Mass.: Harvard University Press, 1965.

Gosnell, Patricia Aran. *The Puerto Ricans in New York City*. New York: New York University (an abridgement of a dissertation in the Department of Sociology), 1949.

Hancock, Ralph. *Puerto Rico: A Success Story*. Princeton, N.J.: D. Van Nostrand Company, Inc., 1960.

Handlin, Oscar. *The Newcomers: Negroes and Puerto Ricans in a Changing Metropolis*. Cambridge, Mass.: Harvard University Press, 1959.

Hanson, Earl Parker. *Puerto Rico: Ally for Progress*. Princeton, N.J.: D. Van Nostrand Company, Inc., 1962.

———. *Puerto Rico: Land of Wonders*. New York: Alfred A. Knopf, 1960.

———. *Transformation: The Story of Modern Puerto Rico*. New York: Simon & Schuster, 1955.

Heredia, Manuel de. *Luis Muñoz Marin: Biografía Abierta*. Spain: Ediciones Puerto, 1973.

Hernandez Alvarez, José. *Return Migration to Puerto Rico*. Population Monograph Series No. 1. Berkeley: University of California, 1965.

Huebener, Theodore. *Puerto Rico Today*. New York: Henry Holt and Company, 1960.

James, William. *Puerto Rico and Other Impressions*. New York: G. P. Putnams Sons, The Knickerbocker Press, 1903.

Johnson, Chalmers. *Revolution and the Social System*. Hoover Institution Studies 3. Stanford, California: The Hoover Institution on War, Revolution and Peace, Stanford University, 1964.

La Palombara, Joseph, and Weiner, Myron, eds. *Political Parties and Political Development*. Vol. 6. Princeton, N.J.: Princeton University Press, 1966.

Lewis, Gordon K. *Notes on the Puerto Rican Revolution*. New York: Monthly Review Press, 1974.

———— *Puerto Rico: Freedom and Power in the Caribbean*. New York: M. R. Press, 1963.

Lewis, Oscar. *La Vida*. New York: Random House, 1966.

Lloréns Torres, Luis. *El Grito de Lares*. San Juan: Editorial Cordillera, Inc., 1973.

Lockett, Edward B. *The Puerto Rico Problem*. New York: Exposition Press, 1964.

López, Adalberto, and Petras, James, eds. *Puerto Rico and Puerto Ricans*. New York: John Wiley & Sons, 1974.

Maldonado Denis, Manuel. *En las Entrañas: Un Analisis Sociohistorico de la Emigracion Puertorriqueña*. Translated by Roberto Simon Crespi. Havana, Cuba: Casa de las Americas, 3RA. YG El Vedado, 1976.

———— *Puerto Rico: A Socio-Historic Interpretation*. New York: Vintage, 1972.

————. *Puerto Rico: Una Interpretación histórico-social*. Mexico: Siglo XXI Editores, 1971.

Marqués, René. *La Carreta*. 7th ed. Rio Piedras, P.R.: Editorial Cultural, Inc., 1970.

———— *"Un Nino Azul Para Esa Sombra."* *Teatro*. Mexico: Ediciones Arrecife, 1959.

Massa, Gaetano and Vivas, Jose Luis. *The History of Puerto Rico*. New York: Las Americas Publishing Company, 1970.

Mills, C. Wright; Senior, Clarence; and Goldsen, Rose Kohn. *The Puerto Rican Journey*. New York: Harper and Brothers, 1950.

Mintz, Sidney W. *Worker in the Cane*. New Haven: Yale University Press, 1960.

Mixer, Knowlton. *Porto Rico, History and Conditions, Social, Economic and Political*. New York: Macmillan Company, 1926.

Morales Carrión, Arturo. *Puerto Rico and the Non-Hispanic Caribbean: A Study in the Decline of Spanish Exclusivism*. University of Puerto Rico, 1974.

Morison, Samuel Eliot, and Obregon, Mauricio. *The Caribbean as Columbus Saw It*. Boston: Little, Brown and Company, 1964.

Padilla, Elena. *Up from Puerto Rico*. New York: Columbia University Press, 1958.

Pagán, Bolivar. *Historia de Los Partidos Politicos Puertorriqueños*. Vols. 1 and 2. San Juan: Libreria Campos, 1956.

_____. *Puerto Rico: The Next State*. Washington, April 1942.

_____. *Ideales En Marcha*. San Juan: Biblioteca de Autores Puertorriqueños, 1939.

Paz, Octavio. *The Labyrinth of Solitude: Life and Thought in Mexico*. New York: Grove Press, Inc., 1961.

Pedreira, Antonio S. *Insularismo Ensayos de Interpretación Puertorriqueña*. Madrid: Tipografia Artistica 12, 1934.

Picó, Rafael. *Geografia de Puerto Rico*. Part II. Rio Piedras: Geografia Economica, Editorial Universitaria, University of Puerto Rico, 1964.

Ramos de Santiago, Carmen. *El Gobierno de Puerto Rico*. Vol. I. Rio Piedras: Editorial Universitaria, University of Puerto Rico, 1965.

Rand, Christopher. *The Puerto Ricans*. New York: Oxford University Press, 1958.

Rexach, Benitez, Roberto F. *Pedro Albizu Campos. Leyenda y Realidad*. San Juan: Publicaciones Coqui, 1961.

Reynolds, Lloyd G., and Gregory, Peter. *Wages, Productivity and Industrialization in Puerto Rico*. Homewood, Illinois: Richard D. Irwin, Co., 1965.

Ribes Tovar, Federico. *A Chronological History of Puerto Rico*. New York: Plus Ultra Educational Publishers, Inc., 1973.

_____. *The Puerto Rican Woman*. New York: Plus Ultra Educational Publishers, 1972.

Rosario, José C. *The Development of the Puerto Rican Jibaro and His Present Attitude Towards Society*. San Juan: University of Puerto Rico, 1935.

Rosario Natal, Carmelo. *La Juventud de Luis Muñoz Marin*. San Juan, Puerto Rico, 1976.

Sánchez Tarniella, Andrés. *Nuevo Enfoque Sobre el Desarrollo Politico de Puerto Rico*. Rio Piedras, P.R.: Editorial Edil Inc., 1970.

Seda Bonilla, E. *Requium Para Una Cultura*. Rio Piedras, P.R.: Ediciones Bayoan, 1974.

Senior, Clarence. *Santiago Iglesias: Labor Crusader*. Hato Rey, Puerto Rico: InterAmerican University Press, 1972.

Servin, Manuel P. *The Mexican-Americans: An awakening minority*. Beverly Hills: Glencoe Press, 1970.

Silen, Juan Angel. *Hacia Una Visión Positiva del Puertorriqueño*. Rio Piedras, P.R.: Editorial Edil Inc., 1970.

Steward, Julian, et al. *The People of Puerto Rico*. Urbana, Illinois: University of Illinois Press, 1956.

Thomas, Piri. *Down These Mean Streets*. New York: Vintage Books, 1974.

Tugwell, Rexford G. *The Art of Politics as Practiced by Three Great Americans: Franklin Delano Roosevelt, Luis Muñoz Marin, and Fiorello H. LaGuardia*. Garden City, New York: Doubleday & Company, Inc., 1958.

_____. *The Sticken Land*. Garden City, New York: Doubleday & Company, Inc., 1947.

Tumin, Melvin M., and Feldman, Arnold S., *Social Class and Social Change in Puerto Rico*. Princeton, N.J.: Princeton University Press, 1961.

Van Middeldyk, R. A. *The History of Puerto Rico*. New York: D. Appleton and Company, 1903.

Vivas, José Luis. *Historia de Puerto Rico*. New York: Las Americas Publishing Company, 1962.

Wagenheim, Kal. *Puerto Rico: A Profile*. New York: Praeger Publishers, 1973.

Wells, Henry. *The Modernization of Puerto Rico: A Political Study of Changing Values and Institutions*. Cambridge, Mass.: Harvard University Press, 1969.

Wilgus, A. Curtis, ed. *The Caribbean: Its Hemispheric Role*. Vol 17, Series 1. Gainesville, Florida: Center for Latin American Studies, University of Florida Press, 1967.

## ARTICLES, PAMPHLETS, AND UNPUBLISHED WORKS

Alvarez Silva, Héctor. "Observations on the Study of the Economy of the Republic of Puerto Rico." Prepared for the Status Commission meeting held February 8–9, 1966, in Washington, D.C., and revised at a later date.

Anderson, Robert W. "Puerto Rico Between the United States and the Caribbean." Paper presented at the Conference of Contemporary Trends and Issues in Caribbean International Affairs, Port of Spain, Trinidad, May 23–27, 1977.

_____. "The Puerto Rican Mainstream: The Spirit of Insular Politics," San Juan Review 1, no. 9 (October 1964), pp. 18 ff.

Baggs, William C. "Puerto Rico: Showcase of Development." Reprinted from the 1962 Britannica Book of the Year.

Barber, Hollis W. "Decolonization: The Committee of Twenty-four." World Affairs 38, no. 2 (Fall 1975).

Barregan [sic], Daniel. "Quien es Dios en Vietnam?" FUPI, 1966.

Bender, Marilyn. "Integration Found Successful in Symbolic Area Here," New York Times, January 16, 1965, 81:1.

Benitez, Jaime. "Unfinished Notes on Commonwealth." Statement read before the United States–Puerto Rico Commission on the Status of Puerto Rico, San Juan, P.R., July 31, 1965. Mimeographed.

Berrios Martinez, Rubey. "Independence for Puerto Rico: The Only Solution." Foreign Affairs 55 (April 1977).

_____. "The Commonwealth of Puerto Rico: It's Reality in the National and World Community." Divisional Thesis. Yale Law School, New Haven, Conn., 1964.

Boorstin, Daniel J. "Self Discovery in Puerto Rico." Yale Review 45 (1955–56): 229–45.

Buder, Peter. "Revolt for Civil Rights is Aim of 'River Rats' of East Harlem." New York Times, March 14, 1964, p. 11.

Coates, Mary Weld. "What's the Matter in Porto Rico?" Current History 16 (April–September 1922). New York: The New York Times Company, 1922. pp. 108–14.

Constitucion. Federacion de Universitarios Pro Independencia.

Gatell, Frank Otto. "The Art of the Possible: Luis Muñoz Rivera and the Puerto Rican Jones Bill." Americas, Vol. 17, No. 1 (July 1960), pp. 1–20.

Documentos del Noveno Congreso de la Federacion de Universitarios Pro Independencia. Rio Piedras, P.R.: Comite Ejectivo FUPI, 1964.

Estudiante Revolucionario (FUPI) No. 1. Rio Piedras, P.R.: Comite Ejutivo FUPI, Apartado de Correos 2187, Estacion Universitaria, November 1970.

*Estudio Sobre El Impacto de la Immigracion en Puerto Rico.* San Juan: Colegio de Abogadros de Puerto Rico, 1967.

Fliess, Peter J. "Puerto Rico's Political Status Under Its New Constitution." *Western Political Quarterly* 5, no. 4 (December 1952): 635–56.

de Galindez, Jesús. "Government and Politics in Puerto Rico. New Formulas for Self-Government." *International Affairs* 30, no. 3 (July 1954): 331–41.

————. "Independence Rejected: Puerto Rico and the Tydings Bill of 1936." *Hispanic American Historical Review* 38, no. 1 (February 1958): 25–44. Durham, N.C.: Duke University Press.

Gonzalez, Antonio J. "El Desarrollo Economico y la Estructura Economica." University of Puerto Rico, 1965. Paper.

————. "La Economica y el Status Politico de Puerto Rico." *Revista de Ciencias Sociales* 10, no. 1 (March 1966): 5–49.

Hammer, R. "Report From a Spanish Harlem Fortress." *New York Times Magazine.* January 5, 1964, pp. 22, 32, 34, 36, 39.

Hernandez, Frederico Rupert. "The Institutionalization of Political Parties in Developing Areas: A Case Study of the Partido Popular Democratico in Puerto Rico." Thesis, Department of Government, Harvard College, April 1, 1966.

Huntington, Samuel P. "Political Development and Political Decay." *World Politics* 17, no. 3 (April 1965): 386–430.

————. "Political Modernization: America vs. Europe." *World Politics* 18, no. 3 (April 1966): 378–414

*Informe del Compañero Presidente Alberto Pérez.* Federacion de Universitarios Pro Independencia XI Congreso. Mimeographed.

Juventud Estado librista. Universitaria. *El Estado Libre Asociado Realidad Puertorriqueña,* 1967. Pamphlet.

Karpatkin, Marvin M. "Puerto Rico: How Much Independence Does It Want?" *New Republic,* May 7, 1966, pp. 12–15.

Kazin, Alfred. "In Puerto Rico." *Commentary* 29, no. 2 (February 1960): 108–14.

Larrabee, Harold A. "The Enemies of Empire." *American Heritage* 11, no. 4 (June 1960): 28–33, 76–80.

Lewis, Gordon K. "Puerto Rico: A New Constitution in American Government." *Journal of Politics* 15 (Fall 1953): 42–66.

Maldonado Denis, Manuel. "La Resistencia al Colonialismo Sixto Alvelo." *La Escalera* 1, nos. 5–6 (June–July 1966).

_____. "Ideologies and Attitudes Among theSpanish Speaking 'Intelligentsia' in the Caribbean." Paper presented at the Annual Meeting of the American Sociological Association in Chicago, Illinois, August 30 to September 2, 1965.

_____. "Declinar del Movimiento Independista Puertorriqueño?" *Revista de Ciencias Sociales* 9, no. 3 (September 1965): 285–302.

Maldonado Sierra, Eduardo, and Trent, Richard D. "The Sibling Relationship in Group Psychotherapy with Puerto Rican Schizophrenics." *American Journal of Psychology* 117 (1960–61): 239–43.

Mari Bras, Juan. "The Struggle for Puerto Rican Independence," *Black Scholar* 8 (December 1976).

Marinello, Juan. "Recuerdo y Homenaje: Pedro Albizu Campos." *Pabellon* Albizu's fild, Harvard Archives, date unavailable.

Marqués, René. "El Puertorriqueño Docil (Literatura y realidad psicológica)." *Cuadernos Americanos* 120 (January–February 1962): 144–95.

_____. "Noted Writer Looks as Kazin's Content." *San Juan Star,* March 8, 1960, pp. 1, 10, 16.

_____. "Pesimismo Literario y Optimismo Politico: Su Coexistencia en el Puerto Rico Actual." *Cuadernos Americanos*, Mexico, 1959, pp. 43–74.

Morse, Richard M. "The Higher Learning in Puerto Rico." *Journal of General Education* 11, no. 2 (April 1958): 83–96.

Muñoz Marin, Luis. "Remarks by the Honorable Luis Muñoz Marin, Governor of the Commonwealth of Puerto Rico, at Harvard University on June 16, 1955."

_____. "Nuevas Caminos Hacia Viejos Objectivos." *El Mundo*, June 29, 1946, pp. 1, 12.

_____. "A Plea for Puerto Rico." *The Nation* 162, no. 19 (May 11, 1946): 571–172.

_____. "Alerta a la Conciencia Puertorriqueña." *El Mundo*. February 7–10, 1946, pp. 1, 20.

_____. "Plight of Puerto Rico." *New Republic* 108 (January 11, 1943): 51–52.

_____. "Porto Rico: The American Colony." *The Nation*, April 8, 1925, pp. 379–82.

Nader, Ralph. "The Commonwealth Status of Puerto Rico." *Harvard Law Record* 23, no. 12 (December 13, 1956): 2–8.

*Nueva Lucha. Revista de discusion politica del MPI*. Year 1, no. 1, San Juan. Libreria Puerto Rico, Calle Humacao 1006, Urbanizacion Santa Rita, November 1970.

Pabón, Milton. "La Integracion Politica en Puerto Rico." *Revista de Ciencias Sociales* 10, no. 2, (June 1966): 131–44.

Partido Independentista Puertorriqueño. Letter to President John F. Kennedy, December 14, 1961. Mimeo.

*Ponencias Presentados al Sexto Seminario Nacional de Dirigentes Del MPI; 20, 21, 22 de enero de 1967; Campamento Yuquiyu, Luquillo, P.R.; El Plebiscito y la Realidad Colonial; Programa y Accion Antiplebiscitaria.* Comision Politica de la Mision Nacional Pedru Albizu Campos; Movimiento Pro Independencia de Puerto Rico. Mimeo.

*Programa Politico Economico y Social del Partido Independentista Puertorriqueño.* 1960. Booklet.

*Puerto Rico Libre: Bulletin of the Puerto Rican Solidarity Committee* 3, no. 2 (September 15, 1975).

*Reglamento.* Partido Independentista Puertorriqueño Aprobado en la Asamblea General Especial celebrado el 29 de septiembre de 1957 con las enmiendas propuestas para ser consideradas en la Asamblea General Especial a celebrarse el 6 de junio de 1965. Mimeo.

Reynolds, Ruth. "Puerto Rico." *USLA Reporter* 2, no. 2 (April 1968): 11–14.

Rothenberg, Albert. "Puerto Rico and Aggression." *The American Journal of Psychiatry*. Vol. 120, no. 10 (April 1964): 362–70.

Ruiz, Rafael. "The Independence Movement of Puerto Rico 1898–1964." Master of Arts Thesis 2562, Georgetown University, June 1965.

Ryder, Katharine. "Freedom for Puerto Rico." *Current History* 5, no. 26 (October 1943): 121–23.

Serrano Geyls, Raul. "An Introduction to the Study of the Party System of Puerto Rico." Unpublished study. May 1955.

Stycos, J. Mayone. "Family and Fertility in Puerto Rico." *American Sociological Review* 17 (1952): 572–80.

"A Talk With the Candidates." *San Juan Review* 1, no. 9 (October 1964): 12, 16, 25.

*The Time for Independence: Political Thesis—Pro Independence Movement of Puerto Rico* (La Hore de la Independencia, Tesis Politica del MPI). Translation based on the original Spanish edition published at San Juan, Puerto Rico, in 1963. First edition, 1964.

*Viva Puerto Rico Libre. Puerto Rico. A Colony of the United States.* Puerto Rico Youth Movement, New England Free Press, 1969.

Wells, Henry. "La Consecución del Gobierno Propio en Puerto Rico." Editorial del Departamento de Instrucción Publica, Estado Libre Asociado de Puerto Rico, San Juan, P.R. Serie I, no. 81, 1955.

_____. "Ideology and Leadership in Puerto Rican Politics." *American Political Science Review* 49, no. 1 (March 1955): 22–39.

_____, and Anderson, Robert W. "Government Financing of Political Parties in Puerto Rico." A Supplement to Number Four, 1966. Princeton, New Jersey: Citizen's Research Foundation.

# INDEX

apparel industry: decline, 46; tied into American import system, 149–50

Arawak Indians: description, 3; population decline, 3

Arecibo Resolution, 32

Arroyo, Waldemiro, leads independence group in plebiscite, 131

back-migration, 117, 119–20

Barceló, Antonio: breaks with Muñoz over Tydings bill, 27, 103; dies, 27; link with sugar interests, 19; testifies against statehood bill, 107

Bell, C. Jasper, Representative, and Bell Committee, holds up Elective Governor Act, 33

Benitez, Jaime: blames Communists and Nationalists for 1948 student strike, 80; as Chancellor, refuses to allow Albizu to use University auditorium, 33; defines essential ingredient of commonwealth, 159

Berríos Martínez, Rubén: becomes PIP leader, 47; civil disobedience on Culebra, 47–48

Betances, Ramon Emeterio, founds 1868 Revolutionary Committee, 6

Borinquen, Taino definition, 3

boycott of 1967 plebiscite, 135–37 (see also Sovereigntist Antiplebiscite Concentration)

Burton, Representative Philip, in Congressional Hearings on New Pact, 157–58

capital intensive industry: consequence is high unem-

ployment, 47; new pattern, 46–47

Castro, Fidel, makes Cuba a symbol, 45; seen as sinister presence, 45

Chardón, Carlos, Dr.: Chancellor of the University of Puerto Rico recommends economic changes, the Chardón Plan, 23; changes in Plan, programs questioned, reduced or eliminated, 24; opposition to Chardón Plan, 23–24; President supports Chardón Plan, 23

Chardón Plan (see Chardón, Dr. Carlos

Charter of Autonomy, 1897: description, 9; Luis Muñoz Rivera negotiates, 9

coffee: agricultural development, 5; crop flourishes, 5–6; grower, 5–6

Coll y Cuchi, José: helped found Nationalist Association, 20 (see also Nationalist Party)

colonialism: creates mentality of inferiority, 81, 133; similarity to sexism, 81

Columbus, Christopher: describes Puerto Rico, discovers Puerto Rico, 1

Committee of Twenty-four (see United Nations Committee on Decolonization)

commonwealth: idea, 34–35, 128; interim solution, 34–36, 128; status alternative, 35–36, 128; term, 34, 128; United States is killing commonwealth, 159 (see also Commonwealth Constitution; in the nature of a contract)

Commonwealth Constitution: changed by Senate, 36;

# ABOUT THE AUTHOR

ROBERTA ANN JOHNSON is a visiting professor in politics at the University of California, Santa Cruz. She was coordinator of women's studies and lecturer in political science at San Francisco State University, and from 1972–74 she was assistant professor of political science at the University of Missouri, Kansas City.

Dr. Johnson is the author of numerous articles on minorities and women and is an office-holder in various professional and academic organizations. She holds a B.A., magna cum laude, phi beta kappa, from Brooklyn College and an M.A. and Ph.D. in political science from Harvard.